Portuguese Film, 1930–1960

Portuguese Film, 1930–1960:
The Staging of the New State Regime

Patricia Vieira

Translated by Ashley Caja

BLOOMSBURY
LONDON • NEW DELHI • NEW YORK • SYDNEY

Bloomsbury Academic
An imprint of Bloomsbury Publishing Plc

1385 Broadway	50 Bedford Square
New York	London
NY 10018	WC1B 3DP
USA	UK

www.bloomsbury.com

Bloomsbury is a registered trade mark of Bloomsbury Publishing Plc

First published 2013

© Patricia Vieira, 2013

All rights reserved. No part of this publication may be reproduced or transmitted in any form or by any means, electronic or mechanical, including photocopying, recording, or any information storage or retrieval system, without prior permission in writing from the publishers.

No responsibility for loss caused to any individual or organization acting on or refraining from action as a result of the material in this publication can be accepted by Bloomsbury Academic or the author.

Library of Congress Cataloging-in-Publication Data
Vieira, Patricia I., 1977-
Portuguese film, 1930-1960, : the staging of the new state regime / Patricia Vieira.
  pages cm
Includes bibliographical references and index.
ISBN 978-1-62356-863-4 (hardback)– ISBN 978-1-62356-899-3 (e-pdf)– ISBN 978-1-62356-735-4 (e-book) 1. Motion pictures–Portugal–History–20th century. 2. Motion pictures in propaganda–Portugal–History. 3. Fascism and motion pictures–Portugal–History. I. Title.
  PN1993.5.P6V55 2013
  791.4309469–dc23
  2013020324

ISBN: HB: 978-1-6235-6863-4
e-pdf: 978-1-6235-6899-3
e-pub: 978-1-6235-6735-4

Typeset by Fakenham Prepress Solutions, Fakenham, Norfolk NR21 8NN
Printed and bound in the United States of America

To Michael, my companion in this and so many other cinematic adventures

Contents

Acknowledgements		ix
Introduction: Cinema in the New State		1
1	Propaganda in the New State: *The May Revolution* (*A Revolução de Maio*)	25
	Propaganda in Portuguese cinema	25
	Salazar's truth as ideology	29
	The primacy of art: António Ferro's politics of the spirit	33
	The staging of the leader	37
2	Poets on the Silver Screen: *Bocage*, *Camões*, and the Heroes of the Regime	57
	Literature and film in the politics of the spirit	57
	The heroes of the New State	59
	Against political inconstancy: The hero as a serious man	66
3	Rural Life in Cinema: In Defense of a Natural Society	81
	Regional and folkloric films	81
	A natural cinema	83
	The countryside and the city	94
	Capitalism, Communism, Corporatism	100
4	The Miracle of Salazarism: *Fátima, Land of Faith* (*Fátima, Terra de Fé*)	125
	Fátima in the New State	125
	Reason, faith and politics in cinema	127
	Balancing reason and religion	131
	Beyond reason and faith: The danger of nihilism	137
5	Gender Stereotypes in New State Cinema	151
	Women in New State films	151
	Singing as a transgression	157
	Fado, fatalism and the Portuguese *femme fatale*	165

6	The Empire as Fetish: *Spell of the Empire* (*Feitiço do Império*)	177
	Portugal and its colonies	177
	The magic of Africa	179
	The empire as a fetish	183
	Spell of the Empire and colonial propaganda	187
7	The Spirit of the Empire in *Chaimite*	203
	Spirituality and materiality in Salazarism	203
	The spirit of Portuguese colonization	206
	The politics of the spirit in *Chaimite*	208

Epilogue: New State Cinema Today	233
Bibliography	239
Index	249

Acknowledgements

The writing and publication of this book counted on the support of several people and institutions. The grants from the Graduate School of Georgetown University in 2008 and 2009 allowed me to complete the research for this study. I would like to thank the Portuguese National Archive of Moving Images (Arquivo Nacional das Imagens em Movimento), the Lisbon *Videotheque*, and the Library of the Portuguese *Cinemateque* for facilitating my access both to films and to bibliography.

The translation of the book into English was funded by the BMW Center for European Studies and the Department of Spanish and Portuguese at Georgetown University. I would like to thank Ashley Caja for doing a wonderful job in producing an accurate and very readable translation. Katherine Vadella provided invaluable assistance in revising the complete English manuscript. All images reproduced in the book are part of the Collection of the Portuguese *Cinematheque*—Cinema Museum (Cinemateca Portuguesa—Museu do Cinema). I thank the *Cinematheque* for the permission to reprint the images included in the book.

The support of my colleagues at Georgetown, in particular Vivaldo Santos, Michael Ferreira and Alfonso Morales-Front was greatly appreciated. I would also like to thank my editor at Bloomsbury Press, Katie Gallof, for backing this project. I am grateful to my family for their help with the practicalities of constant travel between Lisbon and Washington. This book is dedicated to my husband, Michael Marder, with whom I watch so many films.

Introduction

Cinema in the New State

In 1937, António Ferro, director of the Portuguese Secretariat of National Propaganda (Secretariado da Propaganda Nacional), organized a semi-private screening of the film *The May Revolution* (*A Revolução da Maio*, António Lopes Ribeiro) for António de Oliveira Salazar, the country's prime minister and *de facto* leader. The movie, which was about to premiere in national theaters, was produced to celebrate the Revolution of 28 May 1926 that put an end to the Portuguese First Republic (1910–26) and paved the way to the institutionalization of the New State's (Estado Novo; 1933–74) authoritarian regime.[1] It remains to this day the only Portuguese fiction film that openly conveys political propaganda. Curious about Salazar's reaction, the next day Ferro enquired about his opinion of the film and Salazar replied: "I liked that film a lot. I liked it too much, perhaps, because I could not sleep afterwards. This morning I could not work like I normally do. […] I ask you, therefore, not to push me into this type of distractions any more."[2]

This episode, narrated by Ferro, then in Berne, to the French journalist Christine Garnier, is in itself proto-cinematographic and touches upon key questions for the understanding of the films produced during the first decades of the New State.[3] Ferro, stereotyped as the herald of the Portuguese artistic vanguard, displayed before the head of the government the most recent cinematographic production of the regime. Salazar, playing the public persona that he himself created, marked by conservatism and by a withdrawal from mundane pleasures, reacted with a mixture of fascination and sleeplessness to the modernity represented by the film and decided to abstain from future screenings. But is the film an *avant-garde* work worthy of Ferro's innovative plans? Or, despite certain Eisensteinian overtones in the montage, is it merely a movie shored up by conventional technique and narrative? Moreover, was it really cinema, as a relatively new medium of expression, that troubled Salazar, or rather the plot of the movie, which chronicles the preparation of a communist *coup d'état* in Portugal? Isn't Salazar's comment, rather than being a provincial reaction to cinema, evidence of a clear vision of the threats to the security of the New State, a vision that led him to fund other works of propaganda? Finally, by admitting to being impressed by what he saw, was Salazar not recognizing, albeit in a negative way, the power of film and the need to put it at the service of the regime?

The production of a film like *The May Revolution* became possible with the creation of the Secretariat of National Propaganda (SPN) in 1933, which in 1944 would turn into the National Secretariat of Information, Popular Culture, and Tourism (Secretariado Nacional da Informação, Cultura Popular e Turismo; SNI).[4] The objective of the SPN/SNI, led by António Ferro from its inception until 1949,[5] was to foster Portuguese and international support for the political project of the New State. Salazar recognized that, in politics, "[…] the only thing that exists is what the public knows exists,"[6] and he saw the Secretariat as an instrument for the political education of citizens, so that they learned the foundational tenets of his government—distilled in the trilogy "God, Nation, Family"—and then regulated their concrete existence in accordance with this dogma.[7]

As in Fascist Italy or in Nazi Germany, cinema was a fundamental part of Salazar's propagandistic efforts.[8] In 1935, António Ferro inaugurated the Traveling Cinema (Cinema Ambulante), which showed propaganda films all over the country. With regard to production, the SPN/SNI was responsible above all for documentaries that addressed topics as varied as the completion of public works, political events, military parades, sporting events, and festivals.[9] Some documentaries were medium- or feature-length, such as *The Exhibition of the Portuguese World* (*A Exposição do Mundo Português*, 1941) and *The Inauguration of the National Stadium* (*Inauguração do Estádio Nacional*, 1944), both directed by António Lopes Ribeiro, but the majority were short films. Many of these were part of the newsreel *Portuguese Journal* (*Jornal Português*), with 95 editions produced between 1938 and 1951 and substituted in 1953 by *Images of Portugal* (*Imagens de Portugal*).[10] The regime's propaganda services were also responsible for a few feature-length fiction films, including *The May Revolution*, and funded countless other cinematic works produced by private companies.

The attention that the SPN/SNI paid to cinema is usually attributed to the work of António Ferro, an intellectual and former member of the modernist literary group *Orpheu*. Ferro was a film enthusiast and wrote several essays on cinema.[11] Inspired by French writer Paul Valéry, he designed the so-called "politics of the spirit" that placed art at the service of New State propaganda in order to generate enthusiasm for the regime among the Portuguese. Cinema, "which exerts such a considerable influence in the renewal of the soul of a nation and in the projection of its character,"[12] was one of the areas covered under his politics of the spirit.[13] In a 1947 speech, Ferro described the important mandate attributed to cinema in the context of national propaganda:

> In fact, Portuguese cinema has, among others, two great and noble missions: a significant educational mission within the Country (both in the aesthetic and the moral sense) and a difficult foreign mission of bringing to other nations the knowledge of our life, our character and the heights of our civilization.[14]

Unlike Ferro, Salazar was not a cinephile, and he considered cinema to be terribly expensive, as he confessed to Lopes Ribeiro. However, he acknowledged the potential of film as a means to disseminate the ideology of the New State and to bring the regime's values closer to the largely illiterate Portuguese population. Lopes Ribeiro himself testified to Salazar's interest in cinema. He reported that the statesman watched every Portuguese movie and visited several studios, in addition to adopting measures to promote the creation of a domestic film industry such as tax exemptions for cinema professionals.[15] Be it out of aesthetic inclination, as in the case of Ferro, or out of pragmatic considerations, as with Salazar, the New State regarded cinema as a priority, and its leaders undertook multiple efforts to stimulate, direct, and control movie production in Portugal.

In terms of legislation, the military dictatorship that followed the 1926 coup and, later, the New State took several measures both to protect and to stimulate the domestic film industry. In 1927, shortly after the end of the First Republic, Decree No. 13 564, better known as the "Law of the 100 Meters," was issued. This piece of legislation made it mandatory to show a Portuguese film of at least 100 meters, which had to change every week, during all cinematographic events, and additionally exempted from taxes all new films printed in Portugal. The immediate consequence of this law was a substantial increase in the production of short films that were shown before feature-length movies. However, given that these works were solely designed to meet the 100 meters requirement stipulated by the law, the films were acquired at an extremely low price and, therefore, quality suffered considerably.[16] In 1933, Ordinance No. 22 966 made it mandatory for Portuguese distributors to acquire sound films produced in domestic studios. The government established annually the amount of footage to be purchased. The same Ordinance also exempted from taxes the recently created Tobis Portuguesa, a company funded by the state with the aim of developing sound cinema in Portugal.[17] Though the latter measure contributed to the establishment of Tobis as the main film company in the country, the former was never implemented.

The New State's legislation on cinema culminated in Law 2 027 of 18 February 1948—otherwise known as the Protection of National Cinema Law—that, along with other provisions, created a SNI-administered Cinema Fund. The goal of the Fund according to its Article 1 was to "[…] protect, coordinate and stimulate the production of domestic cinema […] keeping in mind its social and educational function, as well as its artistic and cultural aspects."[18] It is significant that the social and educational function of film or, in other words, its instrumentalization as a vehicle for propaganda, is mentioned before its artistic aspects.[19] In his presentation of the Law, António Ferro did not hide the SNI's bias when it came to distributing the Fund's future subsidies, emphasizing that the works funded would be those that followed the parameters established by the institution: "Naturally, this criterion will lead us to protect in principle and as a matter of principle, certain producers and filmmakers who adapt better to our own criterion."[20] The decisive criterion to which Ferro alludes here is the subject-matter of each production. He established a categorization of the various films produced in the country and defined from the outset which works were more likely to be subsidized, namely, historical films, documentaries, and, to a lesser degree, films of a poetic nature and films about daily life.[21] Commercial films, especially the comedies that explore "the *backwardness*, the crassness that remains in the life of our streets," would not be funded.[22] Aesthetic and ideological concerns intertwine in the criteria mentioned by Ferro. While the SNI sought to fight "bad taste," artificiality, vulgarity, and "easy answers," it was also concerned with creating a "healthy" cinema,[23] in other words, a cinema that was both artistically accomplished and politically aligned with the worldview of the New State. Thus, it is not surprising that preference was given to historical films permeated by nationalism that praised famous figures from the past, and to documentaries frequently made with clear propagandistic intentions.

In retrospect, it becomes clear that the Protection of National Cinema Law did not produce the expected results. Ferro himself predicted this situation in a 1949 speech in which he announced that he was resigning from his position at the SNI and referred to the bureaucratic delays in the implementation of the Law.[24] In fact, the number of Portuguese films that premiered annually decreased during the second half of the 1940s, prolonging the death throes of domestic production until 1955—Portuguese cinema's *annus horribilis*, when not a single feature-length film was released.²⁵

In a text published shortly after the implementation of the Law in 1951, Manuel de Azevedo presciently described the reasons that would lead to the failure of the Fund. He criticized corruption in the allocation of film subsidies, which were often awarded to directors who had given little proof of their talent, and pointed out that independent producers were unable to afford the high production costs prevalent in the country (access to studios, laboratories, etc.) when they lacked government financing.²⁶ Citing from an article he published in *Mundo Literário*, Azevedo concluded that "cinematographic production was split in two; a part will resort to the fund and will be guided and supervised by the SNI; and another part [will remain] defenseless and without opportunities, independent but condemned."²⁷ While independent cinema was gradually asphyxiated due to exorbitant production costs, the SNI-financed films became more and more formulaic, repeating clichés and following conventions so as to receive state support.

Beyond the legal provisions for cinema that, despite their scarce practical results, stood as evidence of the government's efforts to promote the film industry, the New State also created film awards. These were similar to the literary prizes awarded by the SPN after 1934 and rewarded the most distinguished works, actors, and technicians in any given year. Distributed by the SNI from 1944 onwards and continued by the SEIT until the early 1970s, the film awards—divided into the categories of best picture, best actor, best actress, best photography, best adaptation, the Paz dos Reis prize for best documentary, and honorable mentions in each category—were a way simultaneously to stimulate film production and to steer Portuguese cinema to topics consistent with the regime's values.²⁸ Ferro's statement from 1935 about literary prizes would later also apply to the cinema awards:

> The *broadly constructive* intentions of our awards are, then, easily understandable. To avoid having them be classified as a puzzling matter, the competitors should just remember that the S.P.N. is an agency of the Council Presidency and that the Council President is Salazar. Whoever does not agree with these principles—and with any action that derives from them—only has one path to follow: not compete for our awards.²⁹

The literary prizes, like the film awards later on, promoted the political, social, and even moral order established by Salazar, meaning that works that went against the principles of the New State were automatically rejected. This is why, until the 1950s, awards were predominantly given to historical films such as *Camões* (Leitão de Barros, 1946), *Friar Luís de Sousa* (*Frei Luís de Sousa*, António Lopes Ribeiro, 1950), and *Chaimite* (Jorge Brum do Canto, 1953) that were directed by the three filmmakers who worked most closely with the regime and that followed Ferro's plan to promote this film genre.[30] It is also the reason why Jorge Brum do Canto, whose work promoted the values of the regime, was the filmmaker who received the most awards, and fado singer Amália Rodrigues was the only person to receive three best actress awards—a response to the national and international popularity of fado, which the propaganda machine exploited to support Salazarism.

We have established the New State's undeniable interest in developing Portuguese cinema. This intent was translated into the direct production of films, particularly documentaries, by the propaganda services of the regime; into financial incentives, subsidies and prizes; and into attempts to make the distribution and exhibition of domestic productions mandatory by defining quotas. It behooves us now to consider the status of the films produced during the New State. If *The May Revolution* and the SPN/SNI documentaries were clearly propaganda works, what was the relationship between the state and the other fictional films released during the first decades of Salazarism? Given the government's intervention in the film industry, would not all cinema from this period be, in one form or another, a means to disseminate propaganda?

To answer these questions, we will have to formulate, albeit briefly, our understanding of the term propaganda. Without entering into a detailed discussion of the vast research on the subject,[31] for the purposes of this study we subscribe to the definition proposed by Garth Jowett and Victoria O'Donnell and grounded in a communicative model: "Propaganda is the deliberate, systematic attempt to shape perceptions, manipulate cognitions, and direct behavior to achieve a response that furthers the desired intent of the propagandist."[32] Here, propaganda is understood as a specific form of persuasion that may include elements as innocuous as some of the rules of classical rhetoric, but also the appeal to emotion and the subconscious, as well as the use of information—be it truthful, misleading or even false—in an attempt to influence the opinions and actions of certain individuals or groups. This definition derives from the first use of the word in the sense that we attribute to it today. The precursor of the modern meaning of propaganda emerged in 1622, in a Papal Bull by Pope Gregory XV, wherein he created the *Sacra Congregatio de*

Propaganda Fide (The Sacred Congregation for the Propagation of the Faith). Charged with the Church's missionary activities, the *Congregatio* was conceived as an instrument to combat the spread of Protestantism both in Europe and in the colonies.[33] Although Jowett and O'Donnell's definition of propaganda encompasses activities such as advertisement or public relations, in our analysis of cinema during the New State we will focus on political propaganda conveyed by the state or by governmental organizations. In the case of Salazarism, these include, first and foremost, the SPN/SNI, but also the military, the various state ministries, the General Agency of the Colonies (Agência Geral das Colónias), and youth associations such as the Portuguese Youth (Mocidade Portuguesa).

We now find ourselves in a position to revisit the aforementioned questions and reformulate them in a more precise manner. Was cinematic production from the 1930s to the 1950s, as a whole, used as a means of persuading the public to adhere to the principles of Salazarism, to recognize the advantages of the regime, and to mold behavior in accordance with the values of the New State?

Historians and film critics unanimously agree that the ideological manipulation of film in Portugal was not comparable to the instrumentalization of cinema that took place under the yoke of the powerful propaganda machines of Fascist Italy and Nazi Germany. For Jorge Leitão Ramos, even Spanish cinema under Franco had a more obvious propagandistic slant than Portuguese productions.[34] João Bénard da Costa goes even further, declaring that one cannot interpret the most remarkable films of the New State as mere vehicles for the official ideology: "We don't find in Salazar's regime [...] a monolithic cultural policy that would allow us to see the art from this era as the reflection of a propaganda apparatus. [...]."[35] Indeed, the production of feature-length, fictional propaganda films during the New State resulted in only two works: *The May Revolution* and *Spell of the Empire* (*Feitiço do Império*, 1940), a film also directed by Lopes Ribeiro and produced by the General Agency of the Colonies that praised the Portuguese colonization of Africa. Despite promotional efforts, the presence of renowned politicians at the premieres, and positive reviews by the majority of critics, both films had little success at the box office, an outcome which probably discouraged the regime from investing in this type of cinema. The remaining fictional, feature films from this period were produced by private companies without direct interference from the state and therefore were not, strictly speaking, works of propaganda.

Nevertheless, the fact that propaganda was limited to only a few fictional feature-length films does not mean that New State filmography was completely independent from political power. On the one hand, the specificity of cinematic production, which requires a large investment of capital, meant that private filmmakers and producers were often forced to resort to state subsidies. They depended on grants such as those offered by the National Cinema Fund and therefore had to follow the directives announced by the authorities. On the other hand, the easy access of a large segment of the public, including those who were illiterate, to Portuguese cinema meant that the films produced and screened in the country were subject to strong censorship.

The definition of the criteria for film exhibition preceded the military coup of 1926 and, even after that date, the first legislation to this effect was predominantly concerned with moral issues. Yet, Decree No. 13 564 of 1927, which established the General Inspection of Entertainment (Inspecção-Geral dos Espectáculos), banned not only films that went against the moral order, but also those that put into question the "political and social regime."[36] The exercise of censorship was carried out after the premieres, subjecting theaters to hefty fines when they screened films that violated the norms defined in the Decree.[37] The political implications of censorship became clearer in 1929, when the General Inspection of Entertainment, until then under the jurisdiction of the Ministry of Public Education, moved to the Department of the Interior as a consequence of the recognition of the "social and political importance" of its activities.[38] In 1944 the services of the General Inspection of Entertainment were integrated with the recently created SNI, and in 1945, during the regime's post-war consolidation, a Censorship Committee was created, upon which the permission to screen any film on Portuguese territory depended.[39]

The state did not establish objective criteria for censorship, but criticism of public figures, government policies, or the Portuguese Empire, as well as allusions to poverty or leftist ideology were certainly grounds for cutting scenes from a film or for banning it altogether. Works that challenged the parochial Salazarist morality and films that explicitly showed sexuality were also often targeted by censorship. Beyond the countless foreign films that were prohibited or mutilated,[40] many domestic productions were censored. One of the most notorious examples is Manuel de Guimarães's *Lives Adrift* (*Vidas sem Rumo*, 1956), a film that was so disfigured by censorship that it could not be screened.[41]

Constrained by censorship's omnipresent gaze and by financial contingencies that led to the self-censorship of producers and filmmakers, whose work often depended on subsidies granted by governmental institutions, New State filmography ended up conforming to the regime's values, or, at the very least, not disputing Salazarism's foundational principles. Historian Luís Reis Torgal describes this situation in terms of the film industry's adoption of an "indirect or contextual ideology—in regards to subject-matter [...], atmosphere [...], social morality [...]."[42] Jorge Leitão Ramos advocates an even more radical position when he describes the mark that Salazar left on all domestic sound films: "Because of what he did, because of what he ordered to be done, and because of what he did not allow to be done, all sound cinema in Portugal *until long after 1974* was influenced by Salazarism."[43] However, Ramos is careful to point out that "even films that best convey the ideals of the regime (given that those seeking to combat it are almost non-existent) do not do so [...] in an inflamatory and direct way [...]."[44] In other words, returning to the question raised above, we do not have, with regard to feature-length fiction films, an industry with a blatantly propagandistic slant, but rather films that fit into the worldview of the New State and that reproduce Salazarist principles through their settings, choice of characters, and even the narrative plot.

In this book we discuss a selection of films produced between the 1930s and the 1950s with the aim of examining the reciprocal relationship between cinematographic language and the rhetorical and discursive construction of the ideology of the Portuguese New State. Leaving aside purely documentary production, less complex due to its more obvious instrumentalization for propaganda purposes, we focus on fictional feature-length films. Our study concentrates on the confluence between the image of the country represented in these works and the portrait of Salazar's government elaborated by the ideologues of the regime. In other words, the films are not considered as mere sociological documents that reveal the way of life of this period or as an illustration of specific government policies or practices—although both of these approaches are possible and, in some cases, justified—but instead as representations of a fantasized country. New State cinema offers us not so much an image of what Portugal was but of what it should have been, a paradigm conveyed to the population through artworks, so that the Portuguese progressively sought to conform to this ideal. Accordingly, the purpose of the book is not to undertake a history of cinema and describe the development of film during the first three decades of the New State. Such a project has been, moreover, already carried out by Alves Costa, Luís de Pina, José de Matos-Cruz, and João Bénard da Costa, among others. Rather, we have adopted a thematic approach to the film industry that allowed us to identify the guidelines of Salazarism as they were portrayed in cinema.

In a study that juxtaposes two distinct types of discourse, namely the political–ideological and the artistic–cinematographic, the question of whether or not the influence of the former on the latter is unilateral necessarily arises. In other words, are we not adopting an excessively mechanistic conception of cinema as a mere reflection of the New State's worldview? Or, better yet, are we not espousing a modified version of the oft-criticized Marxist model for understanding art, substituting here the economic base with political ideology, which ineluctably determines the superstructure—in this case, cinema?

If the relationship between artworks and the socio-ideological context wherein they originate is, in general, the subject of much controversy, the matter is even more complex in societies where a concerted effort is undertaken to determine the content of art. With regard to film, Siegfried Kracauer is situated at one of the extremes of this debate since he considers that "all Nazi films were more or less propaganda films—even the simple entertainment films which seem to be remote from politics."[45] For Kracauer, seemingly apolitical cinema was used as a vehicle to disseminate Nazi propaganda and, for this reason, any film from the period can only be understood when analyzed through the perspective of Hitlerism. Viewed in this light, films become, simultaneously, historical documents and case studies that illustrate the characteristics of German totalitarianism.[46] On the opposite end of the interpretive spectrum we find an emphasis on the aesthetic value of cinema, an application of the concept of "art for art's sake" to film analysis. In line with this position, films should be primarily appreciated in and of themselves, with particular attention paid to the language and the style with which the various actors in the process of film creation operate, and not as a reflection of a given social environment or ideological system.

In the chapters that follow, we will consider films from the first decades of the New State from two distinct angles. First, as aesthetic objects that dialogue with the cinematographic trends of their time and express the artistic vision of the actors, filmmakers, and technicians who created them. Second, as the products of an industry subject to the constraints of Salazar's regime, which saw cinema as a means for disseminating its principles, and thus established a set of mechanisms that aimed to stimulate but also control film production. Cinema from this period could be mapped along a continuum that extends from films that are most openly propagandistic to those that deviate or even seem to contest—albeit covertly, due to the control of censorship—the hegemony of the New State. This diversity discourages the adoption of a uniform pattern of interpretation, suggesting instead the need for an interdisciplinary approach, as well as a comparative perspective. An analysis of the filmography from this period needs to consider not only the styles and plots of the different films but also the similarities and differences between cinematographic language and the intellectual and socio-political discourses from the time, thus allowing us to highlight one interpretive element or another, depending on the work or the subject under discussion.

As we explore Salazarist film, the key features of the New State, as well as its tensions and contradictions, begin to emerge. Cinema does not simply reproduce a set of values, but also brings to light the paradoxes of a government in which multiple agents—from the Church to the Armed Forces, from old Republicans to Integralists, etc.—are vying for their share of political influence.[47] The films highlight the absence of a unified, timeless New State ideology and reveal instead a bric-à-brac of doctrines and political practices amalgamated in order to produce a unified whole. Cinema was one of the means used by the regime to create an illusion of coherence and ideological harmony, but at the same time it also exposed, often inadvertently, the inconsistencies inherent in Salazarism.

Our interpretation of cinema during the New State oscillates between an appraisal of these movies as vehicles for the dissemination of an ensemble of ideas that we will call, for the sake of convenience, Salazarist "ideology", and a resistant reading of the filmography of this period. The latter presupposes that films, beyond being both aesthetic objects and products of an industry—with a commercial component and susceptible to greater or lesser political control—also function as repositories of a society's fictions, of its desires and expectations, and of its (often unconscious) fears. In this sense, we endorse Marc Ferro's position, according to which cinema allows for a "counter-analysis of society," based not only on the explicit content of each film but principally on what it hides, on its lapses or assumptions: "These lapses of a creator, of an ideology, or a society constitute privileged significant signs that can characterize any level of film, as well as its relationship with society."[48] Despite the fact that Ferro's interest in cinema is limited to its use as a historical document, his emphasis on lapses, on latent or avoided themes, can be transposed onto our analysis. Moving beyond history, including the history of ideas, this study highlights the mutual influences of cinema as art and industry, on the one hand,

and New State ideology, on the other. In this context, psychoanalysis provides us with a series of useful interpretative tools, which we complement with historical and discourse analysis, as well as with a detailed examination of the cinematographic object in itself, in order to paint a comprehensive portrait of Portuguese cinema as the staging of the New State regime.

The films discussed in this book include adaptations from novels and plays, like *Severa* (*A Severa*; Leitão de Barros, 1931), based on a play by Júlio Dantas, and *Spell of the Empire* (*Feitiço do Império*; António Lopes Ribeiro, 1940), whose plot draws inspiration from a homonymous novel by Joaquim Pereira Mota Júnior. We also analyze historical films, some of which were adapted from nineteenth-century novels, while others focus on the life of important figures in Portuguese culture or narrate decisive events in the country's history, like *Camões* (Leitão de Barros, 1946) and *Chaimite* (Jorge Brum do Canto, 1953). In addition, we interpret dramas, including *Wild Game* (*Gado Bravo*; António Lopes Ribeiro, 1934), *Fátima, Land of Faith* (*Fátima, Terra de Fé*; Jorge Brum do Canto, 1943), *Black Mantels* (*Capas Negras*; Armando de Miranda, 1947), or *Ribatejo* (Henrique Campos, 1949). Finally, we also look at fictionalized documentaries such as *Maria of the Sea* (*Maria do Mar*, 1930) and *Up and Away!* (*Ala-Arriba!* 1942), both directed by Leitão de Barros.

Although foreign cinema, in particular American cinema, always dominated the Portuguese market,[49] especially after the late 1940s when the crisis in national production became more pronounced, and although overtly propagandistic films enjoyed, as we have already mentioned, little success with the public, many of the films that we will analyze in the following pages were box office hits. A noteworthy example is *Severa*, the first Portuguese sound film, which ran for more than 6 months and was seen by an estimated 200,000 viewers. This success was repeated with *Black Mantels* and *Fado, the Story of a Songstress* (*Fado, História de uma Cantadeira*; Perdigão Queiroga, 1948), to mention only examples of movies about fado.

The popularity of many of these films led to a flourishing of the film industry in the first decades of the New State.[50] The genre that contributed the most towards this achievement was certainly the so-called Portuguese-style comedy (comédia à portuguesa), which had a brilliant start with *Song of Lisbon* (*A Canção de Lisboa*; Cottinelli Telmo, 1933). The comedy reached its climax, in terms of production, in the first half of the 1940s, afterwards rapidly declining, with *The Great Elias* (*O Grande Elias*; Arthur Duarte, 1950) as its swan song. Comedies privileged the parochial experience of Lisbon's *petite bourgeoisie*, which constituted the vast majority of Portuguese filmgoers. Employing actors who were already famous in theater, like Beatriz Costa and Vasco Santana, the movies centered on misunderstandings and mistaken or switched identities. Their plots, which captured the urban bourgeoisie's aspirations to wealth and social ascent, progressively became fixed in increasingly schematic and repetitive patterns. At times compared to the White Telephone films in Mussolini's Italy, the Portuguese comedies were an escapist cinema, in which the conflicts, in themselves superficial—unrequited love, a hoax laid bare, the impossibility of obtaining tickets to see a soccer match—dissolved to the beat of popular marches and were resolved by the marriage of the leading male and female characters. Avoiding references to either the political situation[51]—the apogee of this genre coincided with the Second World War—or the serious social problems that affected the country during this period,[52] the comedies forged the image of a poor but happy Portugal and of a Lisbon organized like a village, where a few meager trademarks of modernity (cabarets, automobiles, electricity, etc.) peacefully coexisted with a traditional, patriarchal, and hierarchical social structure.

In this book we do not undertake a detailed analysis of the Portuguese-style comedy as a genre, but instead include commentaries about some of these films in the various chapters. This decision is justified, on the one hand, by the existence of several studies that examine different aspects of this group of movies, such as Paulo Jorge Granja's essay "Portuguese-style Comedy or the Black-and-White Dream-Making Machine of the New State" ("A Comédia à Portuguesa ou a Máquina de Sonhos a Preto e Branco do Estado Novo"), in which the author shows how the comedies conveyed the conservative values of the New State. On the other hand, we opted for a thematic approach in the chapters that follow, choosing to organize the films according to the topics that we deem central to the filmography of the period, and incorporating, when relevant, an analysis of some of the comedies in the various sections of this study.

Chapter 1, "Propaganda in New State: *The May Revolution*," discusses the different meanings of the concept of propaganda in the New State through a detailed analysis of the regime's propagandistic efforts as exemplified in António Lopes Ribeiro's film *The May Revolution*. For Salazar, propaganda was, above all, meant to convey information and to disclose the truth. Conversely, António Ferro believed that works of propaganda should present an ideal version of reality, and that society should progressively seek to approximate this ideal. The chapter ends with a commentary on how the figure of Salazar is presented in

Lopes Ribeiro's film, which uses documentary images in order to promote the population's identification with their leader.

Chapter 2, "Poets on the Silver Screen: *Bocage*, *Camões* and the Heroes of the Regime," examines two films directed by Leitão de Barros, *Bocage* and *Camões*, which lend a cinematic voice to António Ferro's wish to promote historical cinema based on national literature. Both movies have poets as heroes and suggest that the New State was the climax of a series of glorious accomplishments and illustrious personalities that reach their apogee with Salazar. However, by presenting the protagonists' amorous fickleness as the cause of their misfortunes, these films may also be interpreted as an admonition to the too sentimental and often frivolous Portuguese public. The movies condemn the political inconsistency of the Portuguese and call for fidelity to Salazar's regime.

Chapter 3, "Rural Life in Cinema: In Defense of a Natural Society," analyzes the so-called "regional or folkloric films" that have rural Portugal as their background. These movies depict an idealized version of rural life, where social cohesion and solidarity enable the inhabitants of the countryside to overcome the difficulties created by nature. In contrast to the rectitude and the purity of rural life, the city emerges as an unhealthy environment, permeated by foreign habits, and as the source of immorality. The New State implicitly presents itself as a translation of the naturalness of rural life into political terms, and corporatism is shown to be the most natural way to organize society.

The centrality of Fátima for the Church during the New State is the topic of **Chapter 4**, "The Miracle of Salazarism: *Fátima, Land of Faith*." Brum do Canto's film focuses on the Faith/Reason dichotomy that has structured the debate about the miracles of Fátima since the First Republic. It ends with the film's protagonist, a famous doctor and professor at the University of Coimbra, concluding that religion is not incompatible with scientific reason. The doctor's conversion to Catholicism at the end of the movie prevents his fall into nihilism and signifies his reintegration into the traditional society of the New State. The film equates the miracle of this conversion with the political miracle of Salazarism and thus inscribes the regime in a teleological, religious history of Portugal.

Chapter 5, "Gender Stereotypes in New State Cinema," addresses the image of the woman in Salazarist film, focusing particularly on movies about fado singers. The New State reduced women to their roles as wives and mothers since, for Salazar, feminine independence and women working outside of the home endangered social stability. Films about female singers showed the reverse side of the official image of the submissive woman, in that female artists transgressed the norms imposed on the majority of Portuguese women. These singers paid for their violation of the prevailing codes of behavior with ostracism, exile, and even death at the end of the movies.

The last two chapters deal with the representation of the colonial empire in New State cinema. **Chapter 6**, "The Empire as Fetish: *Spell of the Empire*," shows how the Portuguese African colonies may be read, from a psychoanalytical perspective, as a fetish, since their territorial extension and economic relevance compensate for metropolitan Portugal's geopolitical insignificance. The protagonist of *Spell of the Empire*, a man of Portuguese descent who lives in the United States, becomes fascinated by Portuguese Africa. He learns to appreciate the country of his ancestors through its colonies, which are portrayed as the material embodiment of the Portuguese impetus to conquer and civilize.

The book closes with **Chapter 7**, "The Spirit of Empire in *Chaimite*," in which we examine Salazar's emphasis on the spirit as the bedrock of his political project and the implementation of this spirituality in the African colonial empire. Criticizing materialism, which brought the Western world to its decline, Salazar highlights spiritual values as the cornerstone of the regime. This spirituality is manifested overseas through the civilizing influence on and Christianization of the colonial regions. In *Chaimite*, a film directed by Jorge Brum do Canto, spiritual values confer upon the colonizers a moral superiority that distinguishes them from their enemies. The Portuguese moral supremacy helps them to win difficult battles and to defeat the African insurgents, adherents to a reprehensible materialism that does not allow them to appreciate the advantages of colonization.

Notes

1 In 1926 a military coup ended the Portuguese democratic First Republic (1910–26) and inaugurated a period of military dictatorship (1926–33). The Portuguese New State was the authoritarian regime that followed the military dictatorship. António de Oliveira Salazar was the founder of the New State and he served as prime minister of Portugal until 1968, when he was sidelined because of an illness and replaced by Marcelo Caetano. Caetano governed until the end of the New State with the 1974 Carnation Revolution, which paved the way to democracy. The

influence of Salazar's personal style of governing was so great in the New State that the thirty-five-year period during which he served as prime minister is often called Salazarism.

2 "J'ai pris goût à ce filme. Trop peut-être, car je n'ai pu dormir, ensuite. Ce matin-là, je n'ai pu travailler comme d'habitude. […] Je vous prie donc de ne plus me pousser à ce genre de distraction." Garnier, *Vacances avec Salazar*, 97. In this quote, Garnier does not refer explicitly to *The May Revolution*, merely mentioning "a Portuguese film" (97). João Bénard da Costa tells the same story in an interview with Maria do Carmo Piçarra, in which he identifies *The May Revolution* as the film that had troubled Salazar. Bénard da Costa heard the story from António Lopes Ribeiro, who told it to several other people. As a result, the case became known and interpreted as symptomatic of the relationship between Salazar and cinema. According to Bénard da Costa, Salazar told Ferro, when asked his opinion of the film: "I liked it a lot, a lot. But the film troubled me a lot and at night I couldn't sleep because I was thinking about it. Don't take me to see more of such things." ("Gostei muito, muito. Mas o filme perturbou-me muito e de noite não consegui dormir a pensar naquilo. Não me leve mais a ver coisas daquelas.") *Salazar vai ao Cinema II*, 130. I thank Maria do Carmo Piçarra for referring me to the source of this episode.

3 Christine Garnier collected a series of her interviews with Salazar and with some of his close associates, as well as her impressions about the statesman gathered during two stays in Portugal, in the book *Vacances avec Salazar*, published in France in 1952.

4 The change in name from SPN to SNI resulted from the transformations that took place in European politics toward the end of the Second World War, when the word "propaganda" fell out of favor. The Secretariat of the State for Information and Tourism (Secretaria de Estado da Informação e do Turismo, SEIT) replaced the SNI in 1968. We will refer to these institutions by their respective acronyms. When speaking of the actions of the regime's propaganda services from the 1930s to the 1940s in general, we will use the abbreviation SPN/SNI.

5 After António Ferro, the SNI knew a number of directors, including José Manuel da Costa, Eduardo Brazão, and César Moreira Baptista. The reason for António Ferro's removal from the SNI is unknown. Fernando Guedes mentions that the most common explanation for his replacement refers to health issues. However, the author questions this explanation and states that the reason is likely to have been the change in the international political situation after the defeat of Fascism in the Second World War (32). Heloísa Paulo points out that Ferro's departure from the SNI is frequently interpreted as a sign of the increasing distance separating the institution from the values of the regime (98). In a speech given during the inauguration of the exhibition "14 Years of Politics of the Spirit" ("14 Anos de

Política do Espírito") in 1948, Ferro himself lists some of the reasons why the activities of the SPN/SNI could not have a broader reach, including lack of trust in his policies and the misunderstanding with which some of his projects were received (*Política do Espírito, Apontamentos*, 18–20).

6 "[…] só existe o que o público sabe que existe." Salazar, "Propaganda Nacional," in *Discursos (1928–1934)*, 259–68.

7 Salazar, "Fins e Necessidade," in *Discursos e Notas Políticas (1938–1943)*, 196–9, 210. According to Salazar, the SPN/SNI is not an institution created to praise the government, but rather to show facts and educate the Portuguese: "[…] the Secretariat calls itself *of national propaganda*. Whoever understands well the meaning of this will grasp that it is not an institution to praise the government […]; will realize that the Secretariat is not an instrument of the Government but rather an instrument of governance in the highest meaning that the term may have." ("[…] o Secretariado denomina-se da *propaganda nacional*. Quem penetrar bem o seu significado, entenderá que não se trata duma repartição de elogio governativo […]; compreenderá que o Secretariado não é um instrumento do Governo mas um instrumento de governo no mais alto significado que a expressão pode ter.") "Propaganda Nacional," in *Discursos (1928–1934)*, 262.

8 In an article titled "Cinema and Dictatorships" ("O Cinema e as Ditaduras") and published in *Cinéfilo* magazine on 16 May 1936, J. Natividade Gaspar speaks to this issue: "The Portuguese dictatorship also seems willing to address the question of film with a focus that was absent in the preceding forms of government […]. We are therefore not far from recognizing the advantages of dictatorial regimes in the field of cinema." ("Em Portugal a ditadura parece também disposta a encarar a causa cinematográfica com uma atenção ausente nas precedentes formas de governo […]. Não estamos pois longe de reconhecer as vantagens dos regimes ditatoriais no campo do cinema.") Cited in Morais, "Vinte Anos de Cinema," in *Estado Novo*, 194. Cinema was already recognized both by totalitarian governments and by democracies as an effective means of propaganda at least since the First World War: "The cinema, by this time [1919], was manifestly *the* medium of the urban working masses and it was recognised as inherent in the medium that it operated over the way individuals perceived their own relationship to the world in which they live and its capacity to envision different worlds." (Pronay, "Introduction," in *Propaganda, Politics and Film*, 16.)

9 In Franco's Spain, cinematographic propaganda also meant primarily documentary films, especially after the creation of *Noticiarios y Documentales Cinematográficos* (NO-DO) as part of the Vice-Secretariat of Popular Education in 1942. These documentaries were the only ones that could be produced in Spain and were screened in all movie theaters.

10 For a detailed analysis of the *Portuguese Journal*, see Maria do Carmo Piçarra's study *Salazar vai ao Cinema. O Jornal Português de Actualidades Filmadas*.
11 In 1917, Ferro gave a talk tiled "The Great Tragic Actresses of the Silent Era" ("As Grandes Trágicas do Silêncio"), later published as a book, and in 1931, he published *Hollywood, Capital das Imagens*, a collection of essays about Hollywood and cinema.
12 "que tão larga influência exerce na renovação da alma dos povos e na projecção do seu carácter." Ferro, *Teatro e Cinema*, 61.
13 See Jorge Ramos do Ó's *Os Anos de Ferro: O Dispositivo Cultural durante a "Política do Espírito" 1933–1949. Ideologia, Instituições, Agentes e Práticas* for a description of the areas of intervention and the mechanisms of the "Politics of the Spirit" as developed by António Ferro.
14 "O cinema português, com efeito, tem, entre outras, duas grandes e nobres missões: uma alta missão educativa dentro do País (no sentido estético e no sentido moral) e uma difícil missão externa levando aos outros povos o conhecimento da nossa vida, do nosso carácter e do grau da nossa civilização." Ferro, *Teatro e Cinema*, 70–71.
15 Torgal, "Introdução," in *O Cinema sob o Olhar de Salazar*, 34–5.
16 Pina, *Documentarismo*, 12.
17 The Portuguese film company Tobis Klang Film was founded in June 1932 and António Ferro was selected as the head of the production committee. Its press release reads: "What moves us, more than any consideration of an industrial or commercial nature, is predominantly a patriotic thought: that of making possible a national art that in many aspects and in many ways can and should have a broad influence on the life and on the progress of the Nation." ("Move-nos muito mais do que quaisquer considerações de carácter industrial ou comercial um pensamento eminentemente patriótico: o de tornar possível uma arte nacional que em muitos aspectos e por muitos títulos pode e deve ter uma vasta influência na vida e no progresso da Nação.") Cited in Ribeiro, *Filmes, Figuras*, 292–3. João Bénard da Costa indicates that Tobis's creation was one of the results of a Commission created in 1930 and formed by Leitão de Barros, Lopes Ribeiro, and Chianca de Garcia, among others, to study the conditions for the creation of a studio for sound films in Portugal. In the Commission's final report from 1931, the filmmakers delineated the foundations for the development of the domestic film industry and even suggested the creation of a Film Archive. Bénard da Costa compares this report to the one produced by the generation of the 1960s and turned in to the Gulbenkian Foundation, a document that led to the creation of the Center for Portuguese Cinema (*Histórias*, 49).
18 "[…] proteger, coordenar e estimular a produção do cinema nacional […] tendo em atenção a sua função social e educativa, assim como os seus aspectos artístico

e cultural." The Law was complemented by Ordinance No. 37 369 and Decree No. 37 370, both from 11 April 1949, which specified the details of the National Cinema Fund's administration and financing (Ferro, *Teatro e Cinema*, 123–31).

19 The preamble of Ordinance No. 36 062, which preceded the already definitive Law 2 027, recognized "the importance of cinema in the life of modern nations, its power of insinuation over people's spirits, its influence as an educational medium, its power as an instrument of popular culture." ("a importância do cinema na vida dos povos modernos, o seu poder de insinuação nos espíritos, a sua influência como meio educativo, a sua força como instrumento de cultura popular"). Here, cinema is seen as a fundamental tool for influencing public opinion.

20 "É natural que este critério nos leve a proteger em princípio e por princípio, certos produtores e realizadores que se adaptem com mais compreensão ao nosso critério." Ferro, *Teatro e Cinema*, 70.

21 Ferro divides national cinematographic production into regional or folkloric films, historical films, crime films, films adapted from novels or plays, comedies, documentaries, films of a poetic nature, and films about daily life (*Teatro e Cinema*, 63–6). He points to Manuel de Oliveira's *Aniki-Bobó* as an example of a film of a poetic nature. Films about daily life were "[…] stories told naturally, as one writes well or paints well, without worrying about the great *moments*, but on the contrary made with everyday nothings […]." (" […] histórias contadas naturalmente, como se escreve bem ou se pinta bem, sem a preocupação dos grandes *momentos*, mas feitos pelo contrário, com os nadas de todos os dias […].") *Teatro e Cinema*, 66.

22 "o que ainda há de atrasado, de grosseiro na vida das nossas ruas." Ferro, *Teatro e Cinema*, 67–9.

23 "mau-gosto"; "soluções fáceis"; "saudável". Ferro, *Teatro e Cinema*, 65–6.

24 Ferro, *Teatro e Cinema*, 82.

25 In addition to the decline in domestic film production in the early 1950s, in 1956 experimental television emissions began at the Feira Popular. The growing popularity of television throughout the 1960s led to efforts to adapt cinema to this new reality (*Cinema Português*, 9).

26 Azevedo, *Perspectiva do Cinema Português*, 41–2.

27 "a produção cinematográfica foi partida em duas; uma que recorrerá ao fundo, orientada e fiscalizada pelo SNI; outra, sem nenhuma defesa nem possibilidades, independente mas condenada." Azevedo, *Perspectiva do Cinema Português*, 39. Azevedo's article is an editorial published on 1 February 1947 in response to Ordinance No. 36 062 of January 1947, which would give way to Law 2 027 of 1948.

28 For a list of the SNI/SEIT's cinematic awards, see the website *Novo Cinema Português (1949–80)*: http://ncinport.wordpress.com/2007/07/16/premios-de-cinema-premios-sni-1944-1953/

29 "As intenções *amplamente construtivas* dos nosso prémios são, portanto, facilmente compreensíveis. Para não serem classificadas como um problema de quebra-cabeças, bastará lembrarem-se os concorrentes de que o S.P.N. é um órgão da Presidência do Conselho e que o presidente do Conselho é Salazar. Quem não concordar com tais princípios—e com toda a acção que deles deriva—só tem um caminho a seguir: não concorrer aos nossos prémios." Ferro, *Política do Espírito e os Prémios*, 18–19.

30 Note that in some years, the SNI/SEIT prizes were not awarded, while in other years they were only awarded in certain categories.

31 The historical period that began at the start of the twentieth century has been called the "age of propaganda" (Pratkanis and Aronson, *Age of Propaganda*), and studies about propaganda abound, particularly after the 1930s. This phenomenon has been analyzed from a variety of perspectives, namely historical, sociological, and political—the academic disciplines that studied this topic the most—but also, more recently, from a psychological (Pratkanis and Aronson, *Age of Propaganda*), communicative (Jowett and O'Donnell, *Propaganda and Persuasion*), and philosophical (Cunningham, *Idea of Propaganda*) point of view.

32 Jowett and O'Donnell, *Propaganda and Persuasion*, 7.

33 The Congregation, whose objective was to "propagate" Catholicism, was preceded by a commission of Cardinals of the same name, created approximately forty years earlier by Pope Gregory XIII. In 1627, Pope Urban VIII established a seminary to educate the young "propagandists," the name attributed to the school's students who worked for the Congregation (Jackall, "Introduction," *Propaganda*, 1). The term "propaganda" soon started to be used in colloquial language to designate the Congregation and was employed during the following centuries to describe evangelization activities. This situation began to change throughout the nineteenth century. The term acquired the meaning that we attribute to it today during the First World War, when several countries involved in the conflict created propaganda mechanisms to ensure their populations' support of the war effort (Reeves, *Power of Film Propaganda*, 11).

34 "O Cinema Salazarista," in *História de Portugal*, 387.

35 The quote continues: "The works that most reflect the official ideology [...] date back to his [António Ferro's] time but [...] these were never the dominant products and it would be brash to see the expression of this ideology in those that were." ("Não encontramos no regime salazarista [...] uma política cultural monolítica que permita rever a arte desse período como o reflexo de um aparelho de propaganda. [...] Se datam do seu 'consulado' [de António Ferro] [...] as obras que mais reflectem a ideologia oficial [...] nunca foram esses os produtos dominantes e é ousado ver nos que o foram a expressão dessa ideologia.") Costa, *Histórias*, 37.

36 "regime político e social." The General Inspection of Entertainment was created by the same Ordinance that instituted the "Law of the 100 meters": Decree No. 13 564 from 6 May 1927.
37 Decree No. 13 564 prohibited the exhibition of films with scenes that contained mistreatment of women, human and animal torture, nudity, lewd dancing, surgeries, executions, brothels, murders, thefts that included tampering with or violation of the home from which the public could assess the means to commit the crime, and the glorification of crime through billboards or photography. In general, the films were not to be "pernicious to the education of the masses" ("perniciosas para a educação do povo"), incite them to crime, or be "detrimental to morality or the existing sociopolitical regime" ("atentatórias da moral e do regime político e social vigorantes").
38 "importância política e social." Decree No. 17 046-A
39 For detailed information about censorship in the New State, see Cândido de Azevedo's *A Censura de Salazar e Marcelo Caetano*. About censorship specifically within the context of cinema, see Lauro António's study, *Cinema e Censura em Portugal*.
40 See António, *Cinema e Censura*, 73–179.
41 Costa, *Breve História*, 109–10.
42 "ideologia indirecta ou contextual—no que respeita à temática [...], ao ambiente [...], à moral social [...]." Torgal, "Propaganda, Ideologia e Cinema," in *O Cinema sob o Olhar de Salazar*, 71. In another essay, when faced with the question of whether New State cinema was an "official cinema" or an "integrated cinema," Torgal responds: "Either way, the truth is that cinema during the New State tried to become part of the regime's basic or contextual ideology or, at the very least, did not wish to deny it." ("Seja como for, o certo é que o cinema no Estado Novo procurou integrar-se numa ideologia básica ou contextual de regime ou, pelo menos, desejou não a negar.") Torgal, *Estados Novos*, vol. 2, 214.
43 "Pelo que fez, pelo que mandou fazer e pelo que não deixou que se fizesse todo o cinema sonoro português *até muito depois de 1974* se confronta com o Salazarismo." Ramos, "Cinema Salazarista," in *História de Portugal*, 387.
44 "mesmo o cinema que melhor veicula o ideário do regime (já que o que procura combater [sic] é quase inexistente) não o faz [...] de um modo inflamado e directo [...]." Torgal, "Propaganda, Ideologia e Cinema," in *O Cinema sob o Olhar de Salazar*, 387–8.
45 Kracauer, *From Caligari to Hitler*, 275.
46 In the Portuguese context, Armindo José Baptista de Morais adopts a similar position: "For us, the possibility of identifying the terroristic violence of fascist discourse within the filmic document proper turns it into an essay about fascism

itself. The direct exercise of this violence, reproduced in a mystified language for the masses, instrumentalizing the syntactic and morphological code of cinema, makes the work produced a fascist one. [...] Collective daydreams, societies' daily mythology, these are social products, and before considering their influence and their effects we have to think that they themselves are effects, that they themselves are influenced." ("Para nós, a possibilidade de definir a violência terrorista do discurso fascista no próprio documento fílmico faz dele um ensaio sobre o próprio fascismo. O exercício directo dessa violência, reproduzido numa linguagem mistificadora sobre as massas, instrumentalizando o código sintáctico e morfológico do cinema, faz da obra produzida uma obra fascista. [...] Sonhos acordados colectivos, mitologia quotidiana das sociedades, eles são produtos sociais, e antes de se considerar a sua influência e os seus efeitos temos de pensar que eles próprios são efeitos, que eles próprios são influenciados.") "Vinte Anos de Cinema," in *Estado Novo*, 190.

47 Rui Ramos states in his *História de Portugal* that, early on in the New State, Salazar was forced to seek support from distinct sectors of Portuguese society in order to consolidate his power (634–8).

48 Ferro, *Cinema and History*, 30.

49 Refer to the statistics presented to this regard by Manuel de Azevedo (*Perspectiva do Cinema Português*, 92), given for 1949–50, and by Eduardo Geada (*Imperialismo*, 190) concerning the period between 1961 and 1975. *O Cinema Português e os seus Públicos*, edited by Manuel José Damásio, presents detailed information about the public of Portuguese cinema but it focuses on a more recent period.

50 A sign of revival of Portuguese cinema after the late 1920s was the boom in newspapers dedicated to film, like Avelino de Almeida's *Cinéfilo* (first series 1928–39), Chianca de Garcia's *Imagem* (1928–32), and Lopes Ribeiro's *Kino* (1930–1) (Costa, *Histórias*, 46). On the other hand, the number of movie theaters increased exponentially in this period, although they screened primarily foreign films.

51 In *Song of Lisbon* we find a brief political reference: Vasco (Vasco Santana) hides behind a coat with a sign that reads "Estado Novo" ("as new", but literally "new state"), in a clear reference to Salazar's government. Also in *The Courtyard of Ballads* (*O Pátio das Cantigas*; Francisco Ribeiro, 1942), released during the Second World War, there is a simulation of a bombing with the explosion of fireworks, and Narciso (Vasco Santana) hides with a group of children in a protected space where the inscription "barca Salazar" ("Salazar's boat") can be read. However, such references are rare, and even if the former could be interpreted as a veiled criticism of the regime, the latter is certainly understood as a praise of Salazar, who had avoided Portugal's entry into the War.

52 Jorge Leitão Ramos mentions an increase in mendicancy, growing infant mortality, low salaries, and prostitution as some of the social problems omitted from the comedies ("Cinema Salazarista," in *História de Portugal*, 389–90). Alves Costa states that apolitical cinema would function within the politics of the regime, aiming "to show the image and the ways that they would have us believe to be those of this good nation—poor but happy, sentimental and impulsive, with eight centuries of history and an empire (to be respected), resigned to and happy with its simplicity, its daily ration of birdseed, bullfighting, fado, and the sun over the Tagus." ("espelhar a imagem e os modos que se pretende fazer crer que são os deste bom povo—pobrete mas alegrete, sentimental e marialva, com oito séculos de história e um império (a respeitar), conformado e feliz com a sua simplicidade, a sua ração diária de alpista, a festa brava, o fado e o sol sobre o Tejo.") *Breve História*, 82–3.

1

Propaganda in the New State:
The May Revolution (A Revolução de Maio)[1]

Propaganda in Portuguese cinema

Salazar frequently described the New State as an apolitical regime. He blamed the excess of political activity during the First Republic for the socio-economic chaos that he encountered when he began to govern: "For many years in this country, politics killed administration: partisan fighting, revolutions, intrigues, […] power for power's sake have proved to be irreconcilable with the resolution of many national problems."[2] Salazarism responded to this impasse with a "politics *without politics*" or, even better, a "Government *without politics*" that "seemed like madness to many and was a blessing for all."[3] In many of his speeches, the statesman criticized the "democratic disorder"[4] motivated by the "absolute sterility of politics considered as an end in itself."[5] He asserted that any multi-party system would unavoidably include lies and mistakes, in so far as each party proclaims that its doctrines are true, but they cannot all be equally valid, given their disparate and sometimes contradictory assertions.[6] Salazar's negative verdict regarding the feasibility of democracy is based on a conception of truth as universal. The democratic system placed this notion in doubt through trivial disputes among political parties, and as a result led to the nation's decline.[7] According to Salazar, "politics"—a term that in his vocabulary was synonymous with democracy's vices—should therefore be replaced with an authoritarian regime grounded in immutable truths.

Salazar claimed that truth was the root of all his governmental decisions: "Like social life, politics and public administration should be based on truth: by temperament, by conviction, by an imposition of conscience, I advocate this way of directing and administering."[8] Salazar's administration was founded upon the belief that "political truths"[9] exist and are as real as scientific laws. The "politics of truth" that Salazar proposed contrasted with the "politics of lies and secrets" of the Republican government that preceded the New State.[10] For the head of government, truth was indisputable, just like other equally eternal values such as the Good or Beauty: "We believe that Truth, Justice, Beauty, and the Good exist; we believe that individuals and nations rise up through the worship of these values, they become noble, become dignified [...]."[11] These qualities, which resemble Platonic ideas in their metaphysical immateriality, are considered so evident that they do not require explications or justifications.

José Gil points out that Salazar developed a "rhetoric without rhetoric"[12] in his speeches, since the veracity of his statements should be so clear to the audience that any persuasive rhetorical device became unnecessary.[13] This discursive simplicity is not overlooked by French journalist Christine Garnier, who reports that "[t]he President, in fact, never endeavored to please the masses. Few words."[14] Thus, when Salazar identified God, Fatherland, Authority, Family and Work as the pillars of his government, he emphasized at the same time that these "great truths" should not be questioned.[15] Rather, Salazar's core values, with their indisputable legitimacy, became a panacea for the crisis that the country traversed—a situation that, in turn, could only be overcome through a limitless trust in these principles. Therefore, Salazar postulated the existence of an apodictic, eternal truth that he established as a measure of all political activity and social structures.[16] Respect for this truth would lead to the Good or, in other words, to a stable and prosperous society.

Although he emphasized that truth is obvious, Salazar admitted that its clarity may be muddled by misrepresentations or abusive interpretations. He considered it the duty of any political regime to inform and guide the public down the path of truth. Within the New State, this task fell to propaganda:

> Some, still, consider propaganda as a subtle instrument that, gathering all of the contributions of science and art [...] changes colors, disfigures the facts [...] *creates a truth*, so clear, so incisive, so evident that everyone will judge it as genuine. [...] this is not what propaganda means to us. / What is it, then? Whenever I spoke of this subject I always linked propaganda to the political education of the Portuguese people, and I assigned it two functions: first information, then political education.[17]

Salazar rejected the notion that propaganda produces a tendentious version of events, and instead he deemed it to be a means of information and political education.[18] As he said in a speech given during the inauguration ceremony of the Secretariat of National Propaganda (SPN), political realities do not correspond to facts, but to the information that the public has access to: "In truth, however, *as far as politics is concerned*, all that *appears to exist*, actually exists. I mean to say, lies, fictions, fears, even if they are not justified, create spiritual states that are *political realities*: we must govern based upon these, with them, and against them."[19] An imbalance between reality and the perception that society has of it sometimes arises, and the role of propaganda is to bridge this gap in order to disseminate the truth. Salazar was careful to distinguish his version of propaganda from the propaganda practices of other totalitarian states of the 1930s, underscoring the need to "disregard identical services in other countries," and to avoid "the exalted nationalisms that dominate them"—probably referring here to the propaganda services of Mussolini's Italy and Nazi Germany.[20] This is consistent with his definition of propaganda as the transmission of the truth, which, since it is evident, does not need artful embellishments.

In the already mentioned speech given for the inauguration of the SPN, Salazar stated that the Institution's main goal would be combatting "error, lies, slander or simple ignorance, from within or abroad" under the banner of truth and justice.[21] Even though a part of Portuguese propaganda was geared towards improving the image of Salazarism abroad via the translation of works about the government's politics, the participation in international exhibitions, and the dissemination of images that highlighted the country's natural beauty or historical sites, the majority of the SPN's resources were channeled to internal matters.[22] Some of its functions included control of the press and coordination of censorship services, organization of pro-government demonstrations, and financing of artistic projects. Cinema also fell within the scope of the SPN's intervention, and the institution financed numerous documentary shorts.[23] It also gave subsidies for the production of feature-length films, the majority of which focused on topics related to national history and popular culture.

The film *The May Revolution* (*A Revolução de Maio*, 1937) was the only fictional feature-length film produced entirely by the SPN. This movie was created to celebrate the tenth anniversary of the 28 May 1926 Revolution that later led to the creation of the New State. It was directed by António Lopes Ribeiro,[24] one of the personalities in cinema at the time who most openly supported the ideology of the New State, for which he received the epithet of "Salazarism's official filmmaker."[25] Lopes Ribeiro was also responsible for various other films with a propagandistic slant, such as the fictional feature-length *Spell of the Empire* (*Feitiço do Império*, 1940), which we will analyze later, and documentaries about landmark events for the regime, such as presidential

Figure 1.1 Advertisement poster for *The May Revolution*

trips to the colonies, the bicentennial celebrations of 1940, and the inauguration of the National Stadium in 1944.[26]

The plot of *The May Revolution* openly discusses a political topic, namely the threat that communism posed to Salazar's regime. It is virtually the only example of an explicitly political fiction film during the first decades of the

New State. Furthermore, the movie stands out for its inclusion of documentary footage in the fictional plot, a technique that Lopes Ribeiro also used in *Spell of the Empire*. *The May Revolution* translates Salazar's notion that the values of the regime were necessarily good and just into cinematographic language, deploying propaganda to inform the public about the truths underlying New State ideology. However, the film also shows that there was not always a peaceful coexistence of differing ideas about propaganda and truth within the regime.

The May Revolution seeks to establish an affective bond between Salazar and the people through the juxtaposition of fictional images with documentary sequences of the statesman being applauded by the multitude, thereby diluting the border between real events and the plot. The goal of this fusion of documentary and fiction is to transform reality itself, using the persuasive power of art to reshape the boundaries of the real. Propaganda is then no longer a mere reproduction of facts, as Salazar intended, since it becomes a method of influencing and even reconfiguring actuality.

Art's role as an ideal model of socio-political reality was the subject of a thesis defended by António Ferro. A modernist intellectual and the director of the SPN from its creation until 1949, Ferro collaborated with Lopes Ribeiro as co-author of the film's screenplay.[27] For Ferro, the existence of a close relationship between the leader and the people was vital for the regime, and art, especially cinema, was the most efficient way to promote this link. Propaganda films like *The May Revolution* should not simply show eternal truths, but rather create their own truths, making it the Portuguese people's responsibility to put this artistic blueprint into practice in their daily lives.

Salazar's truth as ideology

The cinema of the New State systematically employed the *topos* of "conversion" in its attempt to win over the viewers' support for the regime's politics, as the historian Luís Reis Torgal emphasizes in his article about Salazarist cinematographic propaganda.[28] The narrative of *The May Revolution* is no exception to the rule, in that it follows the transformation of the protagonist, César Valente (António Martinez), from a supporter of communism to a staunch believer in Salazarism. Several factors contribute to this transformation, among them his romantic involvement with a young girl, Maria (Maria Clara), whose father died while defending the regime. Yet, the main cause of the protagonist's "conversion" lies in his discovery that the country progressed considerably during the years he was away from Portugal, which coincided with the first decade of the New State.

One of the first steps toward César's transformation occurs when he visits the National Institute of Statistics. The sequence begins with a medium-long shot, filmed from a slightly high angle, in which the protagonist is alone in the middle of an enormous plaza facing a majestic staircase, surrounded by newly constructed buildings. The magnificence of the architecture symbolizes the New State's power and stability, while the insignificance of the main character reveals the futility of any attempt to alter the existing political system, a topic that permeates the entire film. Once inside the Institute, César goes through statistical data about the country's current state and realizes that all areas of activity have gone through a period of enormous progress, from the increase in exports and the elimination of foreign debt to the generalized assistance for impoverished mothers and children. The film alternates between statistical data and a

Figure 1.2 César (António Martinez) contemplates the architecture of the New State in *The May Revolution*

conversation of two men sitting in a café who both criticize Salazar's politics. Each piece of criticism is followed by statistical information that contradicts it in order to highlight the untruthfulness of the comments. This scene illustrates Salazar's idea that the SPN "should strictly limit itself to the facts and preferably use images and numbers as the most striking, most eloquent expressions of the facts of public life."[29] Numbers are shown here to speak for themselves because the truth is transparent and accessible to all. Therefore, any man of good will, like César, will inevitably convert to the principles of the New State upon hearing the truth.[30] As Jorge Leitão Ramos points out, the obviousness of the truth is a fundamental feature of the film,[31] unfolding through statistical evidence (the data from the Institute), material evidence (the country's prosperity), and ideological evidence—the manifest disadvantages of communism when compared to the ideology of the New State.

The May Revolution was shot during the period of the Spanish Civil War, an era when communism was a palpable threat to the regime. In his speeches at the time, Salazar frequently referred to leftist ideas as pernicious doctrines that infiltrate and poison society.[32] In contrast to the indisputable truths of the New State's ideology, communism was regarded as a "great lie"[33] that was incompatible with the spirituality of Western civilization.[34] Therefore, it had to be fought, and Lopes Ribeiro's movie functions as a denunciation of communist falsehood.[35] In the film, the protagonist's initial plan is to overthrow Salazar's government in order to establish communism in Portugal, aided by, among others, a Russian comrade, Dimoff (Eliezer Kamenesky), so as to suggest a conspiracy linked to the Soviet Union. As the plot unfolds, the advantages of the current regime become clearer, leading César to surrender to the virtues of the New State in a sequence of exacerbated nationalism, in which he salutes the national flag instead of hoisting the red flag of communism. On the morning of 28 May 1936—ten years after the military *coup* that led to the institutionalization of Salazarism—the protagonist completes his metamorphosis, under the surveillance of benevolent political police officers who, instead of arresting him, give him a chance to repent for his errors.[36] César surrenders to the evidence of the great truths of Salazarism and becomes a new man, thus exemplifying Salazar's belief that the truth is obvious and easily identified by all good Portuguese men and women.

César's initial mistake, corrected in the last moments of the film, was that of trying to participate in politics, questioning the "truth" of the regime and suggesting that other alternative "truths," such as communism, could be

Figure 1.3 Conspiracy against the New State in *The May Revolution*

introduced into the country. Salazar himself recognized that the national renewal he proposed to carry out required the suppression of "purely political activities," including the freedom of the press, freedom of association and freedom of assembly,[37] and claimed that "true freedom [...] can only exist in the spirit of Men."[38] In Lopes Ribeiro's film, these forbidden political activities emerge in the form of clandestine meetings in scarcely illuminated, sinister basements, during which a group of revolutionaries plan their *coup* to overthrow the regime.

The film also shows the Portuguese attachment to what Salazar called the "hatreds," "battles," and "particularisms" that lead to "intellectual and moral anarchy" in which "everything is slippery and arbitrary" through idle coffeehouse conversations where government decisions are criticized, without any grounds.[39] In contrast to this nefarious multiplicity of political discussions, Salazar aimed for a government that would be purely administrative, without politics. The country would thus operate as "a big family or a big business" that requires "for the defense of its common interests and in order to achieve its common goals, a coordinating head, a center of life and of action."[40] According to Salazar, those who "prefer their freedom of action to obedience or those who opt for the indications of their intelligence over expertly designed directives," like César at the beginning of the film, "are not with us."[41] The abolition of politics in favor of administration requires a blind obedience to the leader, an authority figure that incarnates the unquestionable truths of the state. Opinions that differ from the leader's cannot be tolerated, not just because they weaken his administration with petty, vain politics, but, more importantly, because they are necessarily wrong in that they move away from the eternal, evident truth that underpins the New State.

Salazar's conception of truth encapsulates a paradox that was exacerbated by works of propaganda such as *The May Revolution*. If the truth of the regime's principles was evident, it should have resisted all the lies and slander that the opposition produced in order to denigrate it. The need for propaganda shows that Salazar's version of the truth was far from hegemonic, and testifies to the power of different takes on reality. The government's propaganda efforts obliquely reveal the regime's instability and prove that many Portuguese were reluctant to convert to the virtues of Salazarism. The presentation of the foundational values of the New State as universally true and indisputable was just another propaganda trick, an ideological construction aimed at persuading public opinion that there were no alternatives to the *status quo*.

The primacy of art: António Ferro's politics of the spirit

According to Salazar, the relevance of films such as *The May Revolution* lies in their presentation of the regime's political program as the only possible truth. For Salazar, any artistic creation, especially propaganda, has a didactic function. The statesman condemned the notion of "art for art's sake" and adopted the Platonic idea that artworks do not possess an intrinsic value; they should merely serve as vehicles for the education of the people.[42] António Ferro had a distinct view of the purpose of art, which also comes through in Lopes Ribeiro's film. Ferro was the architect of the so-called "politics of the spirit"[43] that, inspired by the model of Italian fascism, valued art and stressed its significance as a measure of a country's greatness:

> Men of action, leaders, rulers that despise or overlook the fine arts and literature, assigning to them a purely decorative function, a superfluous role, reducing them to a sort of accessory of social life, are wrong. The premeditated, conscious development of Art and Literature is as necessary, in the end, to the

progress of a nation as the development of its sciences, its public works, its industry, its commerce, and its agriculture.[44]

The president of the SPN claimed that art is a concrete fact that needs to be taken into account as a political reality. Ferro considered the politics of the spirit to be essential for the project of national regeneration that the New State sought to implement, and he saw art not as the transitory manifestation of an external truth that resides in the political or social domains, but as the motor of national progress. The centrality of artistic creation for Ferro led António Pedro Pita to compare his position to that of artists like Oscar Wilde, for whom the work of art is truer than existence itself, a notion with roots in the Romantic conceptualization of art and of the artist that extends to Modernism.[45] Ferro recognized that "lying is the artist's only truth,"[46] but he believed that art's potential resided precisely in its infidelity to the facts, in its ability to lie and conjure up a different reality.[47] Artistic creations thereby offer a set of possibilities that should serve as an inspiration and a guide for the regime's politics, given that fiction is, to some extent, more truthful than the prosaic truth of the real. In other words, it is life that should imitate art and not vice versa.

One can conclude from the essay "The Great Tragic Actresses of the Silent Era" ("As Grandes Trágicas do Silêncio"), a version of a conference given by Ferro in 1917, that, for the author, cinema is the highest form of art, since it completely recreates reality: "The Art of the artists on the screen is the true Art because it differs absolutely from Life."[48] The relevance of art for any political project lies in its difference from the real, not in the correspondence between the two. Although he moderated his radical opinions when he took office as the president of the SPN, Ferro did not abandon his belief in art's power to shape social reality. According to this perspective, the purpose of propaganda films like *The May Revolution* is not so much to help the public recognize the veracity of the principles that define the New State as it is to serve as guides indicating a path yet to be trodden. The politics of Salazarism is then not the expression of an eternal truth. Rather, it becomes truer the more it conforms to the paradigm outlined by propagandistic art, which acts as a mediator between the society idealized by the New State and Portuguese reality.

In *The May Revolution* the mediation between art and reality is accomplished by resorting to documentary footage, which is skillfully introduced in the fictional plot of the film to illustrate the population's enthusiastic adherence to the regime. César's trip to the north of the country, where he will receive the necessary arms for the *coup d'état* that will pave the way for a Communist revolution, coincides with the 1 May celebrations. The fictional narrative of the protagonist's travels is crosscut with documentary images of a pro-Salazar parade. The exuberant decorations of the celebrations and the liveliness of the participants contrast with the somber state of mind of the main character and his companions. In the final moments of the film, documentary sequences are introduced once more, this time related to the celebration of the tenth anniversary of the 1926 Revolution. First, we see a commemoration in Braga, where the crowd happily salutes Salazar and President Carmona. Later, César, who had by then become a defender of Salazarism, participates in a demonstration in Lisbon in favor of the regime with his girlfriend, Maria. The film ends with more documentary footage of the commemoration in the capital, which culminates in a nationalistic speech given by Salazar. A part of the speech is heard off-screen while the movie focuses on the enthusiasm of the crowd. The film thus emphasizes the omnipresence of Salazar, who continues to dominate Portuguese society even when he is invisible.[49]

The numerous documentary images showing the people's praise of the leaders of the New State in *The May Revolution* may be seen as a representation of external reality. Alternatively, we could interpret these images as a fictional manifestation of support that the viewers should imitate: just as the masses salute Salazar in the film, so too they should behave in reality. This last hypothesis depends on the assumption that, once confronted with a propaganda film showing pro-government demonstrations, even the most reluctant Portuguese citizens will surrender to the New State, convinced of the benefits of Salazar's government. The belief in the possibility of a transfer of ideas from cinema to practical politics presupposes António Ferro's thesis that life imitates art. The film shows how reality should be, leaving it to the public to try to reach this ideal.

Documentary footage forms a bridge between fact and fiction, and in this process it undergoes a double inversion. The documentary scenes, a version of real events, are first fictionalized through their inclusion in the filmic narrative, and then reintroduced into the world by the power of art, in order to be disseminated in society. The result of this mutation is a transfiguration of reality itself, which should adapt to the model put forth by the movie.

The role of documentary footage in *The May Revolution* is similar to the one played by documentary images in propaganda films produced by other totalitarian states. In his essay on "Propaganda and the Nazi War Film," Siegfried

Figure 1.4 Documentary footage in *The May Revolution*

Kracauer stresses that many of the German fictional propaganda works from the 1930s and 1940s included documentary footage in scenes where fictional material would have been aesthetically more efficient. Kracauer argues that this technique was part of the effort to distort the real that characterizes propagandistic art. If the Nazis merely sought to substitute existing reality with one fabricated by them, it would have been easier to resort to fictional images and superimpose them over actuality. However, this would not have destroyed the real but would have merely banished it, allowing it to persist in the subconscious of the people. Instead, Nazi propaganda used reality, in the form of the documentary, to distort the real, so as to create a new pseudo-facticity of totalitarianism: "Reality was put to work faking itself, and exhausted minds were not even permitted to dream any longer."[50] The documentary images assimilated into fictional films contributed in this way to a modification of reality that made the artificial ideology of Nazism more concrete. The process described by Kracauer corresponds to the technique used in *The May Revolution*. The sequences with documentary footage confer verisimilitude to the film and to the representation of the New State created by it, an image that the citizens should transpose to real life.

According to Kracauer, the desire to emphasize the virtues of Nazi society through cinema often resulted in an exaggeration that laid bare the mechanisms for distorting reality employed by propaganda. On the one hand, the films overstressed German superiority, which could have led the public to doubt the universality of this dogma. On the other hand, the documentary images at times undermined the propagandistic objectives of Nazi cinema, given that the distortion imposed on the documentary scenes became obvious.[51] In *The May Revolution*, the abundance of documentary footage that depicts the masses saluting Salazar could lead the less gullible viewers to question this emphasis and to see the excessive use of this type of sequences as a way to hide the lack of public support for the politics of the New State. Similarly, the disproportionate benevolence of the political police in the film aims to cover up their violent practices.[52] In addition, César's "conversion" to the government ideology suggests that there were many other nonbelievers who might have never become proselytes. As Kracauer indicates, propaganda films risk failure since the public can recognize a regime's flaws precisely in the propagandistic efforts to represent a given political system in a positive light.

The staging of the leader

In *The May Revolution*, one of the goals of repeating documentary footage that shows Salazar smiling and waving to the crowd was to forge a positive image of the head of government, so that the public would identify with the statesman. The relevance of a close connection between a political leader and the people was emphasized by António Ferro in his article "The Dictator and the Crowd" ("O Ditador e a Multidão"), published in 1933 along with a series of his interviews with Salazar.[53] This text stresses that the efficiency of the state and the adaptation of its laws to the country's situation should be complemented by an intimate relationship between the leader and the population, in order to foster the support of the masses for the dictator's political decisions:

> What should the dictator do, then, so as […] not to become a victim of ingratitude on the part of those that he served, those that he saved? Just this: constantly hammer his ideas, strip them of their rigidity, give them life and warmth, communicate them to the multitude. The dictator should speak to the people, and the people should speak to him. The dictator and the people should merge in such a way that the people feel like they are the dictator and the dictator feels like he is the people.[54]

Ferro outlines here the key principles of a populist government: a relationship without intermediaries between the political leader and the masses; the enunciation of government decisions as decisions *for* the people or, in other words, decisions made in order to safeguard the population's interests; and the creation of a strong emotional link between the masses and the leader, which translates into the warm acclaim of the latter as the unquestionable head of the nation. But the success of a dictatorship does not depend only on the crowd's enthusiastic empathy for its leader. That which unites the dictator to the people is more profound and part of the ontology of these two categories. In other words, the dictator should *feel* like he is part of the people, and more importantly, the people should *feel* like they are the dictator, which will only happen if the dictator *becomes* the people and the people *become* dictator, albeit only transiently. According to Ferro, one of the goals of propaganda is precisely to create the illusion of a congenital link between the dictator and the masses, so that the people accept his authority, which is presented as natural and even desirable. This leads the population to feel (or to be) the dictator, and, in this way, identify with his decisions and accept them as their own.

The president of the SPN/SNI continues, in the same text, to describe the building blocks of his propagandistic program:

> Faith is not darkness, but light. [...] The forcible, but necessary, suppression of certain liberties, of certain human rights, has to be filtered through happiness, enthusiasm, faith. [...] If the leader's character is averse to certain contacts, if it is preferable perhaps not to contradict his character so as to not break its fertile integrity, someone or some people should undertake the task of looking after the necessary staging of celebrations of the ideal, those encounters, so necessary in dictatorships, between the crowd and those who govern ...[55]

Ferro notes that some leaders—and here he certainly has Salazar in mind—are averse to contact with the masses. In fact, Salazar, unlike politicians such as Hitler or Mussolini, always cultivated a modest public persona, presenting himself as a near recluse who kept a minimal amount of social contacts, and stressing that he did not have a talent for speaking in public.[56] The separation between the head of the government and the rest of the Portuguese people was accentuated by his professional training as a university professor in an era when a large segment of the population was illiterate, a disconnect that would earn his government the nickname "dictatorship of doctors."[57] Salazar frequently mentioned the divide between him and the rest of his compatriots, and he stressed that he was forced to bear the "cross" of public service and sacrifice his personal life for the good of the state because of his complete commitment to his country.[58] The image of the distant leader, a martyr who renounced the interests of everyday life in order to take the reins of power and whose providential intervention in state matters allowed the rest of the Portuguese to lead tranquil lives without worrying about politics, was therefore cultivated by Salazar himself.[59] In the excerpt reproduced above, Ferro recognizes that the dictator's isolation and his avoidance of contact with the masses creates an aura of intellectual rectitude and moral respectability—of "fertile integrity," in his words—leading the people to view Salazar as untouchable, a public figure that is beyond both individual scrutiny and political scandals. Nevertheless, the director of the SPN finds it necessary to look after what he calls the "staging" of the dictatorship, leaving it to "someone"—to Ferro himself, in this case—to carry out the "celebrations of the ideal," a project that he will concretize through the various activities of the Secretariat of Propaganda, including the film *The May Revolution*.

In the passage cited above, Ferro recognizes that the violence, either physical or discursive (political arrests, censorship, etc.), inherent to a totalitarian regime will only be accepted by the population if it has "faith" in its leader.[60] The obvious use of religious vocabulary here is very appropriate, given that Salazar is someone whom the masses should admire from a distance, but, at the same time, is a figure with whom they should identify. This relationship evokes the manner in which the faithful are encouraged in Catholicism to identify with Christ and to imitate him in their lives. In order to encourage the people to have faith in their leader and to consider him a source of illumination, a dictator would have to multiply his contacts with the masses through parades, speeches, or official visits to several regions and institutions in his country.[61] Yet, this intimacy between the dictator and the people becomes particularly difficult to achieve due to Salazar's aversion to contact with the public. In these circumstances, cinema is a particularly effective instrument to promote the "staging" of the regime, since it makes possible the diffusion of the image of the dictator on a large scale, without him having to actually appear in front of crowds more than on a few rare occasions.

The use of documentary cinema as a way of stimulating the people's quasi-religious adherence to their leader and to the policies of the regime, as well as of underlining the dictator's omnipresence in society, was something that New State propaganda shared with its counterparts in authoritarian Italy, Germany, and Spain. It suffices to think about the title of the first documentary directed by Leni Riefenstahl, *Victory of the Faith* (*Der Sieg des Glaubens*, 1933), a movie that depicts the fifth congress of the Nazi party and is a precursor to the more famous *Triumph of the Will* (*Triumph des Willens*), completed two years later. The documentary images of Salazar in *The May Revolution* are in line with cinematographic practices of the time and correspond to Ferro's efforts to bring the Portuguese population closer to the head of government in order to foster the nation's identification with its leader.

The psychological process of identification with a leader and the concurrent imitation that occurs among equals when they submit to the power of the same authority figure were analyzed by Freud at the beginning of the twentieth century in his studies of group psychology, especially in *Group Psychology and the Analysis of the Ego* (1921). In this work, Freud dissects the phenomenon of identification of group members with their leader since he considers this to be an essential tool for understanding the nature of any human grouping. Identification is a libidinal or affective relationship through which the individual abandons his super-ego and substitutes it with the *group ideal*, represented by

Figure 1.5 Documentary footage of Salazar and President Óscar Carmona in *The May Revolution*

the figure of the leader.[62] The "celebrations of the *ideal*" that António Ferro wished to create in order to encourage the people to embrace the dictatorship can be understood in light of psychoanalysis, to the extent that what is achieved in these commemorations is precisely the celebration of the leader *as an ideal* with whom the people should identify.

According to Freud, the result of identification with the leader is a regression in the mental activity of the group members to earlier phases of the psychic evolution of human beings. This regression is characterized both by an inability to moderate emotions and by a decrease in critical thinking. The mechanism of "regression" that Freud describes is later identified by Kracauer as one of the reactions that the films of the Third Reich sought to encourage:

> Rather than suggesting through information, Nazi propaganda withheld information or degraded it to a further means of propagandistic suggestion. This propaganda aimed at psychological retrogression to manipulate people at will. Hence the comparative abundance of tricks and devices.[63]

The psychological regression and the manipulation that Kracauer mentions coincide with Ferro's definition of the purpose of propaganda in the New State: to generate enthusiasm for the political leader, that is, to strengthen the emotional bonds that link the people to the dictator, while simultaneously diminishing the critical capacity of each person, so that the masses accept the limitations imposed on them by an authoritarian regime. Films that, like *The May Revolution*, contain explicit references to the population's admiration of Salazar, sought to stimulate the identification of the Portuguese viewers with their leader, so that they would unconditionally support the regime.

Freud establishes an analogy between the libidinal bonds that link a leader to his group and the relationship between what he calls the "primordial father" and the "brothers," or members of the group, a configuration that the psychoanalyst mentions in his book about group psychology but that he had already studied in greater detail in his 1913 work *Totem and Taboo*. A parallel reading of these two Freudian texts points to a problem that arises when we try to use the psychoanalytic theory of group relations to understand the mechanisms of modern propaganda. In *Totem and Taboo*, Freud postulates that the beginning of what we call "civilization" and all modern political organization dates back to an initial trauma, the moment when a group of brothers—an imaginary prototype of all later societies—killed their father, driven by the desire to take his place. No authoritarian regime intends for the identification of its acolytes with the figure of the dictator to degenerate into a feeling of hatred towards him, which would drive the members of the community to literally or figuratively kill their leader. Theodor Adorno attempts to resolve this apparent contradiction between Freudian psychoanalysis and the propaganda of totalitarian regimes in an essay in which he discusses the mechanisms of Nazi propaganda. According to Adorno, modern dictators, unlike the ancient kings, present themselves as simple men in order to distance themselves from the Freudian "primordial father"—a technique used by many political leaders even in democracies:

> Accordingly, one of the basic devices of personalized fascist propaganda is the concept of the "great little man," a person who suggests both omnipotence and the idea that he is just one of the folks [...]. The leader image gratifies the follower's twofold wish to submit to authority and to be the authority himself.[64]

Presenting himself as a "great little man," an "everyman" who finds himself, almost accidentally, in a position to govern, the dictator manages to have the people identify with him in their desire to also be a leader. At the same time, he avoids a situation in which the masses develop antagonistic feelings towards him due to his exercise of power. In the case of the New State, Salazar highlighted the distance that separated him from the rest of the Portuguese, but at the same time he sought to present himself as a common man: a simple professor from Coimbra who rose to power against his will and who viewed his political tasks as a burdensome duty that he must fulfill for the good of the country. Salazar also emphasized his humble origins on several occasions, suggesting that his family background allowed him to govern in harmony with the interests of the majority of the people. He claimed that the Portuguese nation saw him as one of its own, instinctively adhering to the politics of the New State.[65] In other words, the population identified with the head of the government, despite the distance that separated it from him, since Salazar was not a professional politician but rather a simple man who, due to his merits, rose to a position of power almost by chance.

The representation of Salazar in *The May Revolution* is consistent with this notion of the "great little man." At times, his only presence is his voice, a way of portraying him as a distant figure who is averse to popular manifestations, but who remains ubiquitous in Portuguese society. On other occasions the statesman is shown to be close to the people, who euphorically applaud him, in order to demonstrate that he is in harmony with the population. He appears in parades, driving along in a car and greeting the crowds nearby, and he always uses simple phrases and expressions, avoiding stylistic flourishes. The film blurs the contradictions of a paradoxical model of authority—strong and simultaneously benevolent—by establishing a balance between Salazar's power and the desire of the Portuguese to identify with him. It strives to create a libidinal bond with the leader, so that people would accept the values of Salazarism without questioning them. In short, Lopes Ribeiro's movie encourages viewers to feel that they are like the dictator, so that they gladly accept the limits imposed on them by an authoritarian government.

The propaganda cinema of the New State glorifies not only Salazar but also other representatives of power. These function as substitutes for the head of government through a subtle manipulation of the viewers, who are led to surrender and, more insidiously, to want to surrender to the power of the authorities. Several films from this period focus on Salazar's surrogates: authority figures who form part of the regime's central institutions, such as the Police, the Catholic Church, and the Army. Members of the police force appear in *The May Revolution* and also in several comedies from the 1930s and 1940s as firm but courteous characters that maintain public order and guarantee respect for the law.[66] Similarly, the Church and the Army, institutions identified by Freud as paradigmatic examples of groups that organize themselves around a leader, appear in films like *Fátima, Land of Faith* (*Fátima, Terra de Fé*, 1943) and *Chaimite* (1953), both directed by Jorge Brum do Canto, as vehicles for spreading the ideology of the New State through their representatives, as we will see in the following chapters.[67] Priests, lieutenants, and generals operate as replacements for Salazar, and they play a role of leadership similar to that of the statesman, either on the spiritual or on the military level. Just like Salazar, the representatives of the Police, the Church, and the Army exercise a diffuse authority in the films. They avoid open demonstrations of power and prefer to present themselves as guides, counselors, or mere observers, so as to establish a close and cordial relationship with their subordinates.

The May Revolution illustrates the coexistence of two distinct visions of the function and objectives of propaganda in the New State, which reflect opposing conceptions of art. On the one hand, the work adheres to Salazar's notion that the truth is obvious. This would mean that propagandistic art should inform and educate the population by disseminating this truth, which coincides with the principles guiding the New State. Thus, the film didactically presents the various benefits brought about by the regime in such a way that the public surrenders to the evidence of the advantages of Salazar's administration. On the other hand, the film adopts the concept of art espoused by António Ferro, according to which works of art are truer than the real world in that they engender a model to be imitated by concrete existence. The great pro-government demonstrations in the movie and the crowd's enthusiastic salutes of Salazar form an artistic ideal that the Portuguese should emulate. The emphasis on facts and numbers that Salazar identifies as the best method of persuasion is substituted, in the version of propaganda that Ferro puts forth, by the manipulation of the unconscious, which, in Lopes Ribeiro's film, is deployed to foster the people's irrational identification with their leader.

The divergences that separate Salazar's concept of propaganda from the notion that Ferro proposes correspond *grosso modo* to the distinction between rational and irrational propaganda, as well as between integration and agitation propaganda, as outlined by Jacques Ellul in his groundbreaking study of propagandistic techniques. Ellul points out that propaganda, beyond appealing to the unconscious, frequently resorts to facts and numerical data that are distorted but retain an appearance of scientific truth in order to demonstrate the superiority of any given system. Furthermore, Ellul stresses that, while many works of propaganda aim for the enthusiastic agitation of the people, their emotional involvement, and their explicit support for an idea, in other cases the goal of propaganda is to achieve silent conformism, stability, social cohesion, and the population's tacit consent of current politics. In the scheme defined by Ellul, Salazar would thus prefer a rational propaganda of integration, while Ferro would opt for an irrational propaganda of agitation. Ellul does not take these categories as gradations in a typology of propaganda genres that would be more or less manipulative and insidious. Rather, these categorizations merely describe diverse techniques—techniques that, as we have seen in *The May Revolution,* are often mutually compatible—employed to manipulate the public's perception of reality, while seeking to reach the broadest possible audience.

Propaganda as understood by Salazar, a conservative Catholic eager to highlight the originality of the Portuguese regime in comparison with other European authoritarian governments, was radically different from the definition of propaganda espoused by António Ferro, a cosmopolitan, *avant-garde* intellectual and unconditional admirer of Mussolini. Both visions of propaganda worked as complementary forms of persuading the Portuguese to comply with the New State that were directed at distinct audiences. If the appeal to the unconscious through the creation of a link between the leader and the people is geared toward the more credulous masses, statistical data, once grasped by reason, would prove the benefits of Salazarism to the more demanding, literate segment of the population. The urgency in winning over public support, be it through Salazar's approach to propaganda or through Ferro's, testifies to the precariousness of the New State, which needs to convert to its dogma all of those who, like César in the movie, believe in alternative political systems. *The May Revolution* aims to persuade the audience that its protagonist only becomes truly human and truly Portuguese when he accepts the values of Salazarism.[68] The film thereby establishes an equivalence between the principles of the New State and authentic humanity and suggests that there is no possible life outside the ideology of the regime.

Notes

1 Some of the ideas from the initial sections of this chapter were developed for the first time in the article "Truth and Art as Ideology: Cinema and Propaganda in the Portuguese New State" published in the academic journal *Clcweb*.11(3). A first version of the last section of the chapter was published in the book *A Cultura Portuguesa no Divã*, edited by Isabel Capeloa Gil and Adriana Martins (51–61). We thank the editors of *ClcWeb* and of *A Cultura Portuguesa no Divã* for permission to reproduce here a longer, revised version of parts of these essays.

2 "Durante muitos anos a política matou neste país a administração: as lutas partidárias, as revoluções, as intrigas, [...] o poder pelo poder revelaram-se inconciliáveis com a solução de muitos problemas nacionais." Salazar, "Momento Político," in *Discursos e Notas Políticas (1935–1937)*, 72. Salazar described with disdain what he considered to be the general political practice: "We have many times shown reluctance in accepting political activity as having an end in itself. All of this clamoring of promises without consistency and demands without seriousness; all of this gushing of ideas without depth and construction of plans without foundations; this systematic, endless discussion of things that cannot and should not be discussed; this obsession with opportunism to which is sacrificed not only truth, which is eternal, but also justice [...]; this undignified running after a meritless notoriety; this igniting of uncontrollable passions; the sick exploitation of the worst sentiments; this strange equivalence between the truth and lies and the inconceivable lawfulness of misrepresentation and fabrication of facts, even when the intellect cannot manage to lend them a whiff of credibility; in short, all of this feverish, and in the end unproductive, agitation that horrifies us is what is called politics in contemporary belief and practice." ("Temos muitas vezes mostrado relutância em aceitar a actividade política como tendo em si própria o seu fim.

Todo esse alarido de promessas sem consistência e de exigências sem seriedade; todo esse borbulhar de ideias sem fundo e arquitectar de planos sem base; essa discussão sistemática e infindável das coisas que não podem nem têm que ser discutidas; essa obsessão de oportunismo ao qual se sacrifica não só a verdade, que é eterna, mas também a justiça […]; esse correr sem brio atrás de uma notoriedade sem mérito; esse atear de paixões incontroláveis; a doentia exploração dos piores sentimentos; essa estranha equivalência da verdade e da mentira e a inconcebível licitude da deturpação ou invenção dos factos, mesmo se a inteligência não consegue imprimir-lhes um ar de credibilidade; enfim, toda essa agitação febril, e ao cabo improdutiva, que nos causa horror, é, na concepção e na prática correntes, o que se chama política.") "Governar Dirigindo," in *Discursos e Notas Políticas (1943–1950)*, 486–7.

3 "política *sem política*"; "Governo *sem política*"; "pareceu a muitos uma loucura e foi para todos uma felicidade." Salazar, "Espírito da Revolução," in *Discursos (1928–1934)*, 320. Salazar ironically referred to his political ineptitude: "It has been repeated so often that I know something about finances, but that I understand nothing about politics, that I really should have already been convinced of it." ("Tanto se tem repetido de mim saber eu alguma coisa de finanças, mas não perceber nada de política, que, em boa verdade, já me devia ter convencido disso.") "Diferentes Forças," in *Discursos (1928–1934)*, 161.

4 "desordem democrática." Salazar, "Educação Política," in *Discursos e Notas Políticas (1938–1943)*, 33.

5 "absoluta esterilidade da política considerada como fim em si mesma." Salazar, "Momento Político," in *Discursos e Notas Políticas (1935–1937)*, 72.

6 Salazar thought that democracy during the First Republic merely substituted "particularisms for other particularisms, ambitions and vanities for other ambitions and vanities (particularismos por outros particularismos, ambições e vaidades por outras ambições e vaidades)," instead of solving the problems that the nation faced ("Espírito da Revolução," in *Discursos (1928–1934)*, 320).

7 Salazar believed that democracy's days were numbered: "I am convinced that within twenty years, unless there is a setback in political evolution, there will not be legislative assemblies in Europe." ("Estou convencido de que dentro de vinte anos, a não se dar qualquer retrocesso na evolução política, não haverá na Europa assembleias legislativas.") "Constituição das Câmaras," *Discursos (1928–1934)*, 386.

8 "Como a vida social, a política e a administração pública devem apoiar-se na verdade: por temperamento, por convicção, por imposição da consciência, defendo esta forma de dirigir e de administrar." Salazar, "Política de Verdade," in *Discursos (1928–1934)*, 24.

9 "verdades políticas." Salazar, "Duas Palavras a Servir de Prefácio," in *Discursos e Notas Políticas (1935–1937)*, vii–xxiii.
10 "política de verdade"; "política de mentira e de segredo." Salazar, "Problemas Nacionais," in *Discursos (1928–1934)*, 10. As Salazar put it, "In an administrative system where lack of sincerity and light prevailed, I said, from the outset, that a *politics of truth* was needed." ("Num sistema de administração em que predominava a falta de sinceridade e de luz, afirmei, deste a primeira hora, que se impunha uma *política de verdade.*") "Política de Verdade," in *Discursos (1928–1934)*, 23. In another speech, Salazar stated: "I always advocated for a politics of the truth, clearly telling the people about the situation in the Country, to accustom them to the sacrifices that one day would have to be made, and that would be all the more difficult the longer we waited." ("Advoguei sempre que se fizesse a política da verdade, dizendo-se claramente ao povo a situação do País, para o habituar à ideia dos sacrifícios que haviam um dia de ser feitos, e tanto mais pesados quanto tardios.") "Problemas Nacionais," *Discursos (1928–1934)*, 10.
11 "Cremos que existe a Verdade, a Justiça, o Belo e o Bem; cremos que pelo seu culto os indivíduos e os povos se elevam, enobrecem, dignificam [...]." Salazar, "Para Servir de Prefácio," in *Discursos (1928–1934)*, lx. In his speeches, Salazar often alluded to the triad formed by truth, beauty, and the good. Another example of this association can be found in the text "O Estado Novo Português na Evolução Política Europeia:" "[…] truth, beauty, and the good—the life of the spirit" ("[...] a verdade, o belo e o bem—vida do espírito.") in *Discursos (1928–1934)*, 344.
12 "retórica sem retórica." Gil, *Salazar: A Retórica da Invisibilidade*, 8.
13 For an appraisal of the rhetorical strategies used in Salazar's speeches, see José Martinho Gaspar, *Os Discursos e o Discurso de Salazar*, 99–132.
14 "Le Président, en effet, n'a jamais fait d'efforts pour plaire à la foule. Peu de paroles." Garnier, *Vacances avec Salazar*, 84.
15 Salazar, "Grandes Certezas," in *Discursos e Notas Políticas (1935–1937)*, 130. In his interviews with António Ferro, Salazar asserted the proximity between truth and authority, in opposition to doubt and even to freedom: "There cannot be freedom against truth, there cannot be freedom against the common interest […] There are many uncertain things in life, but truth, like authority, is absolute. You can revise an idea or a system: you cannot govern in the name of doubt." ("Não pode haver liberdade contra a verdade; não pode haver liberdade contra o interesse comum. [...] Há muita coisa contingente na vida, mas a verdade, como a autoridade, participa do absoluto. Pode rever-se uma ideia ou um sistema: não se pode governar em nome da dúvida.") *Entrevistas*, 160. Salazar also bemoaned the destruction of the "great certainties" of humanity by falsehood: "None or very few moral concepts and useful elements for human work remain—neither treatises, nor truth, nor faith

in the behavior of governments, nor confidence in the feelings of the nations, nor honesty in relationships, not even the relative value of the word upon which the honor of States depends. Almost everything is fictitious, merely superficial, shifting and uncertain in the conscience of governments and of the masses. Lies are fatally wearing down, systematically and on a large scale, the soul of the peoples." ("Dos conceitos morais e dos elementos utilizáveis para uma obra humana, nada ou muito pouco resta de pé—nem tratados, nem verdade, nem fé na atitude dos governos, nem confiança nos sentimentos das nações, nem sinceridade no trato, nem valor mesmo relativo da palavra que empenha a honra dos Estados. Quase tudo é fictício, meramente aparente, movediço e incerto na consciência dos governos como das multidões. E o desgaste fatal da mentira, em grande e por sistema, na alma dos povos.") "Duas Palavras de Prefácio," in *Discursos e Notas Políticas (1935–1937)*, xii–xiii.

16 In his speech "As Grandes Certezas da Revolução Nacional," Salazar affirmed the centrality of truth in his thought and political practice: "Contrary to falsehood—a political school and system of government—truth, truth in words, in acts, in reforms, in laws and in the enforcement of laws." ("Contrariamente à mentira— escola política e sistema de governo—a verdade, a verdade nas palavras, nos actos, nas reformas, nas leis e na sua execução.") in *Discursos e Notas Políticas (1935–1937)*, 139. In his interviews with Garnier, Salazar went back to condemning falsehood: "The world is pleased with living a lie. We, we present reality without artifice." ("Le monde se plaît à vivre dans le mensonge. Nous, nous présentons sans fard la réalité.") *Vacances avec Salazar*, 241. In turn, the French journalist quotes Salazar's friend Augusto de Castro saying about him: "In our century, no one worries about the truth because we are accustomed to not finding it. In Portugal, however, truth maintains its worth thanks to Salazar, who always presents it without artifice or camouflage. In his speeches, in his reports, in his communiqués, one should not look for insinuations, hidden agendas or secret intentions; Salazar is the most direct, clearest, the most truthful possible, without worrying about displeasing. His best political weapon is the truth. This is the reason why we also pay homage to the President." ("En notre siècle, nul se soucie de la vérité, parce qu'on est habitué à ne plus la trouver nulle part. Au Portugal, cependant, la vérité a gardé sa valeur grâce à Salazar qu l'a toutjours présentée sans artifice ni camouflage. Dans ses discours, ses rapports, ses communiqués, il n'y a pas à chercher de sous-entendus, de propôs sibyllins, d'intentions secrètes, Salazar va au plus droit, au plus clair, au plus vrai, sans se soucier de déplaire. Sa meilleure arme politique, c'est la vérité. Voici pourquoi, aussi, nous rendons hommage au Président.") *Vacances avec Salazar*, 99.

17 "Alguns ainda considerarão a propaganda como o instrumento subtil que, recolhendo todos os contributos da ciência e da arte [...] transmuda as cores,

desfigura os factos [...] *cria uma verdade*, tão clara, tão incisiva, tão evidente que todos a hão-de julgar verdadeira. [...] não é isso para nós propaganda. / O que é, pois? Sempre que abordei este assunto tenho ligado a propaganda à educação política do povo português e lhe tenho atribuído duas funções—informação primeiro; formação política, depois." Salazar, "Fins e Necessidade," in *Discursos e Notas Políticas (1938–1943)*, 195.

18 Salazar made the connection between propaganda and education on several occasions. In the speech "A Educação Política, Garantia da Continuidade Revolucionária," the head of the government referred to the topic more than once: "The earlier considerations attempt to demonstrate in one way or another the need to continue, and intensify, the great task of political education of the Portuguese people in harmony with the principles of our Revolution; I call this work *educational work* and not propaganda, which would be only one of the means of achieving this work." ("As considerações anteriores pretendem demonstrar por uma ou por outra forma a necessidade de continuar, intensificando-a, a vasta obra de educação política do povo português em harmonia com os princípios da nossa Revolução; chamo a essa obra *obra de educação* e não de propaganda, pois esta será apenas um dos meios de conseguir aquela.") *Discursos e Notas Políticas (1938–1943)*, 33.

19 "A verdade porém é que *politicamente* tudo o que *parece* é, quer dizer, as mentiras, as ficções, os receios, mesmo injustificados, criam estados de espírito que são *realidades políticas*: sobre elas, com elas e contra elas se tem de governar." Salazar, "Educação Política," in *Discursos e Notas Políticas (1938–1943)*, 27.

20 "abstrair de serviços idênticos noutros países"; "dos exaltados nacionalismos que os dominam." Salazar, "Propaganda Nacional," in *Discursos (1928–1934)*, 62.

21 "o erro, a mentira, a calúnia ou a simples ignorância, de dentro ou de fora." Salazar, "Propaganda Nacional," in *Discursos (1928–1934)*, 268.

22 Paulo, *Estado Novo e Propaganda*, 75–6.

23 Paulo, *Estado Novo e Propaganda*, 81.

24 The offer to direct *The May Revolution* was only extended to Lopes Ribeiro after Leitão de Barros, Jorge Brum do Canto, and Chianca de Garcia had declined to make the film (Ramos, "O Cinema Salazarista," in *História de Portugal*, 394).

25 "cineasta oficial do salazarismo." Ramos, "O Cinema Salazarista," in *História de Portugal*, 394.

26 António Lopes Ribeiro was an active filmmaker and film critic during the New State. He founded and directed three film journals—*Imagem*, *Kino*, and *Animatógrafo*—directed eight feature-length films and several documentaries, many of which at the service of the regime's propaganda (Costa, *Breve História*, 78–9).

27 António Ferro and António Lopes Ribeiro wrote the film's screenplay using the pseudonyms Jorge Afonso and Baltasar Fernandes, respectively.
28 Torgal, "Propaganda, Ideologia e Cinema," in *O Cinema sob o Olhar de Salazar*. Torgal argues in this article that the propaganda of the New State used a religious model, in that it presented itself as an instrument for converting nonbelievers to the virtues of Salazarism. Torgal mentions *The May Revolution* and *Spell of the Empire* (*Feitiço do Império*, 1940), a film also directed by Lopes Ribeiro, as examples of this conversion. In both movies the protagonist goes through a process of metamorphosis in the course of which he becomes a zealous supporter of the New State (*Revolution*) or its colonies (*Spell*).
29 "deve cingirse estritamente aos factos e utilizar de preferência a imagem e o número como as expressões mais frisantes, mais eloquentes dos factos da vida pública." Salazar, "Propaganda Nacional," in *Discursos (1928–1934)*, 266.
30 Salazar established a Manichean distinction between good and bad men. According to him, good men, even when they have been led astray, recognize their mistakes if they are shown the truth. In contrast, bad men are intrinsically corrupt and should not be tolerated: "There are then some souls, perhaps full of sincerity and certainly also filled with illusions, that seek the means to make peace and justice among men, peace and justice as abstract and unreal as their conception of humanity itself. There are still, and above all, active and interested agents, organizers of disorder because of social maladjustment, because of their rebellious instinct, or because of business, who receive and spend the funds they raised, and who are responsible for maintaining the sacred flame of anarchy, generally on behalf of and ordered by foreigners. These people, perfectly conscious of evil, cannot count on tolerance for their ideals, or on freedom for their actions [...]." ("Há depois alguns espíritos, porventura cheios de sinceridade e certamente também cheios de ilusões, que buscam os meios de realizar a paz e a justiça entre os homens, paz e justiça tão abstractas e irreais como a concepção que têm da própria humanidade. Há ainda, e sobretudo, os agentes activos e interessados, organizadores da desordem por inadaptação social, por instinto de revolta e por negócio, recebendo e gastando os fundos angariados, e encarregados de manter, geralmente por conta e ordem de estrangeiros, o fogo sagrado da anarquia. Estes, perfeitamente conscientes do mal, não podem contar nem com tolerância para os seus ideais, nem com liberdade para a sua acção [...]." "Balanço," *Discursos e Notas Políticas (1935–1937)*, 33–4. In *The May Revolution*, the protagonist falls within the first group of idealistic men, who want to achieve good in the name of humanity but who find themselves off the correct path.
31 Ramos, "O Cinema Salazarista," in *História de Portugal*, 395.
32 Salazar, "Fins e Necessidade," in *Discursos e Notas Políticas (1938–1943)*, 204–5.

33 "grande mentira." Salazar, "Governo e Política," in *Discursos e Notas Políticas (1951–1958)*, 305.
34 Salazar, *Para a Compreensão*, 11.
35 Salazar defined communism in the following way: "As a revolutionary movement and as the expression of an aggressive international policy, communism is the great enemy of the moment, and the first contribution that can be made for the world order is to decisively defeat it within our borders. It is a vital and urgent problem to find the appropriate means to do so." ("O comunismo é, pois, como movimento revolucionário e expressão de uma política internacional agressiva, o grande inimigo do momento, e a primeira contribuição que pode dar-se na ordem externa é contê-lo decisivamente no interior. É problema vital e urgente definir os meios apropriados.") "Governar Dirigindo," in *Discursos e Notas Políticas (1943–1950)*, 508–9. The film *The May Revolution* would then be part of the government's efforts to contain the spread of communist ideology in the country.
36 The political police force is represented in the film as an efficient but benign institution. The police officers follow the conspirators' path, all of whom, except for César, are imprisoned at the end. Moreira (Alexandre de Azevedo), the head of police, says that the protagonist is a man who made a mistake and gives him a chance to change his behavior.
37 "activités purement politiques." Garnier, *Vacances avec Salazar*, 240.
38 "verdadeira liberdade [...] só pode existir no espírito dos Homens." Ferro, *Entrevistas*, 160.
39 "ódios;" "lutas;" "particularismos;" "anarquia mental e moral;" "tudo é movediço e arbitrário." Salazar, "Grandes Certezas," in *Discursos e Notas Políticas (1935–1937)*, 128.
40 "uma grande família ou uma grande empresa"; "para a defesa dos seus interesses comuns e para a realização dos fins colectivos, duma cabeça coordenadora, dum centro de vida e de acção." Salazar, "Constitução das Câmaras," in *Discursos (1928–1934)*, 377.
41 "preferem à obediência a sua liberdade de acção nem os que sobrepõem às directrizes superiormente traçadas as indicações da sua inteligência;" "não estão connosco." Salazar, "Diferentes Forças," in *Discursos (1928–1934)*, 183–4.
42 Salazar, "Para Servir de Prefácio," in *Discursos (1928–1934)*, lix–lx.
43 "política do espírito."
44 "Enganam-se os homens de acção, os orientadores, os governantes, que desprezam ou esquecem as belas-artes e a literatura, atribuindo-lhes uma função meramente decorativa, um papel supérfluo, reduzindo-as a uma espécie de sobremesa da vida social. O desenvolvimento premeditado, consciente, da Arte e da Literatura é tão necessário, afinal, ao progresso duma nação como o desenvolvimento das

suas ciências, das suas obras públicas, da sua indústria, do seu comércio e da sua agricultura." Ferro, *Entrevistas*, 226.
45 Pita, "Temas e Figuras," in *O Cinema sob o Olhar de Salazar*, 44–5.
46 "a mentira é a única verdade dos artistas." Ferro, cited in Torgal, *Estados Novos*, vol. 2, 55.
47 At the conference "The Age of the Jazz-Band" ("A Idade do Jazz-Band") held in Rio de Janeiro in 1922, Ferro described a process of renaissance of humanity, which would free itself from its condition through art: "[...] God intended that his children, Man and Woman, follow his path, dehumanizing themselves, becoming gods like the Father ... Man and Woman, however, did not understand this. They remained preoccupied with Humanity, backward, inferior, unworthy of God ... Finally they began to free themselves, to make themselves artificial, to be gods ... The *Jazz-Band* age is the precursor to this renaissance." (" [...] Deus teria desejado que os seus filhos, o Homem e a Mulher, seguissem o seu caminho, desumanizando-se, tornando-se deuses como o Pai ... O Homem e a Mulher, porém, não compreenderam assim. Ficaram-se no preconceito da Humanidade, atrasados, inferiores, indignos de Deus ... Começaram, finalmente, a libertar-se, a artificializar-se, a ser deuses ... *A Idade Jazz-Band* é a Idade precursora deste renascimento.") Cited in Torgal, *Estados Novos*, vol. 2, 66.
48 "A Arte das artistas do écran é a verdadeira Arte porque difere absolutamente da Vida." Ferro, cited in Torgal, *Estados Novos*, vol. 2, 56.
49 Siegfried Kracauer points out that Hitler was almost completely absent from many German war films, like *Victory in the West* (*Sieg im Westen*, 1941), because the dictator wanted to present himself as an omnipresent god that could not always be seen but whose presence was always felt (*From Caligari to Hitler*, 282). José Gil outlines an argument similar to Kracauer's when he interprets Salazar's "rhetoric of invisibility" as a subtle technique used by the statesman to convey his omnipresence in the lives of the Portuguese people even when he was not visible. However, this "rhetoric of invisibility" is at odds with António Ferro's desire to bring the image of the dictator to the masses through cinema.
50 Kracauer, *From Caligari to Hitler*, 299.
51 Kracauer, *From Caligari to Hitler*, 306–7.
52 When António Ferro asked Salazar about the complaints of political prisoners, who claimed that they had been victims of violence, he received the following response: "I want to inform you, however, that we have come to the conclusion that the mistreated prisoners were always, or almost always, dreaded bombers who refused to confess, despite all of the skilled efforts of the Police, where they had hidden their criminal and deadly weapons. It was only after those violent means were employed that they decided to tell the truth. And I ask myself, continuing to suppress such

abuses, if the lives of some children and some defenseless people were not worth it, did not broadly justify, a half dozen thrusts at the right moment against these sinister creatures ..." ("Quero informá-lo, no entanto, de que se chegou à conclusão de que os presos maltratados eram sempre, ou quase sempre, temíveis bombistas que se recusavam a confessar, apesar de todas as habilidade da Polícia, onde tinham escondidas as suas armas criminosas e mortais. Só depois de empregar esses meios violentos é que eles se decidiam a dizer a verdade. E eu pergunto a mim próprio, continuando a reprimir tais abusos, se a vida de algumas crianças e de algumas pessoas indefesas não vale bem, não justifica largamente, meia dúzia de safanões a tempo nessas criaturas sinistras ...") *Entrevistas*, 54.

53 António Ferro's interviews with Salazar were translated and published in several European countries to make the ideology of the New State known abroad. The book was prefaced by European intellectuals like Austen Chamberlain and Paul Valéry.

54 "Que deve fazer, portanto, o ditador para [...] não ser vítima da ingratidão daqueles que serviu, daqueles que salvou? Apenas isto: martelar constantemente as suas ideias, despi-las da sua rigidez, dar-lhes vida e calor, comunicá-las à multidão. Que o ditador fale ao povo e que o povo lhe fale. Que ditador e povo se confundam de tal forma, que o povo se sinta ditador e que o ditador se sinta povo." Ferro, *Entrevistas*, 222–3.

55 "A fé não é a treva, mas a iluminação. [...] A supressão forçada, necessária, de certas liberdades, de certos direitos humanos, tem de ser coada através da alegria, do entusiasmo, da fé. [...] Se a natureza do chefe é avessa a certos contactos, se é preferível talvez não a contrariar para não a quebrar na sua fecunda inteireza, que se encarregue alguém, ou alguns de cuidar da encenação necessária das festas do ideal, dessas entrevistas indispensáveis, nas ditaduras, entre a multidão e os governantes ..." Ferro, *Entrevistas*, 221–2.

56 Salazar, "Para Servir de Prefácio," in *Discursos (1928–1934)*, xlvi. Hitler took lessons from an actor to develop his repertoire of gestures and in 1928 created a school to train members of his party to speak in public. Mussolini adopted gestures and stylized expressions, possibly copied from silent films, which could be decoded even when the leader spoke to large crowds (Clark, *Art and Propaganda*, 49).

57 Salazar, "Independência da Política," in *Discursos e Notas Políticas (1951–1958)*, 71.

58 Garnier, *Vacances avec Salazar*, 84, 90.

59 Salazar recognized that many Portuguese citizens were curious to meet him, given the lack of opportunities to have contact with such an important public figure: "It is also natural that many of you are curious to meet the Finance Minister ... Here he is, and he is, as you can see, a very modest person. He has a precarious health and is never ill; he has a limited capacity to work and he works without rest. How is this miracle possible? Because many good souls of Portugal pray for him, wishing

for him to continue in his position." ("É natural também que muitos de VV. Exas. tivessem curiosidade em conhecer o Ministro das Finanças... Aqui está e é, como vêem, uma bem modesta pessoa. Tem uma saúde precária e nunca está doente; tem uma capacidade limitada de trabalho e trabalha sem descanso. Porquê este milagre? Porque muito boas almas de Portugal oram, anseiam por que continue neste lugar.") "Problemas Nacionais," in *Discursos (1928–1934)*, 10. Salazar stressed here the providential character of his government, which he described as if it were a miracle, an image that he used on countless other occasions.

60 Years later, Ferro highlighted the success of his politics of the spirit, which had led the Portuguese to willingly accept Salazar's government, or in other words, to have "faith" in their leader: "They can struggle to explain his [Salazar's] permanence in power with words that are meaningless in the context of the regime: dictatorship, oppression, violence ... No one can *seriously* believe that Salazar could govern for 20 years (and many more, God willing) if the Nation did not desire it, if Portugal did not want it." ("Podem esfalfarse em explicar a sua [de Salazar] permanência no poder com palavras sem sentido na estrutura do regime: ditadura, opressão, violência ... Ninguém poderá acreditar *a sério* que Salazar pudesse governar 20 anos (e muitos mais se Deus quiser) se a Nação não o desejasse, se Portugal não o quisesse.") *Política do Espírito, Apontamentos*, 23.

61 Ferro emphasizes the need of revamping Salazar's public figure: "[...] Salazar, whose name, so many times pronounced, never gets old [...], because it is renewed, it is illuminated, constantly, through new daily works, new perspectives, highly prophetic words that are being proven true." ("[...] Salazar, cujo nome, tantas vezes pronunciado, nunca envelhece [...], porque se renova, se ilumina, constantemente, através de novas obras quotidianas, de novas perspectivas, de palavras altamente proféticas que se vão confirmando.") *Política do Espírito. Apontamentos*, 20–1.

62 Freud, *Group Psychology*.

63 Kracauer, *From Caligari to Hitler*, 278.

64 Adorno, "Theory and the Pattern," in *The Culture Industry*, 142.

65 Salazar, "'A Regar! A Regar!,'" in *Discursos e Notas Políticas (1943–1950)*, 399.

66 For an analysis of the representation of the police force in the Portuguese-style commedy (comédia à portuguesa), see Paulo Granja's article, "A Comédia à Portuguesa, ou a Máquina de Sonhos a Preto e Branco do Estado Novo," in *O Cinema sob o Olhar de Salazar*, 227–31.

67 Freud describes the workings of the Church and the Military in the fifth chapter of *Group Psychology*.

68 Salazar denigrated the followers of communism, presenting them as anti-spiritual, anti-Portuguese, and anti-human: "The [Portuguese] Youth [is] the nursery of an anti-communist elite merely by being Portuguese, anti-communist by being

spiritual, anti-communist merely by defending freedom of conscience and fighting for human dignity." ("A Mocidade [é] o viveiro de uma elite anticomunista só por ser portuguesa, anticomunista por ser espiritualista, anticomunista só por defender a liberdade da consciência e lutar pela dignidade humana.") "Governar Dirigindo," in *Discursos e Notas Políticas (1943–1950)*, 510–11.

2

Poets on the Silver Screen: *Bocage, Camões,* and the Heroes of the Regime

Literature and film in the politics of the spirit

From its inception, the cultural politics of the Portuguese New State privileged both literature and film as methods to disseminate Salazarist ideals. António Ferro, SPN/SNI director and ideologue of the regime's "politics of the spirit," was a prominent representative of Portuguese literary Modernism. He was the editor of the journal *Orpheu* and the author of several literary works including the novel *Leviana*. At the same time, he was a cinema enthusiast and published several texts about the silver screen over the course of his career.[1] While he was responsible for the propaganda of the New State, Ferro created incentives for literary creation and film production, viewing both as ways to impart enthusiasm for Salazar's political project to the Portuguese people and to persuade them to accept the decisions of the head of the government.[2]

Although he believed that all art should be mobilized to support the New State, Ferro—like his counterparts in other authoritarian regimes—considered film to be the most effective means of communication to influence the masses and thereby convert viewers to the principles of Salazarism:[3]

> [Cinema's] magic, its seductive power, its penetrating force, are incalculable. More so than when we read [...] the image penetrates, it insinuates itself, almost without being noticed, in man's soul. In almost all other means of recreation our intelligence, our own sensibility have to make an effort, have to work more than they do when dealing with cinema; when facing that screen which, for two hours, takes charge of thinking and dreaming for us. [...] The film viewer is a passive being, more defenseless than the reader or the simple listener.[4]

The relationship between films and their audience is considered to be essentially asymmetrical in that the defenseless viewers willingly surrender to the power of the image. Ferro rhetorically feminizes the audience in order to give evidence of the persuasive and propagandistic potential of cinema. In his speech, film assumes the traditional masculine role of a conqueror of the passive masses and takes charge of forming their opinions, thinking and dreaming for them. Defenseless and uncritical, the film viewer becomes the ideal receptor, who suspends the use of her or his intelligence and assimilates the ideology conveyed by cinema almost unconsciously. It is therefore understandable that, in Ferro's view, cinema should be one of the regime's preferred instruments of propaganda used to create the "New Man" of Salazarism.[5]

In the passage transcribed above, Ferro negatively compares literature to cinema, suggesting that the former does not lend itself as effectively to propaganda since it requires a more conscious effort of interpretation and does not possess the same persuasive power as film. Despite this, Ferro believes that "literature [...] is the great source of cinema" because it reveals the nation's personality and reflects patriotic values.[6] Beyond providing plots for fictional films, Portuguese literature should also act as a stylistic example for cinema: "Cinema is, above all, a great book of stories ... It is necessary to know how to tell them with simplicity, without resorting to the usual crutches: folklore, great moments of true or faked dramatics, vulgar humor, misleading situations, etc., etc .... "[7]

According to Ferro, the masterpieces of national literature would aid Portuguese cinema to overcome what he saw as its main flaws: an abundance of useless words and images, pompous tendencies, lack of rhythm, no attention to detail, commercial stories, and vulgar comedies, among others.[8] The narrative coherence and the moralizing plots that characterize good literature should be adopted by cinema, translating the meticulous care for language in literary texts into cinematic terms. The result would be cohesive dialogues, sequential and harmonious rhythms, and careful cinematography. Ferro recognized that some of the flaws in Portuguese cinema were due to a lack of resources, which led to financial constraints outweighing moral and artistic values.[9] The subsidies from the National Cinema Fund (*Fundo do Cinema Nacional*), administered by the SNI, were created with the intention of supporting films that, despite being economically unviable, were considered valuable for the regime, both from an artistic and from a moral point of view.

Ferro's reflections about the advantages of a close relationship between literature and cinema were concretized in the cinematographic practice of the early decades of the New State, as literature became the preferred source of film narratives between the 1930s and the 1950s. For example, the plots of nineteenth-century novels gave rise to films such as *The Rector's Pupils* (*As Pupilas do Senhor Reitor*, Leitão de Barros, 1935), *The Noblemen of the Moorish House* (*Os Fidalgos da Casa Mourisca*, Arthur Duarte, 1938), *Ill-Fated Love* (*Amor de Perdição*, António Lopes Ribeiro, 1943), *The Heiress of the Reeds* (*A Morgadinha dos Canaviais*, Amadeo Ferrari and Caetano Bonucci, 1949), and *Cousin Basil* (*O Primo Basílio*, António Lopes Ribeiro, 1959). Other movies brought plays to the big screen, including *Severa* (*A Severa*, Leitão de Barros, 1931), an adaption of Júlio Dantas's homonymous drama, and *Friar Luís de Sousa* (*Frei Luís de Sousa*, António Lopes Ribeiro, 1950).[10] Some New State films, like *Spell of the Empire* (*Feitiço do Império*, António Lopes Ribeiro, 1940) and *Fátima, Land of Faith* (*Fátima, Terra de Fé*, Jorge Brum do Canto, 1943), were based on Salazarist novels, in these cases narratives that had won literary prizes instituted by the regime.[11] Yet, fictional cinema did not only appropriate novels and plays, but also used poetry as an inspiration for film. Some of these movies focus both on the lives of national poets and on their literary output. Films such as *Bocage* (1936) and *Camões* (1946), both directed by Leitão de Barros, highlight the poetry written by the protagonists and the plot includes readings of some of their best-known compositions. These films fall within Ferro's efforts to create a "poetic atmosphere in Portuguese life"[12] that would translate the achievements of Salazarism in the socio-political domain into the artistic sphere.

The heroes of the New State

Cinema inspired by historical novels and plays or by the lives of renowned writers from the past conjoined Ferro's wish to use literature as a source for national cinema and his preference for historical films. Ferro considered this "bearded cinema," in the words of its detractors, to be "one of the sure, solid paths of Portuguese cinema."[13] He elaborated a typology of the different film genres: regional or folkloric films, historical films, crime films, films adapted from literary works, comedies, documentaries, films of a poetic nature, and films about daily life.[14] Each of these genres was valued differently and a movie's classification could determine whether or not it received funding from the SPN/SNI. For Ferro, comedies were the "cancer of domestic cinema," crime films were dismissed as "weak, unfortunate attempts,"[15] and many of the regional and folkloric movies were accused of including inopportune dances and songs. According to the director of the SPN/SNI, films adapted from novels and plays were a fertile streak of domestic cinema production that should be explored further, while historical films "already [had] prove[n]"[16] to be the genre in which Portuguese artists and filmmakers distinguished

Figure 2.1 Advertisement poster for the film *Camões*

themselves the most. Films inspired by literary works from the past, adaptations of novels or plays with historical plots, and dramatizations of authors' lives fused two of the most promising aspects of Portuguese film production, namely using literature and history as inspiration. Availability of government-awarded funding for such projects explains the production of a great number of movies on these topics.

The central axis of films fictionalizing the lives of authors was the literature–history nexus, as the writers' literary production and their lives became entangled with the unfolding of national history. This identification of an individual hero with the collective destiny of the country was employed as a mechanism to disseminate the regime's ideology.[17] The generous state subsidies given to *Bocage* and *Camões*, the two most expensive films produced in their time, were justified by their value as propaganda.[18] *Bocage*, produced by the Sociedade Universal de Superfilmes, premiered in the São Luíz Theater on 1 December 1936.[19] The film used about 3,000 extras in the scenes filmed in the Queluz Palace; 100 couples danced a minuet in the Palace Throne Room; and a famous opera singer of the period, Tomás Alcaide, was hired to sing

Figure 2.2 Minuet in the Queluz Palace Throne Room in *Bocage*

a romance in a boat as it navigated the canals of the Queluz gardens.[20] The film's prestige led to the release of a Spanish version, *The Three Graces* (*Las Tres Gracias*), produced by Eugénio Gonzalez. It was filmed simultaneously with its Portuguese counterpart by substituting some of the Portuguese actors with Spanish ones, thus initiating a cinematic cooperation between the two countries that would last until the late 1940s.[21]

Camões, produced by António Lopes Ribeiro, was the second installment of the trilogy that Leitão de Barros started with *Bocage*. It premiered in the São Luíz Theater on 23 September 1946. The film marked, in Ferro's words, "a date in the history of our cinema on which it saw large vistas for the first time […]."[22] The film required the construction of vast interior sets as well as the creation of scale model reproductions of several exteriors and the use of numerous costumes.[23] The government considered the movie to be of national interest; Salazar himself wrote a note recommending that the public services support its production.[24] Unlike *Bocage*, *Camões* had considerable commercial success in Portugal,[25] and it received the Best Film Award of the SNI in 1946, along with the Prize for Best Actor for António Vilar and that of Best Actress for Eunice Muñoz, with honorable mentions for Vasco Santana and Paiva Raposo. It was also the first Portuguese film to be selected for the Cannes Film Festival.[26] Both *Bocage* and *Camões* emphasize the heroic, exemplary character of the protagonists, using the identification of writer with fatherland and of poetry with nation, as a way to awaken the patriotism of the Portuguese people, a feeling implicitly linked to Salazarism and its core principles.

Camões and, to a lesser extent, *Bocage* are built upon a a chain of metonymies that culminates in the poets and in the episodes of their lives, the narration of which had been mediated by centuries of historical and literary studies by the time it reached the 1930s and 40s. One of the outcomes of this metonymic operation concerns the reduction of poetry to a mere reflection of the author's life, given that literature is portrayed as an ad hoc response to concrete occurrences and as a direct expression of a feeling. This is the case of Camões's famous poem "Barefoot she goes to the fountain" ("Descalça vai para a fonte") which, according to Leitão de Barros's film, was recited spontaneously by Camões (António Vilar) upon seeing a young woman named Leonor (Leonor Maia) pass by on the way to a fountain in the countryside near Coimbra. Poet and poetry are part of a whole that cannot be disentangled, a notion that has its roots in the Romantic theorization of the genius. According to this conceptualization, the real poet, in his concrete and phenomenological existence, emerges as a channel through which art becomes manifest. His art, in turn, should be understood within the context of the poet's life. In other words, the poet's existence becomes relevant because of the poetry he wrote, but this poetry could only be created as a response to the life of the extraordinary being that was the poet. The merger of the literary work with the writer's persona and the concurrent emphasis on the life of the author are explained by the centrality of the individual hero in Romantic and Post-Romantic culture. This emphasis on exceptional individuals will be appropriated by the New State and placed at the service of its propaganda.

The poet's existence not only encompasses his poetic production, which is subsumed to his life as a mere reflection of his deeds, but is also linked to the being of the nation as an organic entity. This identification of an emblematic poet with the destiny of the nation was an explicit intention of the creators of *Camões*, as the film's producer Lopes Ribeiro stated in an interview to the newspaper *Diário Popular*:

> A living biography of the greatest Portuguese man of the Renaissance. [...] The great epic poet's marvelous life, *living in his time the drama of his age*, to make him on screen what he was, *the image of a genial reality*, made of flesh and emotions, is the desideratum we shall fulfill [...].[27]

For Lopes Ribeiro, Camões represents a synthesis of his time, incarnating both the vices and the virtues of the Portuguese Renaissance. Yet, the film goes even further, transforming the poet into the image not just of a given age but also of the whole of national history. This goal is formulated in an especially clear manner at the end of the film when, in the delirium that precedes his death, Camões contemplates scenes of the Portuguese defeat at the Battle of Alcácer-Quibir (1578). This is followed by symbols of national resurgence, namely, the raising of several subsequent Portuguese flags that appear on the screen juxtaposed with the profile of the writer and accompanied by key dates in Portugal's history: 1640—Restoration of the Portuguese crown after forty years of Spanish rule; 1810—the date that symbolizes the expulsion of the Napoleonic army from the national territory; 1885—the pacification of Mozambique; and finally 1940—the anniversary of the foundation of the country in 1140 and of the 1640 Restoration, a date celebrated in several commemorations organized by the New State. The Republican period, consistently denigrated by Salazar, is conspicuously absent from this list of dates, and the New State of the 1940s appears as the heir to key moments in Portuguese history. Luís de Pina sums up this metonymical confluence of poet, poetry, and nation in the following way:

> [T]he symbols of collective action [were] synthesized here in the life and the art of Luís Vaz de Camões. I have no hesitation in affirming that Leitão de Barros thought of the poet as an image of Portugal. This is the most profound sense of the historical vision of *The Lusiads* in the scene with António Vilar in front of the tapestries of Pastrana, which synthetize Portugal's own history.[28]

What are the ideological goals of choosing a poet, be it Camões or Bocage, and his life—inevitably a historical fiction created over many centuries—as a summary both of this poet's literary work and of national history itself? To answer this question, it is necessary to examine the foundations of the New State's discourse about the national past, which is based upon a displacement of meaning, whereby poet, poetry, and nation become almost synonymous. The emphasis Salazarism places on authors as national heroes is informed by a Hegelian concept of historical progress. For Hegel, Spirit (*Geist*) becomes concrete in the historical evolution of humanity through its materialization

Figure 2.3   The Portuguese flag superimposed on the poet's profile in *Camões*

in men and nations. During the course of this dialectic movement, Spirit frequently becomes incarnate in select individuals who go beyond the contingencies of their beings and whose acts acquire a universal meaning. The actions of these individuals, whom Hegel refers to as "world-historical individuals" (*welthistorische Individuen*), are beyond good and evil. They live for their ideals, which for Hegel represent the absolute unity between a singular character and the universality of Spirit.[29] The Hegelian notion of "world-historical individuals" was adopted later by thinkers such as Thomas Carlyle, who in his book *On Heroes, Hero Worship and the Heroic in History* (1841) highlights the central role of heroic personalities—political leaders but also men of letters—in historical transformation. Friedrich Nietzsche also drew on Hegel to develop the concept of the Superman, an individual who incarnates the potential of his people and who brings to fruition the opportunities of the historical moment of which he is part. Poets like Camões and Bocage are presented in Salazarist films as heroes in the Hegelian or Carlylian sense, or as Nietzsche's Supermen. Their lives and their work epitomize the age in which they live, while at the same time transcending this historical moment and already anticipating the nation's future.

The cult of individual genius, simultaneously spiritual and heroic, that culminates in the New State's veneration of Camões—"One hand the pen, and one the sword employ'd"[30]—was used in Portugal for political purposes since at least the end of the nineteenth century. The celebration of the third centennial anniversary of the poet's death in 1880 was exploited by Republican intellectuals, who took advantage of the opportunity to emphasize the country's decline under the yoke of constitutional monarchy when compared to the Golden Age of Discoveries and presented Republicanism as the solution to the nation's problems.[31] Already during the First Republic, the symbolism of Camões as a national hero was placed at the service of the campaign in favor of Portuguese participation in the First World War. Entering the European conflict was presented as a way to protect the colonies, for which the poet, who had also been a soldier, had fought in the sixteenth century.[32]

Hegel's theory of "world-historical individuals," or "heroes," had a wide circulation in Portuguese intellectual circles in the first decades of the twentieth century. The Republican Alberto Veiga Simões mentioned the existence of "core men" that unite the best qualities of the race in his study about Portuguese literature, *A Nova Geração* (1911), which was influenced by theories of racial and cultural identity based on physiological characteristics.[33] This idea of individuals that synthesize the aspirations of a nation permeated the Portuguese modernist movement and was later adapted by the New State to the new political circumstances.[34]

The notion of the hero or the "core man" was developed under Salazarism by Idalino da Costa Brochado, among others. Costa Brochado, one of Salazar's ideologues, inherited the tradition of venerating Portuguese heroes like Camões, and shaped it to serve the interests of the regime. In his opinion, Portuguese history was determined by a succession of "great men" that represented the aspirations of the Portuguese people in certain historical moments.[35] Salazar appears here as the last avatar of a chain of heroes, which passes through Afonso Henriques, Prince Henry the Navigator, Camões, and Mouzinho de Albuquerque, the latter being the protagonist of another of the regime's films, *Chaimite* (Jorge Brum do Canto, 1953), which we will discuss in a later chapter.[36] It is noteworthy that the same association between the leader and emblematic historical personalities is found, *mutatis mutandis*, in Nazi propaganda cinema. Nazism produced several movies about German heroes from the past—*Bismarck* (Wolfgang Liebeneiner, 1940), *The Great King* (*Der Grosse König*, Veit Harlan, 1942, about Friedrich II), etc.—that suggested the existence of affinities between these men and the *Führer*. Films like *Camões* highlight the relevance of symbolic heroes for the progress of the nation and prepare the audience to accept the political event of the New State as the logical culmination of national history and its triumphs.[37] In this context, we can better understand the Messianism that underlies the cult of Salazar, highlighted by Luís Filipe Meneses in his recent biography of the statesman. Salazar, just like Camões, embodied the spirit of his time and, as he suggested in his speeches, understood the expectations and the will of the Portuguese people, which he translated into concrete policies.[38]

Against political inconstancy: The hero as a serious man

The metonymic identification of poets such as Camões or Bocage with the Portuguese nation in Leitão de Barros's films is a powerful mechanism of ideological manipulation, since it establishes a historical *telos* that culminates in the New State. What remains for us to consider is the question of why should poets, and not prose writers, represent the essence of the nation. Why were films made about Camões and Bocage but not about, for example, Fernão Lopes or Eça de Queirós?

The choice of poets as the heroes of the silver screen is partly due to the Romantic literary tradition, which in Portugal mythified the writer of verses in general and Camões in particular. In the case of Camões, the coincidence of the year of the author's death with the year of the country's loss of independence— the transfer of sovereignty to the hands of a Spanish monarch—certainly contributed to this analogy. If *The Lusiads* were, for Oliveira Martins, the nation's epitaph, then the date of Camões's death symbolically marks the death of the nation, which from that point onward only had a posthumous, phantasmagoric, and decadent existence. It should be stressed that the choice of poets as national heroes was related to the feeling that Portugal found itself in a state of decline, with the films seeking to pinpoint the roots of this phenomenon. The movies suggest the existence of a connection between poetry and Camões's and Bocage's misfortunes, going back once more to a motif dear to Romanticism: the concept of the accursed, unfortunate poet. The parallelism between the poet's fate and national history thus implies an association between the former's misfortunes and the latter's woes, a link that requires a more thorough critical examination.

In both of Leitão de Barros's films, poetry is coupled with Camões's and Bocage's affective inconstancy. In these movies, love is presented as the driving force of the poetic impulse: the majority of the poems recited in the films are responses to circumstances related to the romantic lives of both authors. The filmmaker himself underscores the connection between love and poetry in *Bocage*:

> It is not a biographical film [...]. What is important is the spirit and the nature of the poet and the 'true' psychology of the character. [...] what was taken was what one can and should retain from this genius – *the moments of the poet's pure inspiration, the lover's disconcerting fickleness*.[39]

For Barros, poetic inspiration arises in conjunction with the author's romantic fickleness, forming two sides of the same coin. Thus, from the beginning, the film highlights Bocage's (Raul de Carvalho) exacerbated sentimentality. In one of the first scenes, Bocage tells a friend, upon arriving in Lisbon after a voyage by ship, "Let me go to the tavern, I want the women to see me."[40]

The same emphasis on the writer's romantic adventures is repeated in *Camões* since, in Leitão de Barros's opinion, the poet "lived under the unhealthy influence of romantic ecstasy."[41] The original draft of the film, entitled *Camões, the Rabble-Rouser* (*Camões, o Trinca-Fortes*), focused only on the "poet's agitated youth and his loves,"⁴² in the words of the producer Lopes Ribeiro. Only later was the scope of the movie extended to include the writer's entire life. According to the film, even the impetus that came to Camões in adulthood to write an epic was the result of a romantic episode, namely the poet's expulsion from Lisbon due to his relationship with Princess Maria, King John III's sister. Luís de Pina points out that some critics would have preferred a representation of Camões as a "studious," "well-behaved," "serious Portuguese man." Yet the filmmaker favored a Camões who was "a lover of life, always romantic, lonely, persecuted, defeated, sickly, but who precisely in this, in this baroque excess, in the contrast between a vulgar quotidian and a grandiose vision, in his heart, in the experience of travel and distance, could symbolize Portugal."⁴³

The poets' romantic ties, as represented in the films, involve women from several social classes. Camões courts both Leonor, a peasant woman from Coimbra, and Lady Catarina (Cármen Dolores), one of the Queen's handmaidens, while Bocage falls in love, successively, with the sisters Amália (Maria Castelar) and Márcia (Maria Helena de Matos) of the Lisbon nobility, and with Canária (Celita Bastos), a woman of African descent who sells fruit at the market. The identification of the poet with the nation becomes even more appropriate because these men circulate between the nobility and the people,

Figure 2.4 Bocage (Raul de Carvalho) courts Canária (Celita Bastos) in *Bocage*

relating to members of all social classes, frequenting both taverns and the Court, and indiscriminately favoring both noble and common women.

Although the films stress the two poets' lack of social prejudices, Camões's and Bocage's romantic fickleness is not shown as a positive trait, as is evident from the subtitle of *Camões*: "My Errors, Bad Fortune, Ardent Love" (Erros meus, Má Fortuna, Amor Ardente). In fact, the writer's exile to the Orient results from lack of prudence in choosing Princess Maria, the sister of King Manuel I, as the object of his affections. In the same way, Bocage is expelled from his friend Lieutenant Coutinho's (Tarquínio Vieira) home when the Lieutenant realizes that the poet abused his hospitality by courting his two sisters, one of whom was engaged, while the other was about to take vows and enter a convent. Taking into consideration the identification of the poet–hero with the development of Portuguese history in the filmography of the New State, the writers' romantic inconstancy acquires new significance that goes beyond a strictly biographical interpretation.

We can interpret the writers' romantic debacles and their emotional instability—a result of choosing a series of different women as the objects of their affections—as a commentary about the setbacks of national politics before the New State. For Salazar, political life before he came to power was characterized precisely by instability and disorder, a state of affairs that peaked in the Republican period.[44] Thus, the romantic inconstancy of the poets corresponds to a political inconstancy on a national level, and both are the source of misfortunes. This reading is reinforced by Salazar's opinion that the Portuguese are excessively sentimental, a national character trait with serious political consequences. He stated this on several occasions, among them in his interviews with António Ferro. When Ferro asked him to list the flaws of the Portuguese people, the statesman replied: "[e]xcessively sentimental, abhorring discipline [...] lacking both spirit of continuity and tenacity in action."[45] The excessive sentimentality and lack of tenacity of the Portuguese led to national decline, in the same way that Camões's and Bocage's romantic fickleness caused them countless troubles, despite stimulating their poetic creation.[46]

Salazar's political project included a transformation of Portugal's national character so as to abolish the unhealthy sentimentalism of the Portuguese that hindered their individual and collective development:

> [Ferro] Your aspiration, your willful dream—forgive me if I am wrong—is to change little by little, patiently, our mentality, bringing to an abrupt end the passions of men, atrophying them, silencing them, forcing us to temporarily

move at a slow but safe pace, which will bring down our temperature and cure us from our fever …
Continue …, Salazar answered from the shadows. You may be on the path of truth…[47]

The national *pathos*—exemplified by Camões's and Bocage's romantic inconstancy—appears to be associated with poetic expression in Leitão de Barros's films.[48] Following the literary metaphor of the movie, the country would need to move from poetry to prose, from the brilliance of the moment to a constant effort, from poems to accountants' balance sheets.

Salazar's public image of a modest man, dedicated to work and without known romantic escapades—"hardly sentimental in this as in other areas,"[49] in his own words—was the opposite of the poets portrayed in the films and represented the ideal that the Portuguese should strive to imitate. The head of the government called for the replacement of the inconsistent heroism of the past with dispassionate behavior, the only route to the country's development:[50]

Figure 2.5 One of Camões' feats, fighting alone against several guards at Princess Maria's palace, in *Camões*

Our past is full of beauty, of feats, but we have lacked, especially in the last century, a less brilliant but more tenacious effort, less spectacular but with more perspective. That which appeals only to the heroism of our race without changing the general mentality or our way of doing things may bring us temporary epic moments, but it burns us up in that continuous blaze, later delivering us to an unhealthy fatalism, expressed musically in the *fado*. This is the reason why we are an eternally nostalgic nation, far from reality; we have lived too much, in certain moments, a heroic but false reality.[51]

The adventurous character of the Portuguese resulted in a history rich in episodes of bravery that are the subject matter of Camões's epic poetry. However, it also led the country to the decadence of the First Republic. Salazar contrasted the audacity of heroes from the past with the stability of the New State and the efficiency of his *Realpolitik* in both the social and economic spheres. If Camões' death coincided with the decline of the nation, the New State should be understood as the country's rebirth, this time not under the sign of romantic, socially anarchical sentimentality that the regime uncritically associated with poetry. Instead, this resurgence should have at its base a strong political authority, a solid and cooperative economy, and a clearly defined social hierarchy, in which each citizen had a pre-defined place. Despite their glorification of Camões and Bocage, Leitão de Barros's films are, in the end, a condemnation of the poets' adventurism and a defense of the new model of a pragmatic and prosaic hero as the only viable solution to what Salazar called the national "small problem."[52] The "politics of the spirit" may then be regarded as a way to promote acceptance of the regime's prosaic nature and to compensate for Salazarism's lack of adventurous spirit, sentimentality, and romantic love by generating enthusiasm for the New State.[53]

Notes

1 For an analysis of António Ferro's texts about cinema, see António Pedro Pita's article "Temas e Figuras do Ensaísmo Cinematográfico," 43–7.
2 Ferro, *Entrevistas*, 223.
3 Anatoly Lunacharsky, the first head of the People's Commissariat of the Enlightenment, the Bolshevik institution responsible for propaganda, talked about film along the same lines as Ferro: "Cinema's strength lies in the fact that, like any art, it imbues an idea with feeling and with captivating form but, unlike the other

arts, cinema is actually cheap, portable and unusually graphic. Its effects reach where even the book cannot reach and it is, of course, more powerful than any kind of narrow propaganda." (Lunacharsky, cited in Reeves, *The Power of Film Propaganda*, 4.)

4 "A sua magia [do cinema], o seu poder de sedução, a sua força de penetração são incalculáveis. Mais do que a leitura [...] a imagem penetra, insinua-se, sem quase se dar por isso, na alma do homem. Em quase todos os outros meios de recreação a nossa inteligência, a nossa própria sensibilidade têm de aplicar-se, de trabalhar mais do que perante o cinema, do que em face daquele pano que, durante duas horas, se encarrega de pensar e de sonhar para nós. [...] O espectador de cinema é um ser passivo, mais desarmado do que o leitor ou do que o simples ouvinte." Ferro, *Teatro e Cinema*, 44.

5 Garnier, *Vacances*, 113.

6 "a literatura [...] é o grande manancial do cinema." Ferro, *Teatro e Cinema*, 51.

7 "O cinema é, acima de tudo, um grande livro de histórias ... É preciso saber contá-las com simplicidade sem o recurso das muletas habituais: folclore, grandes momentos de verdadeira ou falsa dramaticidade, graças pesadas, situações equívocas, etc., etc. ..." Ferro, *Teatro e Cinema*, 68.

8 Ferro, *Teatro e Cinema*, 48–51. Ferro also describes the virtues of Portuguese cinema that actually contradict some of the alleged "defects" mentioned earlier: "[…] perseverance, ingeniousness, improvisation (which is also a defect), moral rectitude in the choice and treatment of topics, a certain poetic capacity that is merely hinted at, a certain romanticism, a gift for moving people, a sense of caricature, a fondness for beautiful images, etc., etc. ..." ("[...] perseverança, engenho, improvisação (que também é defeito), limpeza moral na escolha e no tratamento dos assuntos, certa capacidade poética apenas adivinhada, certo romantismo, o dom de comover, sentido caricatural, o gosto pelas bonitas imagens, etc., etc. ...") Ferro, *Teatro e Cinema*, 88.

9 Ferro, *Teatro e Cinema*, 52. Ferro criticizes the search for profits at any cost that precluded investment in quality cinema: "The poor taste of our audiences, which often is not rooted in them but rather derives from being fed easy solutions, could be corrected if there were something in the producers' and exhibitors' heads other than concern for their immediate interests or their purely material profits." ("O mau-gosto das nossas plateias, que não é, muitas vezes, de raiz mas alimentado pelas soluções fáceis, é educável se houver mais alguma coisa na cabeça dos produtores e exibidores do que a preocupação do seu interesse imediato ou dos seus lucros apenas materiais.") Ferro, *Teatro e Cinema*, 66.

10 For a description of the type of literary works adapted to film during the New State, see Luís Reis Torgal, *Estados Novos, Estado Novo*, vol. 2, 202–8.

11 The plot of *Spell of the Empire* (*Feitiço do Império*), written by the director António Lopes Ribeiro, was inspired by a text of the same name by journalist Joaquim Pereira Mota Júnior. Mota Júnior won the contest organized by the General Agency of the Colonies (*Agência Geral das Colónias*) to select the best plot for the film. As for *Fátima, Land of Faith* (*Fátima, Terra de Fé*), the plot was adapted by Catholic writer Mello e Alvim from his homonymous novel.
12 "clima poético dentro da vida portuguesa." Ferro, *Política do Espírito: Apontamentos*, 19.
13 "cinema de barbas"; "um dos caminhos seguros, sólidos, do cinema português." Ferro, *Teatro e Cinema*, 64.
14 Ferro, *Teatro e Cinema*, 63–6.
15 "cancro do cinema nacional"; "fracas e infelizes tentativas." Ferro, *Teatro e Cinema*, 63–5.
16 "já deram largamente as suas provas." Ferro, *Teatro e Cinema*, 67.
17 Ferro reiterates his preference for films inspired by history and literary topics: "The transitory can be found in an eternal work. But the eternal, or at least the consistent, cannot be found in an ephemeral work. Therefore, our producers, our filmmakers should preferably choose the subject-matter for their films from our Nation's history or its literature, which will provide them with topics, as they already have provided, that would not be easy to find in the most vivid imagination." ("Pode ir buscar-se o efémero a uma obra eterna. Mas não pode ir buscar-se o eterno, ou pelo menos, o consistente, a uma obra efémera. Devem, portanto, os nossos produtores, os nossos realizadores escolher os assuntos para os seus filmes, de preferência, na história ou na literatura do nosso País que lhes fornecerão motivos, como já têm fornecido, que não será fácil encontrar na imaginação mais viva.") Ferro, *Teatro e Cinema*, 52.
18 Ribeiro, *Filmes, Figuras*, 353.
19 Only about seventy-eight minutes of the image track and even less of the soundtrack of the Portuguese version of *Bocage* have survived.
20 Matos-Cruz, "Bocage," in *Textos da Cinemateca Portuguesa*, 246; Ribeiro, *Filmes, Figuras*, 360. The historical reconstitution undertaken in the film also made use of the studios of Lisboa Antiga near São Bento, Vasco Regaleira's settings, and an opulent wardrobe that included pieces from the Garnier house in Paris (Pina, *História*, 80).
21 *The Three Graces* (*Las tres gracias*) premiered on 2 December 1936. It was a flop, leaving theaters three days after its premiere (Ribeiro, *Filmes, Figuras*, 360). This did not prevent the continued cinematic collaboration between Portugal and Spain, which was supported by the governments of both countries. For more detailed information on this topic, see Luís de Pina's *História do Cinema Português*, 109–12.
22 "uma data na história do nosso cinema que viu grande pela primeira vez [...]."

Ferro, *Teatro e Cinema*, 72. *Camões* was part of a trilogy by Leitão de Barros that also included *Bocage* and *Marvelous Gale* (*Vendaval Maravilhoso*, 1949), the latter being a joint Portuguese–Brazilian production about the life of Brazilian poet Castro Alves.

23 Ribeiro, *Filmes, Figuras*, 549–51. *Camões* was often criticized for its emphasis on scenography. Thus, Adolfo Casais Monteiro wrote about the film: "Leitão de Barros came to cinema from painting, and he did not succeed in overcoming some limitations that resulted from this move, perhaps because he did not even try. He always saw his films as a succession of 'pretty' pictures; above all, he lacked a cinematographic vision. Each of his films reminds us at all times that he is a specialist in the organization of parades ... His sense of the principles of the fine arts allows him to work with pre-made material, as in the case of *Camões*, with relative ease and great success among the public, who is moved by a story because of the myth therein contained, without being put off by the lack of real cinematographic material." ("Leitão de Barros veio da pintura para o cinema e não conseguiu, talvez por nem sequer o ter procurado, vencer algumas limitações que daí resultam. Viu sempre os seus filmes como uma sucessão de quadros 'bonitos'; falta-lhe principalmente uma visão cinematográfica. Cada filme seu faz-nos lembrar sempre que ele é um especialista na organização de cortejos ... O seu sentido de valores plásticos permite-lhe trabalhar uma matéria já feita, como é o caso de *Camões*, com relativa facilidade e grande êxito entre o público, que se comove com uma história por conta do mito nela contido, sem que de todo lhe pese a ausência de real matéria cinematográfica.") Cited in Costa, *Breve História*, 93. Luís de Pina also notes a "scenographic weight" (peso cenográfico) in the film, due to its excessive emphasis on a baroque setting (*História*, 97).

24 Pina, *História*, 97.

25 *Bocage* was a commercial flop in Portugal and in Spain, but it enjoyed relative success in Brazil, being one of the last Portuguese films to collect considerable profits in the former colony (Ribeiro, *Filmes, Figuras,* 360). Hiring the Brazilian actress Celita Bastos to play the role of Canária was also a strategy to promote the film overseas (Ribeiro, *Filmes, Figuras*, 358). However, *Camões* had little success in Brazil, despite positive reviews in local magazines at the time (Ribeiro, *Filmes, Figuras*, 558).

26 The film was screened in Cannes without subtitles, with a translator explaining the plot. António Ferro comments on this matter: "And if *Camões* did not win the prize that it deserved in Cannes, despite the applause that interrupted the screening, it was just because in that competition and at that moment, pure, elevated nationalism was not in style, because another power, I would not say higher but perhaps stronger, was temporarily on the rise." ("E se *Camões* não ganhou em Cannes o

prémio que merecia, apesar das palmas que interromperam a sua exibição, foi apenas porque, nesse concurso e nesse momento, o nacionalismo elevado, puro, não estava em moda, porque outro poder, não diremos mais alto mas talvez mais forte, transitoriamente se levantava.") Ferro, *Teatro e Cinema*, 72.

27 "Uma biografia viva do maior português da Renascença. [...] A vida maravilhosa do grande épico, *vivendo o seu tempo e o drama da sua época*, torná-lo na tela o que foi, *imagem de uma realidade genial*, feita de carne e de sentidos, é um desideratum que havemos de atingir [...]." Cited in Ribeiro, *Filmes, Figuras*, 549; emphasis added. Ferro also stresses the representative character of Camões as an emblem of his age: "[...] there is no doubt that we are facing a great work, a great cinematic fresco that not only honors national cinema but is also the standard of Portuguese sensibility, a hallmark of its epic, a moving tapestry of its glory." ("[...] não há dúvida que estamos diante duma grande obra, dum grande fresco cinematográfico que honra não só o cinema nacional mas constitui padrão da sensibilidade portuguesa, marco da sua epopeia, tapeçaria movediça da sua glória.") Ferro, *Teatro e Cinema*, 72.

28 "[O]s símbolos de uma gesta colectiva [foram] aqui sintetizados na vida e na arte de Luís Vaz de Camões. Não tenho dúvidas nenhumas em afirmar que Leitão de Barros concebeu a figura do poeta como uma imagem de Portugal, e é esse o sentido mais profundo da visão histórica de *Os Lusíadas* na cena de António Vilar diante das tapeçarias de Pastrana, síntese da própria história de Portugal." Pina, *História*, 97.

29 Hegel, *Reason in History*, 42.

30 "Numa mão sempre a espada e noutra a pena." Camões, *Os Lusíadas*, VII, 79.

31 Meneses, "Camões," in *NUI Maynooth Papers*, 1.

32 In his article "Camões, Portuguese War Propaganda, and the Dream of a Safe Empire, 1914–1918," Filipe Meneses analyzes how the First Republic used Camões's image to justify Portuguese participation in the First World War. According to Meneses, "Camões' life seemed to provide the moral example that should be followed at a time of crisis, and his works contained a vision of greatness which republicans avidly seized as their own, accepting Camões' stirring verse as an alternative to an adequately funded and modern military force, and an efficient colonial policy, both of which were beyond the country's limited means" ("Camões," in *NUI Maynooth Papers*, 2).

33 "homens-núcleo." Torgal, *Estados Novos*, vol. 2, 25–7.

34 See Torgal, *Estados Novos*, vol. 2, 42–54.

35 In a conference given in 1960, Costa Brochado stated: "We are amongst those who believe that the History of a people is the product of the collective soul, intelligence, and action as interpreted by the genius of its cyclical guides. Without a great people, like ours, [...] the epic of the Discoveries would not have been possible;

just like without the driving genius of Prince Henry the magnificent virtues of the Portuguese people would have been worth nothing. [...] Now, Gentlemen, we are at the top of the hill (thanks to Salazar, a perfect guide with a universality that emerges from centuries and centuries) [...]." ("Somos dos que crêem ser a História de um povo produto da alma, inteligência e do braço colectivos interpretados no génio dos seus guias cíclicos. Sem um grande povo, como o nosso [...] não teria sido possível a epopeia dos Descobrimentos; assim como sem o génio condutor do Infante D. Henrique, para nada teriam servido, na História dos Descobrimentos, as virtudes magníficas do povo português. [...] Nós estamos agora, meus senhores, no alto da colina (graças a Salazar, um guia de eleição com universalidade que surge de séculos e séculos) [...].") *Passado, Presente*, 7–8.

36 In a speech given for the celebration of Salazar's birthday, Costa Brochado said: "I even think that April 28th will be designated later in Portuguese history not really as the day of Salazar's birth, but as the day when Providence infused one anonymous Portuguese man's soul with the mysterious secrets and the heroic virtues that the Nation was lacking in the administration of the State, so that it would not flounder once and for all in our time." ("Acho mesmo que o dia 28 de Abril será, mais tarde, assinalado, na História de Portugal, não propriamente como o do nascimento de Salazar, mas como o dia em que a Providência infundiu na alma de um Português anónimo os misteriosos segredos e as virtudes heróicas de que a Pátria carecia, no governo do Estado, para não soçobrar, de vez, em nossos dias.") *Passado, Presente*, 18.

37 According to Luís Reis Torgal, Costa Brochado was a cultural ideologue of the regime who interpreted Portuguese history in a Manichean way in order to present Salazar's government as the nation's salvation and Portugal's last hope after the republican debacle. Costa Brochado's interpretation of history stressed the role of leaders who guide the country towards a grandiose future. According to him, Salazar was a man with a mission of leadership similar to that of Prince Henry the Navigator. See Torgal, *Estados Novos*, vol. 2, 103–17.

38 Christine Garnier highlights the parallels between Salazar and Messianic King Sebastian who, according to legend, would one day return from the dead to lead Portugal into a bright future. Garnier writes: "He [Salazar] thus makes us dream of King Sebastian, the *Desejado*, who was killed by the Moors and who, according to legend, shall return to Portugal on a foggy day." ("Il [Salazar] fait songer ainsi au roi Sébastien, le *Desejado*, qui fut tué par les Maures et qui doit revenir au Portugal, selon la légende, par un jour de brume.") *Vacances*, 76.

39 "Não se trata de um filme biográfico [...]. O que interessa é o espírito e o carácter do poeta e a 'verdade' psicológica da personagem. [...] tomou-se apenas o que desse génio se pode e deve reter—*os momentos de pura inspiração de poeta, a volubilidade*

desconcertante do amoroso." Barros, cited in Ribeiro, *Filmes, Figuras*, 356; emphasis added.

40 "Deixa-me ir para o botequim, eu quero que as mulheres me vejam." Cited in Matos-Cruz, "*Bocage*," in *Textos da Cinemateca Portuguesa*, 246.

41 "viveu sob a influência doentia do êxtase amoroso." Cited in Matos-Cruz, "*Camões*," in *Os Descobrimentos Portugueses*, 46.

42 "agitada juventude do poeta e dos seus amores." Cited in Matos-Cruz, "*Camões*," in *Os Descobrimentos Portugueses*, 46.

43 "estudioso"; "bem comportado"; "português sério"; "amante da vida, amoroso sempre, solitário, perseguido, derrotado, doente, mas que, nisso mesmo, no excesso barroco, no contraste entre um quotidiano vulgar e uma visão grandiosa, no coração, no sentido da viagem e da distância, pudesse simbolizar Portugal." Pina, *História*, 97.

44 Salazar, "Educação Política," in *Discursos e Notas Políticas (1938–1943)*.

45 "Excessivamente sentimental, com horror à disciplina […], falho de espírito de continuidade e de tenacidade na acção." Ferro, *Entrevistas*, 183. Salazar did not fail to list on other occasions the positive qualities of the Portuguese people: "Those qualities that were revealed and became permanent and make us who we are and not someone else: that sweetness of feelings; that modesty; that spirit of humanity, so rare in the world today; that spiritual side […]; that suffering disposition; that bravery without fanfare; that ease in adapting […]; the appreciation of moral values; faith in law, in justice, in the equality of men and of nations; all of these, which are neither material nor lucrative, are traits of the national character." ("Aquelas qualidades que se revelaram e fixaram e fazem de nós o que somos e não outros; aquela doçura de sentimentos, aquela modéstia, aquele espírito de humanidade, tão raro hoje no mundo; aquela parte de espiritualidade […]; o ânimo sofredor; a valentia sem alardes; a facilidade de adaptação […]; o apreço dos valores morais; a fé no direito, na justiça, na igualdade dos homens e dos povos; tudo isso, que não é material nem lucrativo, constitui traços do carácter nacional.") "Princípios e a Obra," in *Discursos e Notas Políticas (1938–1943)*, 403.

46 Salazar still had the same opinion about Portuguese inconstancy in 1953, when he said in a speech: "We are prone to build on fleeting enthusiasms, due to our well-known character, and to abandon the tasks we have just started for others. Now in the work that we strive to do, we must progressively replace improvisation with study, fickleness in feeling with fidelity to a program." ("Somos atreitos, por conhecido modo de ser, a construir sobre entusiasmos efémeros e a abandonar, por outras, tarefas mal começadas. Ora na obra em que nos empenhamos, há que ir substituindo nos hábitos gerais a improvisação pelo estudo, a volubilidade no sentir pela fidelidade a um programa.") "Plano de Fomento," in *Discursos e Notas Políticas (1951–1958)*, 94.

47 "–[Ferro] A sua aspiração, o seu sonho teimoso—perdoe-me se observo mal—é modificar, pouco a pouco, pacientemente, a nossa mentalidade, fazendo parar, bruscamente, as paixões dos homens, atrofiando-as, calando-as, forçando-nos, temporariamente, a um ritmo vagaroso, mas seguro, que nos faça descer a temperatura, que nos cure da febre …
 –Continue …—responde-me da sombra o dr. Salazar–. Talvez esteja a caminho da verdade …" Ferro, *Entrevistas*, 100–1.

48 António Ferro notes the existence of a "certain baroque characteristic of our race" ("certo barroco próprio da nossa raça"), a superabundance, an excessive "verbalism" ("verbalismo") that is manifested both in literature and in cinema, and that is associated with the exaggerated feelings of the Portuguese (*Teatro e Cinema*, 53).

49 "pouco sentimental nesta como noutras matérias." Ferro, *Entrevistas*, 141.

50 In the epilogue to his interviews with Salazar, Ferro compares the statesman to Prince Henry the Navigator, because both are characterized by a distant relationship with the rest of the Portuguese people, which allowed them to be efficient leaders of the country: "It was said that he [Salazar] is outside his race, that he does not understand it. Perhaps they are right, but is this a fault? Was it not this distance from the low point of the race, be it a natural or premeditated distance, what gave Prince Henry the chance to make his dream come true?" ("Diz-se que ele [Salazar] está fora da raça, que não a compreende. Talvez tenham razão, mas será isso um defeito? Não teria sido essa distância da maré-baixa da raça, distância natural ou premeditada, que deu possibilidades a D. Henrique para a realização do seu sonho?") *Entrevistas*, 110. In the same text, Ferro also asserts that one of Salazar's goals as a leader was to bring the nation to "negate its own instincts, save it from its passions" ("negar os seus próprios instintos, libertá-la das suas paixões") 111.

51 "O nosso passado está cheio de beleza, de rasgos, mas tem-nos faltado, no último século, sobretudo, um esforço menos brilhante mas mais tenaz, menos espectaculoso e com maior perspectiva. Tudo quanto seja apelar somente para o heroísmo da raça, sem modificação da mentalidade geral, do nosso modo de fazer as coisas, pode trazer-nos momentaneamente páginas de epopeia, mas queima-nos nessas labaredas contínuas, entregando-nos, depois, a esse fatalismo doentio, de que o *Fado* é a expressão musical. É essa a razão por que nós somos um povo eternamente saudoso, longe das realidades por termos vivido demasiado, em certos momentos, uma realidade heróica mas falsa." Ferro, *Entrevistas*, 98.
 In his interviews with Ferro, Salazar often reiterated this position: "I would dare to say that we are too tied to the memory of our heroes—incidentally, never loved and venerated in excess—too enslaved to a collective ideal that always revolves

around a glorious past and its unparalleled heroisms. Our heroic past weighs too much on our present. We may have had Vasco da Gama, João de Castro, Afonso de Albuquerque, the triumphs, the dazzling glories of India, but behind our backs, English merchants, incomparably less illustrious, created for England a great Empire without realizing it. [...] In wanting to cling to the ideas of heroic times, we run the risk of appearing to be idle hands in a new world that does not understand us." ("Por mim atrevo-me a dizer que estamos demasiadamente presos à memória dos nossos heróis—nunca, aliás, querida e venerada em excesso—demasiadamente escravizados a um ideal colectivo que gira sempre à roda de glórias passadas e inigualáveis heroísmos. O nosso passado heróico pesa demasiado no nosso presente. Se nós tivemos Vasco da Gama, João de Castro, Afonso de Albuquerque, os triunfos, as glórias fulgurantes da Índia, por detrás de nós, comerciantes ingleses, incomparavelmente menos ilustres, criaram para a Inglaterra, sem dar por isso, um grande Império. [...] A querermos agarrar-nos às concepções dos tempos heróicos, corremos o risco de aparecermos como braços desocupados num mundo novo que não nos entende.") *Entrevistas*, 247–8. In his conversations with Christine Garnier, Salazar again mentioned the Portuguese inconstancy and the country's rapid transition from heroism to decadence: "Among us—Salazar replied—the average, a balanced temperature, normality are not the rule. Heroic periods are followed at an incredible speed by catastrophic depression, collective discouragement, national heartache." ("Chez nous, répond Salazar, la moyenne, la température équilibrée, la normalité ne sont pas la règle. Aux périodes héroïques succèdent avec une rapidité incroyable la dépression catastrophique, le découragement collectif, la tristesse nationale.") *Vacances*, 113.

52 "caso comezinho." Salazar, "Propaganda Nacional," in *Discursos (1928–1934)*, 263. Salazar defined the transformation that he sought to operate in Portuguese habits in terms of a "cure" for national "ills," including inconstancy and sentimentality: "Little by little we are getting cured from these ills; with countless difficulties, incessantly fighting against bad tendencies and bad habits, we have insisted that the old man definitely be abandoned and we have sought to build a political and social order that would not encourage the growth of defects and vile passions, but rather the best use of the good qualities of the Portuguese people." ("A pouco e pouco nos vamos curando desses males; com dificuldades sem conta, a lutar incessantemente contra más tendências e maus hábitos, temos insistido em que se dispa definitivamente o homem velho e procurado construir uma ordem política e social que não seja de si mesma incitamento à expansão dos defeitos e das paixões vis, mas à maxima utilização das qualidades dos portugueses.") "Funções," in *Discursos e Notas Políticas (1935–1937)*, 4–5.

53 Ferro, *Entrevistas*, 221.

3

Rural Life in Cinema: In Defense of a Natural Society

Regional and folkloric films

One of the most prolific strands of Portuguese cinema in the first decades of the New State was that of "regional or folkloric films." António Ferro used this expression to refer to a set of productions whose plots develop, at least in part, in a rural environment, and highlight local traditions and customs.[1] Ferro proved to be rather critical of certain aspects of these movies, sarcastically nicknamed "hick flicks" by some critics, since they forged a somewhat exotic image of everyday village life. For instance, they often included long scenes portraying regional folklore and music without great concern for ethnographic truth. However, if Ferro reproached the "dances and songs [...] clearly hammered into" some of these films, he did not fail to appreciate movies that dealt with rural life, so long as "regionalism or folklore does not become forced and therefore artificial."[2] The President of the SPN/SNI condemned the addition of artificial elements to these movies, and warned that even local folklore, when shown in excess, could destroy the simplicity that was the main charm of these productions.[3]

Ferro's rejection of artificiality in the artistic context echoes Salazar's longing to organize Portugal, in socio-political terms, "as much as possible, according to a *natural plan*—that is, respecting the spontaneous grouping of men around their interests and their activities in order to bring these together within the State," as he states in the pamphlet *Como se Levanta um Estado*.[4] Salazar believed in the existence of a natural order, which the structure of Portuguese society should mirror as closely as possible. For him, the social organization that is most harmonious with natural laws is found in the countryside, whereas the artificial life of the city is the origin of all social ills: "Misery seems to be a discharge of progress, of civilization. Its incurable tragedy develops [...] in the cities, in the large capitals, [which are] all the more callous and harsh the more they are civilized."⁵ Therefore, it was appropriate for New State films dealing with the rural world to highlight its advantages over urban culture, to reproduce natural rhythms, and to avoid artificiality. These movies' educational and propagandistic value is derived precisely from their faithful representation of rural life, a social model for all Portuguese people.

The "regional or folkloric films" produced during the New State do not form a homogenous group. They represent a variety of regions—from Minho to the Algarve, from fishing villages to mountainous areas—adopt different styles, depending on the filmmakers' vision, and lean toward one film genre or another, ranging from movies that are predominantly documentary to others featuring a complex fictional plot. However, it is possible to recognize some fundamental traits that unite the various films of this type, characteristics that reflect the central values of the New State's worldview. First, all of these productions more or less explicitly praise the simplicity of village life, frequently represented in a stylized and idealized way. Nature is portrayed both as a source of sustenance for the community and as a force that destroys human endeavors in Leitão de Barros's *Maria of the Sea* (*Maria do Mar*, 1930) and *Up and Away!* (*Ala-Arriba!*, 1942), in Jorge Brum do Canto's *The Song of the Earth* (*A Canção da Terra*, 1938) and *Wolves of the Mountain* (*Lobos da Serra*, 1942), and in Henrique Campos's *A Man from Ribatejo* (*Um Homem do Ribatejo*, 1946). Yet, the image that prevails is that of nature as a nurturing mother that rewards the arduous work of those who trust her, despite occasional setbacks.

Along with the praise of rural life, the notion that the countryside is a repository of the true traditions and values of the Portuguese people appears in films like António Lopes Ribeiro's *Wild Cattle* (*Gado Bravo*, 1934), Leitão de Barros's *The Rector's Pupils* (*As Pupilas do Senhor Reitor*, 1935) and *Maria Papoila* (1937), and Chianca de Garcia's *The Village of White Clothes* (*Aldeia da Roupa Branca*, 1939). These films contrast the countryside with the decadence of city life, influenced by foreign customs that lead to moral corruption and the dissolution of the ties uniting the members of the community. Finally, in films like Henrique Campos's *Ribatejo* (1949) and in Jorge Brum do Canto's late work, *The Iron Cross* (*A Cruz de Ferro*, 1967), we find a critique of two characteristics of capitalism: the excessive accumulation of wealth and the unbridled pursuit of profits. Rejecting a communitarian social model akin to communism, which would entail the abolition of private property and an equalitarian division of labor, these films outline a corporatism *in nuce*, based on solidarity and mutual help as ways of overcoming economic difficulties while keeping the social hierarchy intact.⁶

A natural cinema

The ideological foundations of Salazarism were rooted in the idea that society was the reproduction of nature in the realm of human relations. For Salazar, economics and politics necessarily depended upon the "natural conditions of the existence of a people,"[7] which were determined, in turn, by "natural" social groups such as the family, the different professions, or the Church.[8] The eternal and indisputable "great truths" that formed the core of the New State's ideology—religion, nation, family, etc.—presumably emanated from the concrete reality of the human condition: "What I wanted was […] to find the confirmation of some unchanging and eternally valid truths in the governing of nations, because they corresponded *to the very nature of the human soul*."[9] In the rhetoric of its leaders, the New State was the incarnation of a natural order, i.e. the translation of an original and spontaneous *modus vivendi* that already existed *de facto* in Portugal into institutional and legal terms: "To summarize: we seek to construct the social and corporatist state in close relation to the *natural constitution of society*."[10] Salazar presented himself as a simple interpreter of the truths that underpin the Portuguese nation as a community.[11] The regime's success, its relative stability and longevity, which are opposed, as Salazar repeated countless times, to the disorder of the Republican period that preceded it, would stem from its "naturalness," from its conformity with the natural order that served as its inspiration.[12]

This emphasis on naturalness, which for the leaders of the New State was epitomized in Portuguese rural life, cannot be fully explained by the personality cult of Salazar that would prompt his collaborators to praise his village origins. It is true that Salazar spoke with pride of his humble family history: "[…] I am rural—by origin, by blood, by temperament—attached to the land, the source of men's happiness and of their nourishment."[13] However, the rhetoric of naturalness instrumentalized by the regime's propaganda had an eminently political reach. If one accepts the premise that the New State was in agreement with the natural condition of the Portuguese people, the regime appears to be not only inevitable, but also the best possible political system for Portugal. Salazar's aversion to social change was therefore justified by the fact that the organization of Portuguese society was the most natural way of living. Small adjustments made to the government were nothing more than strategies to reach an increasingly more perfect harmony between nature and the nation.

The popularity of "natural cinema"—films about village life—in the 1930s and 1940s was simultaneously a symptom and a consequence of the emphasis placed by the regime on "living naturally." This expression could serve as a complement to "living habitually," which was Salazar's wish for the country, as he confessed to Henri Massis.[14] On the one hand, the number of movies on this topic shows that the intellectual climate was favorable to this narrative genre. On the other hand, several of these projects were the result of direct support from the state. This was the case of SPN-sponsored *Up and Away!*, which became the first Portuguese movie to win an international competition when it was awarded a prize at the Venice Biennale in 1942. Both *Up and Away!* and *Maria of the Sea*, also directed by Leitão de Barros, follow one of the paths trodden by cinema about the rural environment, namely the documentary style. The plot is used merely as a guiding thread for the presentation of images of nature and of the habits of the local population.

The SPN/SNI produced several short documentaries that highlighted the characteristics of different regions of Portugal. These works, divided into two series—*Portuguese Journal* (*Jornal Português*, 1938–51) and *Images of Portugal* (*Imagens de Portugal*, 1953–70)—were part of the efforts developed by the regime's propaganda to highlight the positive aspects of rural life. Beyond cinema, the New State promoted countless other cultural and artistic activities related to this topic, including the Competition for the Most Portuguese Village of Portugal, the *Verde Gaio* Ballet Company, and the Museum of Popular Art, inaugurated in 1948.[15] Unlike the SPN/SNI shorts, Leitão de Barros made, in the wake of the short documentary *Nazaré, a Fishermen's Beach* (*Nazaré, Praia de Pescadores*, 1927), two feature-length films that are not purely documentary, but rather fictionalized documentaries: *Maria of the Sea* and *Up and Away!*[16] While the fundamental concern of both movies is with showing images of nature and the everyday life of the inhabitants of the fishing villages Nazaré and Póvoa do Varzim, respectively, many scenes from the films are organized around a tenuous plot based on a love story. Barros's movies are further distinguishable from most purely propagandistic films for their technical rigor, their careful framing, and the beauty of their photography. For these reasons, they were very well received among film critics at the time.[17]

The main character of these films is the sea: the fishermen's livelihood depends on it, and the rhythm of fishing and of the tides determines the customs and rituals of the population of these regions. The movies' plots reflect the entanglement of the villagers' lives with nature and the sea. For instance,

Figure 3.1 Arrival of a fishing boat in *Maria of the Sea*

the misunderstanding between the families of the protagonists Maria do Mar (Rosa Maria Monteiro) and Manuel (Oliveira Martins) in *Maria of the Sea* is caused by a shipwreck in which Manuel's father, a fisherman working for Maria's father, is a victim. The enmity between their families leads the young couple to hide their love and marry against their mothers' will. In *Up and Away!*, João (João Moço) courageously saves Julha's (Elsa Bela Flor) father from drowning when he is fishing in the sea during a storm. This act of bravery redeems the young man in the eyes of the community, allowing him to marry Julha in the film's *denouement*. Defiance of the inexorable laws of nature, represented by the greed of some fishermen who go to sea during stormy days, is punished with shipwrecks and with death in the films. Forgetting these laws entails similar risks, as we can see in a central sequence of *Maria of the Sea*, in which the young woman overlooks the force of maritime currents and goes swimming with her friends. When she gets caught in a whirlpool, Manuel saves her from drowning. Here, as in *Up and Away!*, it is a rescue from the dangers of the sea that leads to the union of the protagonists.

In these movies, nature appears both as the source of the community's livelihood and as the cause of its suffering, a motif repeated in several other films from this period. For instance, *The Song of the Earth*, Brum do Canto's film about his native Porto Santo, deals with the drought that periodically strikes the island and its consequences for the local population. Similarly, in *Wolves of the Mountain* and in *A Man from Ribatejo*, a flood puts the peasants' lives in danger, devastates the harvest in the former and the pastures and herds in the latter film. Natural disasters, whether they are maritime storms, droughts, or floods, disturb village tranquility. Yet, they are not a justifiable reason for abandoning the countryside or the sea. On the contrary, the films urge fidelity to an ancestral way of life and show how the catastrophes disrupting rural routine can be quickly overcome by a cohesive community with the help of nature itself.

The Song of the Earth is an indictment of the emigration of many inhabitants from Porto Santo. One of the first scenes of the film portrays the departure of two young men who are going to America in search of employment because they cannot grow enough food during the drought. This decision to leave Portugal is condemned by several characters over the course of the movie. Caçarola (Óscar de Lemos), who emigrated to the US and Brazil only to later return disillusioned to his birthplace, says that hunger and unemployment also exist in these countries. He complains of the nostalgia he felt when he was far from home, and advises the other men from the village not to leave. As the drought deepens, the protagonist himself, Gonçalves (Barreto Poeira), considers leaving the village and his beloved Bastiana (Elsa Rumina) in order to try his luck in America. At the end of the film, when the drought is over and the island is enjoying a period of prosperity, a letter from the two young men who emigrated arrives. In their message they express regret for having departed and complain of being homesick. At that point, Gonçalves reflects that he too was "about to lose faith," but that in the end he realized "the land gives you labor—that it does—but sooner or later it also gives you everything."[18] The film endorses agriculture as the most suitable activity for the Portuguese and stresses that, despite the obstacles, farming is a gratifying occupation.

In *The Song of the Earth*, the drought is exacerbated by João Venâncio's (António Moita) greed. Refusing to sell his well water to Gonçalves, he tries to buy his cattle that are about to die of hunger at very low prices. Just like in Leitão de Barros's films, in which the goal of increasing the volume of the catch is responsible for shipwrecks and for the deaths of several fishermen, the unrestrained drive for profits, more than the forces of nature, is identified in

Brum do Canto's movie as the chief cause of the tragedy that strikes the inhabitants of Porto Santo.

In *Wolves of the Mountain* we also find an unambiguous condemnation of a group of smugglers' desire to get rich. Having given up on farming, they risk their lives to cross the Serra do Soajo in order to get to Spain, where they obtain products that they resell in Portugal at a large profit. On one of the occasions when they return with their merchandise, several smugglers are killed by the border police, which leads Joaquim (Carlos Otero) to give up this business. The plot reaches its climax when António (António de Sousa), recently married to his beloved Margarida (Maria Domingas), sees their arduously raised crops destroyed by a flood. Without money and without the willpower to clean the fields, António is persuaded by the smugglers of the region to join their group. In a breathtaking sequence, we witness António's death and Margarida's desperation, represented through distorted images that visually express her state of mind. In the end, the viewers realize they were witnessing António's dream, a premonition that leads him to give up smuggling and return to agriculture. Upon arriving at his plot of land, António finds the entire village gathered there in a manifestation of solidarity to help the young couple recover from the tragedy caused by the flood. While the peasants clean the soil from the debris left by the water, the chief of police and the village priest—the two main authority figures in the movie—comment on recent events. The priest concludes that farming is the best path to happiness, in that God himself ordered humanity: "Till the land with the sweat of your brow."[19]

The rejection of wealth and excessive profit in the films of this period is consistent with the principles defended by Salazar. In line with traditional Catholic doctrine, he often condemned money as a force that corrupts morals and criticized the "suicidal economics" that disconnected "wealth from the interests of human life," as well as the "production of the superfluous," "artificial consumption," and "fictitious necessities." Salazar stressed the need to make "money modestly serve work"[20] and summarized his economic tenets in the following way: "In short: riches, goods, and production are not ends in themselves: individual interests and collective interests have to be achieved; they mean nothing unless they are subordinate to the conservation of human life."[21] The new economy developed by the New State therefore opposed the desire to obtain excessive profits fueled by superfluous consumption.[22] This economic structure should be predominantly rural, based on small- or medium-sized properties, and it should concentrate on meeting the population's basic needs,

Figure 3.2 The community united for the marriage of the protagonists in *Wolves of the Mountain*

not on the accumulation of capital or large-scale industrialization. The "family couple" (casal de família) an institution enshrined in the 1933 Constitution, is an example of the measures adopted by the government to encourage farming. It protected small- to medium-sized farms in an effort to prevent both the fragmentation of arable land and its transfer into the hands of large landowners. The goal was to prevent internal migration to the cities and to encourage the development of traditional rural family communities.[23]

If excessive wealth leads to the perversion of human nature in the sense that, for Salazar, that which is natural is what is strictly necessary, poverty becomes a value that should be preserved: "I owe to Providence the grace of being poor: without valuable possessions, I am attached to the wheel of fortune by very little, nor have I ever needed profitable jobs, riches, ostentations."[24] For Salazar, rural work on small farms was the occupation that best suited human nature. In the countryside one leads a poor, albeit not miserable, life, a humble condition that should be praised:

> Agricultural labor, under the torrid sun and the impertinent rain, is then above all a calling of poverty; but its pride comes from the fact that it is the only thing

that feeds man and allows him to live. When we govern a country, and are faced with difficult markets, impractical seas, hungry mouths not knowing where the next bite of bread will come from, it is the poor land, the humble land that rises to the culmination of unknown heroisms and priceless values.[25]

The result of agricultural work, strictly dependant on natural cycles—from the "torrid sun" to the "impertinent rain"—is an honorable poverty, a situation presented as a social ideal both in Salazar's rhetoric and the films of this period. Salazar defined the land as "poor" and "humble," adjectives that acquired here a positive connotation, since the land became the country's salvation in periods of economic crisis.

"Regional or folkloric films" present village life, fueled by an economy based on small- or medium-scale farming, herding, and fishing, as a model for the rest of the country. In these movies, natural disasters do not lead to the population's estrangement from nature or from the activities that depend on it. On the contrary, such events acquire a quasi-religious meaning, since the main characters must overcome these ordeals by making the correct decisions—in other words, those that are consistent with the values disseminated by the regime—in order to reach happiness. It is in light of this conception of nature that one must interpret the marriage of the protagonists in *Up and Away!* after the rescue from the shipwreck, the prosperity of the married couple after setting aside the idea to emigrate in *The Song of the Earth*, and the happiness of António and Margarida in *Wolves of the Mountain* once António resists the temptation of becoming a smuggler. The films present catastrophes as tests of the moral qualities of the people affected by them, and stress that nature, despite occasional convulsions, rewards those who trust in it to make their livelihood. It is up to human beings to persevere in their activities, even when they are confronted by adversity, to resist the temptation of easy but dishonest profits, and to show solidarity with other members of the group, thus forming a prosperous and cohesive community.

There are clear parallels between the conception of the natural world in New State films and national politics. Like the nature portrayed in the movies, the Salazarist government is at times the source of situations that displease the population, for example, the practice of censorship and other limitations on individual freedom. However, although they may harm individual citizens, the state's laws and the decisions of the government, just like nature itself, are socially beneficial in the end. The role of Mother Nature, who generates her children's livelihood, is thus complemented by a paternalistic view of the state that ensures the country's socio-political wellbeing. The certainty that nature will provide sustenance, the praise of agriculture, and the importance of community cohesion that we find in these films is transposed, in a political context, into confidence in government resolutions, valorization of work, and solidarity among the various classes comprising Portuguese society. The ideology of the New State therefore arises as the necessary counterpoint to the so-called natural conditions of the nation.

In films about rural life, the plot provides an excuse to film both natural beauty and the traditions and festivities of the different regions where the action unfolds. This aim is clear in productions with a large documentary component, like *Maria of the Sea* or *Up and Away!* Leitão de Barros acknowledges this goal when he states:

> *Up and Away!* It will be a film about the habits, laws, customs, and traditions of the fishermen of Póvoa [...] The film will evoke some of their traditional ceremonies: the tribunal of the "men of respect," the crafting of the indispensable betrothal net, [...] their most important and significant festivities [...].[26]

But even in fictional films like *Wolves of the Mountain* (*Lobos da Serra*) and *A Man from Ribatejo* (*Um Homem do Ribatejo*), we often find scenes with a documentary penchant. For example, the former includes a long sequence that shows the procession of the Lady of Peneda, while in the latter we see images of the traditional running of the bulls.

The popularity of film productions that depict a typically Portuguese environment, composed of natural wonders, local traditions, and monuments, dates back to the beginning of cinema in Portugal. The "typically Portuguese" films that highlighted popular culture, understood as synonymous with rural life, abounded in the 1920s. National film critics considered them to be preferable to foreign cinema, which led to a denationalization of the Portuguese people and a perversion of the country's customs.[27] The emphasis placed on popular culture became even more pronounced in the cinema of the New State, in response to Salazar's ambition of presiding over a "re-Portugalization of Portugal," to use his own words,[28] excising nefarious influences from the country and searching for inspiration for his politics in tradition:

> We are trying to make a political creation that is structurally Portuguese. [...] the principal source of our teachings, and the source of inspiration of the great lines of our political construction, has been our history, tradition, temperament—Portuguese reality, in short.[29]

Rural Life in Cinema: In Defense of a Natural Society   91

Figure 3.3   Marriage rituals in *Ala-Arriba*

The New State saw in history and in ancestral customs the source of inspiration to build a stable political regime. This is something Salazarism had in common, local nuances notwithstanding, with Fascist Italy and Nazi Germany.[30] As Salazar put it: "We hope that the greatest merit of our institutions is that they bear the mark of their Portuguese origins."[31] These words implicitly criticize the First Republic, whose support base was mostly urban. According to Salazar, the Republic had failed precisely because it sought to subject Portugal to an artificial political regime that originated abroad and therefore did not respond to the country's needs. Unlike Republicanism, Salazar's government was truly Portuguese because it was grounded in national reality. Instead of importing policies and ideas, the New State sought to "impose Portugal on the Portuguese" in order to "earn the Portuguese the respect of the world"[32] by eliminating the Republican vices that had distanced the nation from its traditional culture.

The country to be imposed on the Portuguese was rural Portugal, where farmers supposedly lived in a perfect symbiosis with nature, disturbed only occasionally by brief incidents: droughts, floods, or storms. These events were then normalized through the efforts of the community, which became more cohesive once it overcame the ordeals imposed upon it by the environment. The nature posited by the New State is not a completely foreign entity, divorced from the life of human beings who would only be able to contemplate the natural sublime with a mix of fascination and terror. Instead of a wild nature, an idea that originated in Romanticism and has found in Caspar David Friedrich's famous painting "Wanderer above the Sea of Fog" its most accomplished visual expression, Salazarism presents a domesticated natural environment adapted to human life. Rousseau's "noble savage" immersed in a virgin nature gives way to the villager, who is just as natural because he is the result of a synthesis uniting humans and the environment. The villager creates a landscape transformed by local customs and traditions and spiritualized by human action, which in turn is more spiritual the more it approximates the natural world.[33] This nature, indistinguishable in the end from the traditions and customs of rural communities, is what Salazar took as a source of inspiration for his politics.

In the "natural films" of the New State, the representation of the environment overlaps with human concerns, namely the expectations of the fishermen, shepherds, and peasants who depend on nature. The majestic images of the stormy sea captured by Leitão de Barros in *Maria of the Sea* and *Up and Away!* only make sense when embedded in the drama of the fishermen who lose their lives during maritime storms. The projection of human hopes in the images of nature is even more obvious in *The Song of the Earth*, more specifically in the sequence following Caçarola's announcement that rain clouds are approaching Porto Santo. All the village farmers run to their fields, carrying hoes and ready to plow the land to later sow new crops. However, the clouds end up dissipating, and they pass without bringing rain. In a pungent image of desperation, the peasants are filmed in a medium-long shot on the island's dry, rough land. They stand with hoes over their shoulders, turned in the direction of the white clouds that move quickly through the blue sky. Once again, the community appears here united, with its members' bodies in the same position as they literally face their difficulties. People are only reconciled with the natural environment in the end of the film when the drought gives way to abundant rain.

If the images of nature are colored by human events, the costumes and celebrations that punctuate the rhythm of village life in the films conversely depend on the natural environment. Thus, songs and dances often accompany farming activities, and processions, pilgrimages, or other festivities normally occur after the harvest. In *A Man from Ribatejo* (*Um Homem do Ribatejo*), for instance, the wedding celebration is interrupted by the news of the death of a

Figure 3.4 The peasants of Porto Santo wait for rain in *The Song of the Earth*

peasant who had been gored by a bull. The films thus portray a natural order that originates not in nature or in socio-political life, but rather in the entanglement of these two spheres.

The New State wishes to establish a link between Portuguese politics and the natural world, offering the country a calm life with only minor transformations that do not disturb the tranquil existence of the nation. Salazar describes this goal to Christine Garnier, when the journalist mentions the almost stifling calm that she found in Portugal:

> [Salazar] What impression did Portugal leave with you, madame?
> [Garnier] An impression of calm, Mister President. Too much calm. Some would say paralysis.
> [Salazar] This calm that strikes you is purposeful, he responded. [...] In fact, I think that the fever and permanent frenzy in which some regimes keep their people is an unhealthy and hardly natural thing. [...]
> [Garnier] However, nature is not in permanent rest, I said.
> [Salazar] Evidently—Salazar admitted. But look at how she behaves. The seasons mark differences, but nevertheless they follow each other with impressive

regularity. […] I also earnestly hope that our little piece of the earth holds on to this precious good […]: the sweetness of a tranquil existence.[34]

Nature changes, but each season returns with predictable regularity. In the same way, the social progress purportedly brought by the regime—in the economy, education, medical access, colonial administration, etc.—was simply a way better to perpetuate the Portuguese way of life. Therefore, Salazar did not stand for immobility, but rather advocated changes that developed like a spiral, moving inward to come ever closer to the center: the full essence of being Portuguese.

Several "regional or folkloric films" echo Salazar's view that change should result in greater social tranquility. *The Iron Cross* follows the construction of an elaborate irrigation system that will bring water from the river to the fields, thereby transforming the ancestral enmity opposing the two villages of the region and resolving the precarious situation of the community of Valado. In the case of *The Village of White Clothes*, the purchase of a truck to replace the traditional oxcarts leads to the return of Chico (José Amaro) from the city to his hometown, where he takes back his position as heir to his father's property. These examples show that the ideology of the New State does not condemn technological development *per se*. What it denounces is the materialism of modern urban society, because the latter subordinates spiritual endeavors to profit, leads to the dissolution of moral values, and consequently disturbs the "tranquil existence" that Salazar wanted for the country.

The countryside and the city

The conflict between the values of rural Portugal and the ways of city life, influenced by foreign customs that destabilize the natural order, serves as the background for several New State films.[35] This "ideological war"[36] is highlighted in *Wild Cattle*, a film that emphasizes the incompatibility of the moral rectitude that prevails in the Ribatejo meadowlands with the bohemian decadence of urban areas. Manuel Garrido (Raul de Carvalho), a well-known bullfighter, is seduced by a Viennese cabaret actress, Nina (Olly Gebauer). Soon after their first encounter in Lisbon, she arrives at his house in Ribatejo after getting lost during a road trip. Despite the protests of Manuel, who is faithful to his Portuguese fiancée Branca (Nita Brandão), Nina stays in Ribatejo and ends up establishing herself in the bullfighter's house. Both his best friend and the workers on the homestead, who gather in a spontaneous manifestation of protest against the "blondie," tell Manuel to kick Nina off the property. Likewise, Branca visits Nina and tries to persuade her to leave, resorting first to pleas and then threats. The local community thus unites in an attempt to expel the foreign element from the heart of their village and to restore the lost tranquility. At the end of the story, Nina returns to Lisbon, where she is murdered by an old lover. This outcome is an obvious expression of divine justice with misogynistic undertones, which can be found in various other films, as we will see later. The allure of cosmopolitan Lisbon, a stage for artists with dubious morals that endanger the bullfighter's integrity, is overcome. The movie ends with the marriage of Manuel and Branca in their village church, an event that brings back the calm that Nina's arrival had disturbed.

The contrast between city habits and the simplicity of rural life is also a central theme in Leitão de Barros's *The Rector's Pupils*, a film adaptation of Júlio Dinis's homonymous novel.[37] The movie depicts young Daniel (Paiva Raposo), a doctor who has recently graduated from the University of Coimbra, as he adapts to daily life in the village where he was born. Influenced by the student lifestyle he picked up at the university, Daniel considers the routine of the countryside to

Figure 3.5   Peasants in the Ribatejo meadowlands in *Wild Cattle*

be too monotonous, and therefore decides to court his brother's girlfriend Clara (Maria Paula), putting the girl's honor into question and endangering the peace of the community. The predicament is resolved by Clara's sister, Margarida (Leonor d'Eça), whom Daniel ends up marrying once he recognizes the moral superiority of village existence. The film includes several scenes that show the rituals associated with farming and popular culture—grape harvesting, the shucking of the corn, folkloric gatherings, etc.—in a picturesque manner. These scenes led the Inspector-General of Entertainment to consider the movie to be a "beautiful expression of national art"[38] (as the viewer can read on screen before the credits), in that it highlighted the positive elements of the Portuguese countryside.

In another of Barros's films, *Maria Papoila*, the criticism of city mores is even more scathing. The movie tells of the adventures of a shepherdess from Beira, played by Mirita Casimiro, who decides to leave her village for Lisbon, where she gets a job as a maid in a pension. There she meets the soldier Eduardo (Eduardo Fernandes), with whom she begins to fall in love because she thinks that he too hails from humble origins. Upon finishing his military service, Eduardo, the son of a wealthy bourgeois family, abandons Maria Papoila for a rich and sophisticated girlfriend. When he is accused of robbery, Eduardo chivalrously refuses to provide his alibi because he would have to confess that he had spent the night with his girlfriend. Since her honor is at stake, she does not testify on behalf of her boyfriend, so as not to reveal her secret. Maria Papoila will be the one who saves Eduardo when she lies and says that he spent the night with her, which proves that he could not have been the author of the crime. Maria thus shows that she has the moral rectitude absent in Eduardo's girlfriend, a woman accustomed to the hypocrisy of city life.

Maria Papoila criticizes both licentious city customs, epitomized in this case by the nocturnal encounters between Eduardo and his girlfriend, and the pretense inherent in the social relationships of members of the bourgeoisie, which contrast with the purity of feelings of people from the countryside. This gap between the conduct of the wealthiest classes and village simplicity is another version of the opposition between city and countryside. In fact, the "people," frequently mentioned in a flattering way in the rhetoric of the leaders of the New State, are elevated to the position of a transcendent category, systematically linked to rural life. This "great mass of people, although illiterate," possessed, in Salazar's words, "strong national consciousness—the most secure base of our independence as a nation."[39] Furthermore, the "people" displayed a

Figure 3.6 Maria Papoila (Mirita Casimiro) and Eduardo's girlfriend in *Maria Papoila*

moral rectitude that did not exist in the city: "Mountain air does not just kill the germs in the chest; it cleans the intellect. City hypocrisy cannot breathe in these altitudes. And the truth flows, like the purest fountain, from the heart and the lips of men."[40] Significantly, this praise of mountain air and many other texts in a similar vein were drafted by intellectual urbanites, who travelled to Portuguese villages in order to get in touch with the cradle of the nation.[41] These intellectuals, part of the urban bourgeoisie, were charged with the task of showing to the rest of the country, especially to city dwellers, the superiority of rural life.

In the New State, the rural population came to symbolize the entire Portuguese nation, so that even when the popular culture of the city was mentioned, it was represented in reference to the countryside. This explains why the Lisbon neighborhoods where urban comedies take place resemble small isolated villages in an expanding metropolis.[42] Following this trend, António Ferro resorts to rural metaphors when he describes the capital: "[…] young men and young women of our neighborhoods […]. You are Lisbon and its charm of cocklofts … stolen from God, you are Portugal and its Virgilian simplicity (the countryside, the spirit of the countryside, lives in our cities …), you are the

Portuguese race, the Portuguese people, with its eternal demeanor of a nativity scene [...]."⁴³ Salazarism posits the countryside as a model for Portuguese cities, transplanting the bucolic atmosphere attributed to rural existence to an urban environment.⁴⁴ In *Maria Papoila* we find precisely this intention of bringing village simplicity to the city and of moralizing urban customs through Maria's courageous example.

The schism between the tranquility of rural life and the moral decadence of the great metropolis outlined in the films of the New State has a long tradition, that goes back to bucolic poetry. Cultivated in the literature of Classical Antiquity, the bucolic genre is associated with the myth of the Golden Age, which paints agricultural societies in idyllic colors, while also praising the Horatian *aurea mediocritas*. Both *topoi* were widely used during the Portuguese Renaissance by authors such as Sá de Miranda or Luís de Camões. Later Portuguese literature often went back to this glorification of rural life. One noteworthy example is Eça de Queirós's *The City and the Mountains* (*A Cidade e as Serras*), a novel in which the protagonist abandons a sumptuous life in Paris to settle in the small village of Tormes, where he becomes a rural landowner.

In the wake of this tradition of praise for bucolic life, the modernization associated with the cities is understood by the New State as detrimental to Portugal. It is perceived as a process that emasculates the nation, not only in moral but also in physical terms. Salazar states that the "disturbing, devastating action of mostly the large urban agglomerations significantly diminishes the potential for procreation of the Race and its conditions of physical resistance."⁴⁵ In his interviews with Ferro, Salazar, whom Ferro nicknamed the "farmer minister,"⁴⁶ also mentioned more than once the hazards of city life: "In the cities—Salazar continued—the man who stops working finds himself completely helpless and risks dying of hunger. [...] Because of this we always defended a modest family life, where the necessary is never lacking, [...] yet without excessive, inhuman aspirations."⁴⁷ The city, the flipside of the idealized rural *locus amoenus*, is to blame for all of the negative aspects of Portuguese society, from immorality to hunger.

Despite the New State's rhetorical denigration of urban centers, Salazar recognized that industrialization and the cities were unavoidable evils for the material progress of Portugal, which should be counterbalanced by the spirituality of the rural world:⁴⁸

> It is known that industry has superior profitability to agriculture and that only industrialization can decisively elevate the standard of living [...] On the other

hand, we believe that agriculture is the guarantee *par excellence* of life itself, due to its greater stability, its natural rootedness in the land and its closer connection to food production; and it is an inexhaustible source of strength for social endurance given the way in which it shapes men's souls. Those who do not let themselves get obsessed with the mirage of unlimited moneymaking, but instead aspire above all to a life that, though modest, is sufficient, healthy, and earthbound, would never be able to [...] follow a path in which agriculture gave way to industry [...].[49]

The New State, like Hitler's Nazism or Mussolini's fascism, espoused a contradictory position in relation to modernity. These forms of government recognized the need for technical progress and modernization while condemning the urban lifestyle that comes with industrialization.[50] Salazarism looked upon city life with suspicion since it led to the dismantling of traditional social ties and established hierarchies, thus promoting a democratic leveling of society that endangered the structure of the regime.[51] Conversely, agriculture was considered to be humanity's calling. As such, it was regarded both as an element of social stability and as a source of spiritual values superior to material progress. Therefore, one of Salazar's main concerns was to preserve the traditions of rural life, "[...] the freshness, like the fountains that spring from the earth, the natural simplicity, the human and Christian fraternity of the Portuguese people, without impeding all the benefits of progress, all the purely material improvements [...]."[52]

Notwithstanding Salazar's preference for a predominantly rural model of development, the New State sought, in practical terms, to establish a precarious balance between farming and industrialization:[53]

> We are neither satisfied by wealth, nor by the luxury of technology [...], if the wing of the spirit does not touch them and subordinate them to the service of an ever more beautiful, elevated and noble life. Without getting detracted from the activity that gives everyone a greater share of goods and, with these, more material comfort, our ideal is to escape the materialism of our time: make the fields more fertile, without silencing the songs of the girls; weave cotton or wool on the most modern loom, without weaving class hatred into the threads and without removing our old patriarchal spirit from the workshop or the factory.[54]

The New State wanted Portugal to enjoy the advantages of technical progress while avoiding its consequences, such as class struggle or the end of patriarchal society. Industry was tolerated because of its potential material benefits, but the preservation of rural life and its traditional values continued to be a government priority—an ideological position that would become increasingly untenable as the country's urbanization accelerated.[55]

The *denouement* of Chianca de Garcia's *The Village of White Clothes* alludes precisely to this desire to reconcile the city's material progress with village life. The film ends with an element from the city—a modern truck—arriving at the village, where it replaces the traditional ox-carts in the transportation of people and goods. Contrary to what happens in *Maria Papoila*, where the female protagonist moves to Lisbon, here we see an object associated with an urban setting, namely the truck, taken to the countryside, adapted to local needs, and integrated into the village economy. Again, the film portrays the city as an unhealthy environment that leads to the degeneration of the moral fiber of the villagers in general and of men in particular. Just as in *Wild Cattle*, the protagonist of *Village*, Chico, falls in love with a city artist, in this case the fado singer Hermínia Silva. This makes him consider abandoning his childhood sweetheart Gracinda (Beatriz Costa) and his family business in order to continue working as a taxi driver in Lisbon.

We should note the symbolism codified in the very title of the film. The village has "white clothes," in contrast to the city's dirty laundry that the rural washerwomen collect to purify in the village stream, as Beatriz Costa describes in the song from the opening sequence of the movie.[56] Replacing ox-carts with the truck in the small business of Chico's father is a compromise solution to the opposition between city and countryside. This ploy will bring the young man back to his home, uniting the material benefits of technical progress with rural community values in a utopia of coexistence of two conflicting social models.

Capitalism, Communism, Corporatism

Despite the concessions to modernity that were part of several films produced from the 1930s to the 1950s, there is a conspicuous absence of industrial settings in the movies from this period. Although the industrial proletariat was in its infancy at the time and was limited to the large urban centers, it was not represented even in the comedies that were set in the city of Lisbon.[57] On the one hand, the exclusion of industrial workers from cinema has to do with the regime's emphasis on rural life as the most "natural" and therefore most perfect form of social organization. According to this perspective, the proletariat was an artificially created group that resulted from a degeneration of the ideal society because it entailed the separation of the workers from their natural environment.[58] On the other hand, the lack of visibility of the urban working classes is a consequence of Salazar's aversion to communism, which he considered to be "an *anti-natural* and profoundly anti-economic theory."[59] For Salazar, communism represented the victory of materialism, divorced from all spiritual and moral concerns, and it was a system that razed both social hierarchies and established authorities. As such, it was a force that operated against nature, and the New State sought to fight it at all costs. The invisibility of the proletariat in cinema conveyed the message that the problem of class struggle, the motor of the communist revolution, simply did not make sense in the Portuguese context.[60] *The May Revolution* (*A Revolução de Maio*, 1937) is the only film from the first decades of Salazarism that explicitly refers to communism. Yet, as we saw above, it does so with the intention of disparaging communist ideas in order to dilute the potential threat that this form of political organization posed to the regime.

The rare occasions when films depict workers protesting their bosses' decisions take place in rural areas, more specifically in the great estates in central and southern Portugal, where the distance separating wage laborers and landowners was more pronounced. This is the case in Henrique de Campos's film *Ribatejo*, in which Miguel (Alves da Costa), who had been a foreman before being replaced by António (Virgílio Teixeira), leads a group of peasants in a rebellion against the owner of the estate, Belinha (Eunice Muñoz), allegedly because the peasants do not want to be managed by a woman. The revolt is orchestrated by the overseer Fernando (José Gamboa), whose goal is to persuade Belinha to marry him and hand over the administration of the property. Armed with hoes, rods, and other work tools, the insurgents meet at the door of Belinha's house in a sequence that clearly alludes to the excesses of the Bolshevik Revolution. Yet, Belinha is not intimidated by the crowd. She confronts the workers with a speech in which she claims that their uprising stems from the fact that a vast majority of them are not from Ribatejo but from other regions of the country, and thus do not have ties that bind them to the land. Her tirade immediately provokes the repentance of the peasants from Ribatejo, who accuse the others of inciting them to rebel against the landowners. This intervention calms down the rest of the insurgents, who realize their mistake and quickly return to their homes.

This episode of *Ribatejo* makes it clear that workers should be embedded in their natural environment because, as Belinha suggests, it is the separation of the peasants from the land they till that leads to their revolt.[61] The threat of a communist uprising, portrayed in the film through the farm workers' rebellion, can thus be avoided through the anchoring of farmers in their homelands and, when this is not possible, through the creation of social ties based on solidarity. In the film, both Miguel, the leader of the revolt, and Fernando, who incited the protest, are outsiders who are maladjusted to Ribatejo customs. Neither understands the local traditions, and as a result, both reject the social hierarchy of the region. Additionally, Fernando, who prefers Lisbon to Ribatejo, is addicted to gambling, a hobby that he finances with the money he steals as the overseer of the estate. Once again, vice is associated with city life, and contrasts with Belinha's moral rectitude as a true Ribatejo native. The film also precludes the possibility of a feminist interpretation of the character of Belinha as a powerful businesswoman, insofar as she merely represents the class to which she belongs. She emphasizes that the decisions she makes are a mere extension of the wishes of her deceased father, whom she replaced as the administrator of the estate.

Ribatejo stresses the centrality of the cooperation between landowners and workers, which is presented as the main pillar of rural society. This view of work relations is related to Salazar's idea that the economy should be based on

Figure 3.7 The corruption of rural customs due to the negative influence of city-dwellers in *Ribatejo*

a family model, with the boss assuming a position similar to the father of the family.[62] The understanding of the economy in the New State thus goes back to the etymology of the word, which in Ancient Greece referred to the law and administration of a house or property. Aristotle had already warned his readers in the first paragraphs of *Politics* of the danger of transferring the methods of administering a house—*oikonomia*—to the governance of a nation. Despite Aristotle's admonishment, the New State encouraged the Portuguese from early on to respect and obey their superiors as if they were fathers who, in exchange for this submission, should protect their employees and provide them with a salary that allowed for a minimally dignified life.[63] Employer paternalism replaced the nonexistent schemes of state-provided public assistance, which contributed to an even greater dependence of employees on their bosses.[64] The New State, which projected the "natural" family structure on to all other social organizations, discarded profit as the main incentive for economic activity, and instead insisted that the economy should center on the administration of resources in order to achieve a balance among different social groups.[65] Work—any sort of work—was valued as the contribution of each individual toward the common good. The importance of a stable society was emphasized, to the detriment of social mobility that could only be achieved through the accumulation of wealth.[66]

With this organic view of the economy as the base of an authoritarian and hierarchical society, in which each worker had a predefined place, Salazarism distanced itself from both the communist model and the capitalism of liberal democracies.[67] If, for Salazar, the "liberal economics that gave us super-capitalism, unbridled competition, economic amorality, the commodification of labor, and the unemployment of millions of men, is already dead,"[68] and communism is the "great evil of our time," corporatism emerges as the only alternative to these two evils.[69] He justified the regime's corporatism in the following way:

> Economic liberalism died, and therefore we are not free to decide to have or not to have some kind of organization. We have to adopt one. Why did we go to a corporatist organization? Because it seemed to us that it was a desirable synthesis of interests, a meeting point of qualified representatives, and the possibility of reaching an understanding that would overcome class struggle.[70]

Salazar summarizes here the advantages of corporatism: this system avoids the Scylla of an economics based on speculation and "money despotism" that subordinates both the individual and the collective to the incessant search for wealth;[71] and the Charybdis of communist materialism, according to which man is completely determined by economic conditions, making class struggle inevitable in the context of the ongoing exploitation of the proletariat. Inspired by the Church's social doctrine[72] but also by Italian fascist corporatism, the corporatist organization of the New State wished to stimulate solidarity and cooperation among the Portuguese people. Its aim was the creation of a cohesive national identity: "[…] *corporatism* […] is like the active conscience of our solidarity with the land, work, and life, i.e. with our Nation — our family that does not die."[73]

Salazar emphasized that the corporatist state should lead the Portuguese to consider their country as one big family. A corporatist nation is the most natural organization, since it reproduces the social relations that take place in a private context. The argument of "naturalness," in opposition to the artificiality of capitalism and communism, is once again used here to justify the politics of the New State: "We want to move to a new economy, *working in unison with human nature*, under the authority of a strong State that defends the higher interests of the Nation […]."[74] For Salazarism, corporatism was not only the most natural system of economic organization, but also the one that best promoted the spiritual calling of the Portuguese people: "In the organization of economic corporations […] the interests of production have to be subordinated, not only to those of the national economy as a whole, but also to the spiritual goal or superior destiny of the Nation and the individuals that comprise it."[75] More than an economic principle, corporatism was thus seen as the organizational principle of the whole of society, both in material terms and in its spiritual or moral aspects.[76] Even though it was never systematically implemented over the entire national territory, and in spite of it becoming increasingly outdated after 1945, corporatism continued to be the regulating principle of Portuguese economy, and it determined the regime's socio-economic discourse well after it became obsolete.

Corporatist ideals of cooperation and social stability pervade all the "regional or folkloric films" produced with the support of the New State. These movies highlight the relevance of mutual help, which was the only way for rural communities to overcome difficulties, as we have seen in *The Song of the Earth* and *Wolves of the Mountain*. Also, the films underscore the importance of cohesion and harmony between employers and employees, which is presented as the most secure path to prosperity. Despite oblique allusions to various economic issues, films from the time rarely depict socio-economic structures different from those of Salazarism. Even in *The May Revolution*, communism is portrayed through the characters' dialogues in an abstract way and never as a palpable reality. In the context of this nearly complete absence of alternatives to the prevailing economic model in Portuguese cinema, the film *The Iron Cross* (1967) acquires particular relevance. One of Jorge Brum do Canto's later productions, the movie juxtaposes the divergent economic practices of two neighboring villages isolated in the mountains of the Trás-os-Montes region.[77]

Filmed when the New Cinema (Novo Cinema) movement was in full swing, *The Iron Cross*, a production of Tobis Portuguesa subsidized by the National Cinema Fund, adopts a nostalgic aesthetic, using almost exclusively black and white images in order to indicate that the action took place in a remote past.[78] The plot centers on the conflict between two villages: São Damião, located on the slope of a mountain, whose population raises livestock; and Valado, located in the valley of that same mountain, which lives off agriculture. Valado depends on São Damião because the herders control the river that irrigates the fields in the valley. Consequently, Valado pays the people of São Damião a tribute in foodstuffs each month in order to continue receiving water. The film highlights the pride and arrogance of the community of São Damião, which treats its neighbors from Valado disrespectfully because they consider farming to be degrading in comparison to herding. Significantly, the leader of São Damião is a man, Marcial (Jorge Brum do Canto), while a woman, Dionísia (Cremilda Gil), heads Valado, since the men from the village spend a large part of the year working in Spain. Thus the film establishes from the beginning a contrast between the feminized Valado, an emasculated community that slavishly obeys the will of the shepherds to whom they are subjected, and the virility of São Damião.

This situation begins to change when Manuel (António Machado Ribeiro), Dionísia's son, falls in love with Rosa (Ângela Ribeiro), the daughter of Marcial. The shepherds of São Damião soon find out about the relationship between the young couple, tie Rosa up, shave off her hair, and promise to kill her child when it is born as a punishment for her having dishonored her race by establishing a relationship with a man from another village. Rosa manages to flee and joins Manuel in Valado. When São Damião demands that Valado hand over the criminal or else they would cut off the water, the valley community, in an unusual act of disobedience and courage, refuses to comply with their neighbors' demands. This marks the beginning of the end of São Damião's exploitation of Valado and an inversion of the power relation between the two communities.

The conflict separating the two villages reproduces the logic of the Hegelian dialectic of the master and the slave. The decision of the people of Valado to confront the shepherds is based on the realization that, while their village depends on the water that São Damião provides for the irrigation of their lands, São Damião needs the agricultural products they give in return. When the farmers understand that their condition of near slavery, working incessantly for São Damião, makes the village of herders dependent on their work, they take the first step toward an inversion of their dependency. In other words, the farmers realize that their slavery enslaves the masters themselves, who need the slaves to do the work that they cannot perform. There is therefore a symbiotic connection uniting the two communities. As the inhabitants of Valado put it: "The day when people can live without each other is the day the world will end."[79] The tragedy of São Damião is that it only grasps this truism at the end of the film, when Valado's independence is already irreversible.

Deprived of the water supplied by the herders, the farmers find themselves in the predicament of needing an alternative source of irrigation. They decide to join together to build an oxen-powered waterwheel to transport water from a nearby brook to the fields. After several days of intense work, their efforts are finally rewarded, providing them with a new method of irrigation and giving them autonomy from their old masters. Just like other Portuguese films about rural life, Brum do Canto's movie emphasizes the cooperation among the villagers of Valado, which allows them to overcome the problems they face. Their solidarity contrasts with the discord reigning in São Damião, where a group of villagers undermines Marcial's leadership, which results in the death of an outsider. Once this group of stray herders acknowledges their mistake, they repent and finally submit to Marcial's authority in end of the film.

In an obvious reference to the political situation in Portugal at the time, the film stresses the importance of obedience to the leader. Even when members of the group do not agree with Marcial's decisions, his choices prove to be the wisest, whereas any act that questions his leadership ends in tragedy. In the last sequence of the film, the people of Valado and São Damião gather to pray around the iron cross that marks the dead outsider's grave. These final images suggest that the two villages will reconcile and resume their relationship, but this time on equal footing.

Figure 3.8 The women of Valado unite to build an irrigation system for the village in *The Iron Cross*

In São Damião's exploitation of Valado's agricultural work in *The Iron Cross*, we glimpse a critique of the abuses of capitalism, which Salazarism accused of reducing one's neighbor to an instrument in the accumulation of wealth. The herders, who are in a position of power because they control the water in the mountains, resemble capitalists, who use their position as masters of the means of production to rule over the proletariat. Just like capitalists, the shepherds lead a parasitic life, taking advantage of the benefits that their position of superiority grants them. The social organization of the village of Valado, on the contrary, can be interpreted as an example of a proto-communist community grounded in the principles of solidarity and shared labor, as the participation of all villagers in the construction of the irrigation system demonstrates. However, it would be a mistake to consider Brum do Canto, a filmmaker sympathetic to the regime, a defender of the Bolshevik mindset. In fact, we find profound differences between the utopian solidarity of Valado and socialism. The farmers do not try to undermine the social hierarchy of the two communities; they merely distance themselves from their neighbors in order to free themselves from oppression. Furthermore, the collaboration of the villagers of Valado in the construction of the new irrigation system does not eliminate private property, since the fields remain in the hands of the different families in the village. It is also significant that the film does not end with the proto-communism of Valado but rather with the union of the two rival villages kneeling in front of an iron cross, a symbol of divine authority that stands above and beyond the quarrels that separate the neighboring communities.

To summarize, and here once again Hegelian dialectics will prove to be a useful interpretative tool, we can see the capitalist aspects of São Damião as the first moment in a process of social transformation, which will go on to a second stage with the proto-communism of Valado. The synthesis of the two villages, which is invoked only in the last minutes of the film, would be corporatism, following the pattern postulated by the ideologues of the New State. Corporatism has a strong leader, as in the organization of the shepherds of São Damião, but it replaces economic exploitation with the emphasis on cooperation and mutual help characteristic of Valado. Therefore, in *The Iron Cross* Brum do Canto illustrates different forms of socio-economic organization. He shows the advantages of each one of these, but takes care to veil the confrontation between capitalism and communism with a plot presented as an oral legend passed on from generation to generation (as the voiceover informs us at the beginning of the film). The temporal distance between the alleged time of the narrative and the present day muffles the potential political implications of the movie, which allows Brum do Canto to conjure up an utopian community with corporatist undertones without the danger of a comparison between this idealized society and the Portuguese reality of his time.

The "regional or folkloric films" produced during the New State created an image of village communities that was consistent with the model of rural life advocated by the regime. These films show how farming, livestock raising, and fishing, carried out in harmony with the rhythm of the seasons in villages ruled by principles of solidarity and cooperation, were the basis of an economic system consistent with the characteristics of the Portuguese people. They underscore the role of Mother Nature as provider of nourishment, and draw an implicit parallel between this caring nature and a paternalistic state authority concerned with the wellbeing of the nation. Contrasting with this idyllic conception of rural life, the city is identified as the source of all vices and the port of entry for foreign customs that distort national traditions and pervert the morals of the Portuguese. The attributes of large cities—the constant search for profit, the desire for easy wealth, capitalist exploitation of labor, and class struggle—are compared to the rural corporatist *ethos*. The latter strives for a perfect equilibrium among the various components of the national economy, leaving inevitable labor disputes to be resolved by fostering ties of dependency between employees and employers. Corporatism reproduces a "natural" family model, with the boss occupying a position equivalent to the *pater familias*.

One of the most striking comments about the image of rural Portugal disseminated by Salazarist ideology can be found in a song performed by Beatriz Costa in the role of the villager Gracinda in *The Village of White Clothes*. She compares city women to village women and states that the "city princesses" are "paper dolls," adding that "only our quality withstands wear and tear."[80] Repeated by a chorus of young villagers, these lines form part of Gracinda's efforts to persuade Chico to abandon his lover in the city and return to his homeland. It is significant that city women were nicknamed "princesses," spoiled by the relative material comfort of urban life, while village women, robust and pure, resemble the white linen that they wash in the river. Similarly to the linen, these tireless women withstand all ordeals, persevering in their work with a smile and a song on their lips, just like Gracinda herself. To be able to "withstand wear and tear" is precisely what the New State considered laudable in the rural condition. Like the village women and the rural population in general, the regime wanted Portuguese society to remain steadfast in the face of all economic pressures, comply with authority figures, and perpetuate ancient customs and social structures. As the films demonstrate, the challenges that arise from natural conditions, as well as any signs of socio-political discontent, should be quickly neutralized and reintegrated into the natural order of things. *The Village of While Clothes* suggests that the most praiseworthy virtue of the Portuguese people is "to withstand wear and tear" like white pieces of linen.

Notes

1 Ferro, *Teatro e Cinema*, 63.
2 "fitas de saloios"; "bailaricos, as cantigas [...] nitidamente metidos a martelo"; "o regionalismo ou o folclore não se tornem forçados, portanto artificiais." Ferro, *Teatro e Cinema*, 63, 67.
3 According to Ferro, simplicity and naturalness are essential in any type of movie: "Cinema is, above all, a great book of stories ... It is necessary to know how to tell [these stories] with simplicity, without resorting to the usual crutches: folklore,

great moments of true or faked dramatics, vulgar humor, misleading situations, etc., etc. ..." ("O cinema é, acima de tudo, um grande livro de histórias ... É preciso saber contá-las com simplicidade sem o recurso das muletas habituais: folclore, grandes momentos de verdadeira ou falsa dramaticidade, graças pesadas, situações equívocas, etc., etc. ... ") Ferro, *Teatro e Cinema*, 68.

4 "tanto quanto possível, *num plano natural*—quer dizer, respeitando-se o agrupamento espontâneo dos homens em torno dos seus interesses ou das suas actividades para os enquadrar no Estado." 76; emphasis added. *Como se Levanta um Estado* was a booklet drafted at the request of French publishing house Flammarion for the occasion of Portugal's participation in the International Exhibition of Paris in 1937. It was comprised mainly of excerpts from Salazar's speeches. The booklet had two goals: to summarize the politics of the Portuguese New State and make them known to an international audience; and to complement the Portuguese Pavilion in the International Exhibition (*Como se Levanta um Estado*, 9–10).

5 "A miséria parece uma secreção do progresso, da civilização. A sua tragédia sem remédio desenvolve-se [...] nas cidades, nas grandes capitais, tanto mais insensíveis e duras quanto mais civilizadas." Ferro, *Entrevistas*, 171.

6 Salazar considered social hierarchy to be natural: "[...] the Nation is an organic whole, composed of individuals who are differentiated because of their diverse skills and different activities and placed in a hierarchy through natural differentiation [...]." ("[...] a Nação é um todo orgânico, constituída por indivíduos diferenciados em virtude de aptidões diversas e actividades diferentes, hierarquizados na sua diferenciação natural [...].") Ferro, *Entrevistas*, 240.

7 "condições naturais da existência dos povos." Salazar, *Como se Levanta*, 41

8 Salazar, "Corporativismo e os Trabalhadores," in *Discursos e Notas Políticas (1938–1943)*, 357. Salazar contrasted "natural" social groupings with those that are artificially constructed, such as citizens' groups or parties. He wanted to organize Portugal according to "natural" principles, thereby substituting political parties with a corporatist association inspired by the family model (*Como se Levanta*, 70–71). Salazar had already expounded on these ideas in his interviews with António Ferro: "[...] for the good of the national interest, the natural or social groupings of men must be recognized—the family, the society, the professional union, associations with idealistic ends, local governments—but not necessarily the groupings of a political nature and for political ends that are organized to conquer Power and consequently take over the State." ("[...] a bem do interesse nacional, se têm de reconhecer os agrupamentos naturais ou sociais dos homens – a família, a sociedade, o sindicato profissional, a associação de fins ideais, a autarquia local— mas não forçosamente os agrupamentos de natureza e fins políticos, organizados para a conquista do Poder e consequente açambarcamento do Estado.") *Entrevistas*,

240. Salazar even mentions the "natural framework" ("quadro natural") of the division of the world into nations, which is opposed to socialist internationalism (*Como se Levanta*, 93–4).

9 "O que desejava era [...] encontrar a confirmação de algumas verdades imutáveis e eternamente verdadeiras, no governo dos povos, por corresponderem *à própria natureza da alma humana.*" Salazar, "Duas Palavras de Prefácio," in *Discursos e Notas Políticas (1935-1937)*, viii–ix; emphasis added.

10 "Em resumo: pretende-se construir o Estado social e corporativo em estreita relação com *a constituição natural da sociedade.*" Salazar, *Como se Levanta*, 71; emphasis added.

11 Salazar pointed out that his speeches expressed ideas derived from the national consciousness: "The ideas of these speeches are generally known. I could even say that they are not mine, rather they belong to the collectivity, either because I drank them from the depths of the national consciousness or because the Country adopted them and made them its own since they correspond to its state of mind." ("As ideias destes discursos são geralmente conhecidas: posso mesmo dizer que não são minhas mas da colectividade, ou porque as fui beber às profundezas da consciência nacional ou porque, correspondendo ao estado de espírito do País, este as adoptou e fez suas.") "Para Servir de Prefácio," in *Discursos (1928-1934)*, lii.

12 The development of the society of the New State is also presented as "natural:" "When I speak of an age of aggrandizement, I have three things in mind: the *natural* development and expansion of constitutionally based principles that will give us the corporatist State through the fructification of the good seed thrown to the earth [...] and as the *natural consequence* of these achievements, the affirmation of our constructive worth and our civilizing actions that becomes internationally clearer and more striking with time." ("Quando falo duma era de engrandecimento tenho presentes no meu espírito três coisas: o *natural* desenvolvimento e expansão dos princípios que estão constitucionalmente assentes e nos hão-de dar, pela frutificação da boa semente lançada à terra, o Estado corporativo [...] e como *natural consequência* destas conquistas, a afirmação cada vez mais clara e vincada na sociedade internacional do nosso valor construtivo e da nossa acção civilizadora.") Salazar, "Era de Restauração," in *Discursos e Notas Políticas (1935-1937)*, 148; emphasis added.

13 "o rural que eu sou—de raiz, de sangue, de temperamento—apegado à terra, fonte de alegria e do alimento dos homens." Salazar, "A Regar! A Regar!," in *Discursos e Notas Políticas (1943-1950)*, 399.

14 Ferro, *Entrevistas*, 172.

15 In her study on the New State, Heloísa Paulo describes several of the regime's activities designed to support and disseminate Portuguese popular culture: the

Exhibition of Popular Art inaugurated in the SPN's headquarters in 1936; the Paris Exhibition, in which rural Portuguese costumes were displayed; the Contest for the Most Portuguese Village of Portugal; the Living Museum, with people from Portuguese villages performing their daily tasks, which was incorporated in the Exhibition of the Portuguese World; the *Verde Gaio* Ballet Company; the Museum of Popular Art; the Theater of the People; incentives for popular music; the Floral Games; etc. (*Estado Novo e Propaganda em Portugal e no Brasil*, 118–36).

16 The subtitle of *Maria of the Sea* is: "fictionalized documentary of the life of the fishermen from Nazaré."

17 Jorge Brum do Canto, working as a film critic for the newspaper *O Século*, writes the following about *Maria of the Sea*: "Few are the Portuguese films that deserve favorable adjectives. *Maria of the Sea* is one of these few films—we feel happy to say." ("Raros são os filmes portugueses que merecem adjectivos favoráveis. *Maria do Mar* é um desses raros filmes—com sentida alegria o dizemos.") Cited in Ribeiro, *Filmes, Figuras*, 269. *Up and Away!* also received positive reviews, like the following comment by Fernando Fragoso: "*Up and Away!* is the happy materialization of an audacious idea […] *Up and Away!* breaks into new horizons in Portuguese film. Hopefully its example will proliferate and the filmmakers who made it will give us, more often, other 'unfamiliar human landscapes,' other 'ignored scenes.'" ("*Ala-Arriba!* é a concretização feliz de uma ideia audaciosa. [...] *Ala-Arriba!* rasga novos horizontes na cinematografia lusitana. Oxalá o seu exemplo prolifere e os cineastas responsáveis nos dêem, mais vezes, outras 'paisagens humanas desconhecidas', outros 'cenários ignorados.'") Cited in Ribeiro, *Filmes, Figuras*, 444–5.

18 "quase a perder a fé"; "a terra dá trabalho, dá, mas mais cedo ou mais tarde também dá tudo."

19 "Trabalha a terra com o suor do teu rosto."

20 "economia de suicídio"; "a riqueza dos interesses da vida humana"; "produção do supérfluo"; "consumos artificiais"; "necessidades fictícias"; "dinheiro a servir modestamente o trabalho." Salazar, *Como se Levanta*, 106, 122.

21 "Em suma: a riqueza, os bens, a produção não constituem em si próprios fins a atingir: têm de realizar o interesse individual e o interesse colectivo; nada significam se não estão condicionados à conservação da vida humana." Salazar, "Conceitos Económicos," in *Discursos (1928–1934)*, 198.

22 Salazar, "Conceitos Económicos," in *Discursos (1928–1934)*, 213.

23 The "family couple" ("casal de família"), legally instituted by the 1933 Constitution, tried to safeguard traditional community values through the creation of small, indivisible, and inalienable plots of land for agriculture. The Constitution reproduced almost in its entirety a bill presented to the Parliament by the Integralist

Adriano Xavier Cordeiro in 1919, a text that was transformed into a decree in 1920, even though it was never enforced. The New State's recovery of the "family couple" was therefore a concession to Portuguese Integralism (Manique, "O 'Casal de Família,'" *O Estado Novo*, 223–4). As António Pedro Manique explains, "Xavier Cordeiro (as well as the Integralists in general) thus stated that he opposed the ideology of progress and that he stood for a model of society similar to that of the Old Regime, in which the dominance of agriculture over industry, countryside over city, income over profits, would be the primary feature." ("Xavier Cordeiro (bem como os integralistas em geral) assume-se, assim, como opositor à ideologia do progresso e defensor de um modelo de sociedade próximo do Antigo Regime, em que a supremacia da agricultura sobre a indústria, do campo sobre a cidade, da renda sobre o lucro, seria o traço fundamental.") "O 'Casal de Família,'" in *O Estado Novo*, 225. The New State adopted, for the most part, the Integralist rhetoric of the valorization of the rural world.

24 "Devo à Providência a graça de ser pobre: sem bens que valham, por muito pouco estou preso à roda da fortuna, nem falta me fizeram nunca lugares rendosos, riquezas, ostentações." Salazar, "O Meu Depoimento," in *Discursos e Notas Políticas (1943-1950)*, 351.

25 "Assim, a faina agrícola, sujeita à torreira do sol ou à impertinência das chuvas, é acima de tudo uma vocação de pobreza; mas o seu orgulho vem de que só ela alimenta o homem e lhe permite viver. Quando se governa um país, e se nos deparam os mercados difíceis, os mares impraticáveis, as bocas famintas sem saber de onde há-de vir um bocado de pão, a terra pobre, a terra humilde, sobe então à culminância dos heroísmos desconhecidos e dos valores inestimáveis." Salazar cited in Melo, *Salazarismo e Cultura Popular (1933-1958)*, 46.

26 "*Ala-Arriba!* Ele será um filme sobre os hábitos, leis, costumes e tradições dos pescadores da Póvoa, [...]. No filme evocar-se-ão algumas das suas cerimónias tradicionais: o tribunal dos 'homens de respeito,' o fabricar da rede indispensável ao noivado, [...] as suas mais importantes e significativas festas [...]." Cited in Ribeiro, *Filmes, Figuras*, 441.

27 Baptista, *Tipicamente Português*, 83–5. Those who praised typically or characteristically Portuguese films considered these movies to have two main goals: on the one hand, they showed the Portuguese city-dwellers a country that was unknown to them; on the other, they promoted the country's image abroad (Baptista, *Tipicamente Português*, 87–9). Tiago Baptista points out that cinema lovers' praise for typically Portuguese films can be interpreted as a reaction to the invasion of domestic movie theaters by foreign films. The discourse of the "typically Portuguese" is therefore linked to economic protectionism (*Tipicamente Português*, 89).

28 "reaportuguesamento de Portugal." Salazar, "Breves Considerações," in *Discursos e Notas Políticas (1943–1950)*, 464. Here is the complete citation of the passage in which Salazar refers to the re-Portugalization of the country: "The dignity of the life of the Portuguese nation, the reintegration of Portugal into the universal and spiritual sense of its history; to know and to be able to claim its rights and govern itself according to its feelings and interests; the strengthening of the ties that bind the Portuguese family here and all over the world; the precious freedom to believe in God, raise one's children, live in charity with one's neighbors: in one word, the re-Portugalization of Portugal—none of this was conceivable in the state of disintegration that we had reached, had we not imposed a principle of unity on the consciousness of the Country and a norm of moral responsibility on its leaders." ("A dignificação da vida da nação portuguesa; a reintegração de Portugal no sentido universalista e espiritual da sua história; saber e poder reivindicar os seus direitos e determinar-se conforme os seus sentimentos e interesses; o estreitamento dos laços que prendem a família portuguesa aqui e em todas as partes do Mundo; a preciosa liberdade de crer em Deus, educar os filhos, viver na caridade do próximo; numa palavra, o reaportuguesamento de Portugal—nada disso poderia conceber-se no estado de desagregação a que chegáramos sem que se impusesse à própria consciência do País um princípio de unidade e aos governantes uma norma de responsabilidade moral.") "Breves Considerações," *Discursos e Notas Políticas (1943–1950)*, 464.

29 "Nós tentamos fazer uma criação política estruturalmente portuguesa. [...] a fonte principal dos nossos ensinamentos, a fonte de inspiração das grandes linhas da nossa construção política tem sido a nossa história, a tradição, o temperamento, a realidade portuguesa em suma." Salazar, "A Educação Política", *Discursos e Notas Políticas (1938–1943)*, 31. Salazar repeated this idea in his speech "Independência da Política Nacional—suas Condições," given in 1951 at the Third Congress of National Unity: "[...] the path to follow had to be discovered and opened up, and we had to dive into the wealth of many of our institutions to extract the usable elements from the good Portuguese tradition." ("[...] teve de descobrir-se e rasgar-se o caminho a seguir e mergulhar na riqueza de muitas das nossas instituições para extrair da boa tradição portuguesa os elementos aproveitáveis.") *Discursos e Notas Políticas (1951–1958)*, 56.

30 Heloísa Paulo notes the similarities between Portuguese, German, and Italian cinema in the 1930s and 1940s regarding the valorization of popular culture: "For instance, in the case of cinema, in Portugal, as in Italy and Germany, the use of documentaries and feature-length films as vehicles to convey a 'worldview' that was focused on the glorification of a heroic past, in society's rural roots or in the rescue of folkloric traditions, reflects the search for popular consensus around the ideas of

Fatherland and Nation put forth by the prevailing regimes at the time." ("No caso do cinema, por exemplo, a utilização dos documentários e das longas-metragens como veículos transmissores de uma 'visão do mundo', centrada na glorificação do passado histórico, nas raízes camponesas da sociedade ou no resgate das tradições folclóricas, traduzem, tanto em Portugal como na Itália e na Alemanha, a busca do consenso popular em torno dos ideais de Pátria e de Nação postulados pelos regimes então vigentes.") *Estado Novo e Propaganda em Portugal e no Brasil*, 176.

31 "Desejamos que o maior mérito das nossas instituições seja o de trazer a marca da sua origem portuguesa." Salazar, *Como se Levanta*, 55. Salazar even says in *Como se Levanta um Estado* that the "sole characteristic of this work [of national regeneration] is its classicism" ("única característica desta obra [de regeneração nacional] é o seu classicismo") (33); in other words, he suggests that the New State didn't seek to import ideas foreign to Portuguese culture but rather tried to develop concepts that were already part of national tradition.

32 "impor Portugal aos Portugueses"; "impor os Portugueses ao respeito do mundo" Salazar, "É esta a Revolução," in *Discursos (1928–1934)*, 225.

33 Salazar stressed the relevance of spirituality in the Portuguese New State, which was opposed to the materialism of both capitalist democracies and communism: "Spirituality—source, soul, and life of our History, is what separates us without remission from a civilization that scientifically returns to the jungle. We refuse to feed the poor with illusions, but we want at all costs to protect the simplicity of life, the purity of customs, the sweetness in sentiment, the balance of social relations, that familiar, modest but dignified aspect of Portuguese life from the wave that rises in the world—and through these conquests or re-conquests of our traditions, to preserve social peace." ("Duma civilização que regressa cientificamente à selva separa-nos sem remissão o espiritualismo—fonte, alma, vida da nossa História. Fugimos a alimentar os pobres de ilusões, mas queremos a todo o transe preservar da onda que cresce no mundo a simplicidade de vida, a pureza dos costumes, a doçura dos sentimentos, o equilíbrio das relações sociais, esse ar familiar, modesto mas digno da vida portuguesa – e, através dessas conquistas ou reconquistas das nossas tradições, a paz social.") "A Embaixada," in *Discursos e Notas Políticas (1935–1937)*, 277. Later we will see how the idea of "spirituality" was used to justify the Portuguese colonization of Africa in films like *Chaimite* (Jorge Brum do Canto, 1953).

34 "– [Salazar] Quelle impression emportez-vous du Portugal, madame?
– [Garnier] Une impression de calme, Monsieur le Président. De trop grand calme, peut-être. Certains diraient : engourdissement.
– [Salazar] Ce calme qui vous frappe est voulu, réplique-t-il.[…] Je pense, en effet, que la fièvre et l'exaltation permanente où certains régimes maintiennent les peuples sont chose malsaine et peu naturelle. […]

- [Garnier] La nature n'est pourtant pas en perpetual repos, dis-je.
- [Salazar] Évidemment, reconnaît Salazar. Mais voyez comment elle se comporte. Les saisons marquent les differences et pourtant elles se succèdent avec une impressionnante régularité. [...] Je souhaite ardemment aussi que notre coin de terre garde ce bien précieux [...]: la douceur d'une existence tranquille." Garnier, *Vacances*, 231-2.

35 As Tiago Baptista points out, in the "typically Portuguese" films of the 1920s we already find a demonizing of the city with its cafés, cabarets, theaters, and so on, where morally dubious actions take place (*Tipicamente Português*). This tendency became more pronounced in the "regional or folkloric films" of the New State, in light of the ideal of rural community that was defended by the regime.

36 Morais, "Vinte Anos de Cinema Português," in *O Estado Novo*, 191.

37 The novel was again made into a movie by Perdigão Queiroga in 1961.

38 "uma bela expressão de arte nacionalista."

39 "grande massa do povo, ainda que iletrado"; "firme consciência nacional—a mais segura base da nossa independência como nação." Salazar, "Duas Palavras a Servir de Prefácio," in *Discursos e Notas Políticas (1938-1943)*, ix.

40 "Os ares da serra não matam apenas os micróbios do peito; deixam a inteligência lavada. A hipocrisia citadina não respira, nestas altitudes. E a verdade flui, como nascente puríssima, do coração e dos lábios dos homens." Cited in Melo, *Salazarismo e Cultura Popular (1933-1958)*, 166.

41 The New State propaganda promoted positive descriptions of the rural environment created by city intellectuals that visited Portuguese villages. These descriptions frequently included depictions of the environment, as well as of the House of the People (Melo, *Salazarismo e Cultura Popular*, 164).

42 See Granja, "A Comédia à Portuguesa," in *O Cinema sob o Olhar de Salazar*, 199.

43 "[...] rapazes e raparigas dos nossos bairros [...]. Vós sois Lisboa e o seu encanto de água ... furtada a Deus, vós sois Portugal e a sua virgiliana simplicidade (há campo, alma de campo, nas nossas cidades ...), vós sois a raça portuguesa, o povo português, com o seu eterno ar de presépio [...]." Cited in Melo, *Salazarismo e Cultura Popular (1933-1958)*, 59.

44 Salazar lamented the lack of contact with nature that is characteristic of city life: "For me, a son of the countryside, raised to the murmur of the water for irrigation and under the shade of the groves, it is such a pity that these people from Lisbon spend their hours and days of rest sadly elbowing through the narrow streets, and that they do not have a great park, not a luxurious one, but one with fresh lawns and leafy trees, where they can frolic, laugh, play, breathe pure air and truly have fun in an intimate coexistence with nature! It pains me to know that on Sundays the cafés are filled with young people discussing the mysteries and problems of low politics,

and at the same time see the marvelous Tagus deserted, the children of this country of sailors not rowing or sailing under the incomparable sun by the thousands." ("Que pena me faz a mim, filho do campo, criado ao murmúrio das águas de rega e à sombra dos arvoredos, que esta gente de Lisboa passe as horas e dias de repouso acotovelando-se tristemente pelas ruas estreitas, e não tenha um grande parque, sem luxo, de relvados frescos e árvores copadas, onde brinque, ria, jogue, tome o ar puro e verdadeiramente se divirta em íntimo convívio com a natureza! Que pena me faz saber aos domingos os cafés cheios de jovens, discutindo os mistérios e problemas de baixa política, e ao mesmo tempo ver deserto esse Tejo maravilhoso, sem que nele remem ou velejem, sob o céu incomparável, aos milhares, os filhos deste país de marinheiros.") "Educação Física," in *Discursos (1928-1934)*, 275.

45 "[com a] acção perturbante, devastadora, sobretudo dos grandes aglomerados urbanos, a potencialidade procriadora da Raça e as suas condições de resistência física diminuem sensivelmente." Salazar, "Educação Física," in *Discursos (1928-1934)*, 274.

46 "ministro lavrador." Ferro, *Entrevistas*, 157.

47 "Nas cidades—continua Salazar—o homem que deixa de trabalhar encontra-se completamente desamparado e arrisca-se, de facto, a morrer de fome. [...] Por isso fazemos sempre a apologia da vida modesta, familiar, onde não falte o indispensável, [...] mas sem aspirações excessivas, desumanas." Ferro, *Entrevistas*, 172. Ferro enthusiastically responds to Salazar's comments about the benefits of rural life: "The countryside itself, I conclude perhaps with excessive optimism, is a large set table." ("O próprio campo—concluo talvez com excessivo optimismo—é uma grande mesa posta.") *Entrevistas*, 171.

48 Daniel Melo points out that, for Salazar, the notion of spirituality is associated with traditional rural culture that is respectful of social hierarchies: "The 'spirituality,' another way of referring to traditional culture, is part of a politics that disseminates a certain vision of society, peaceful, disciplined and orderly, in which the logic of social conflict as a factor of social change is unheard of, because this society finds self-fulfillment in the continuation of tradition. In this sense, tradition is a repository of moral teachings that, as a rule, promotes social normalization and apeasement, and constitutes, therefore, a means of achieving social order." ("O 'espiritualismo,' uma outra forma de referir a cultura tradicional, faz parte de uma política que difunde uma dada visão da sociedade, pacificada, disciplinada e ordeira, alheia à lógica do conflito social como factor de mudança social, porque auto-realizada no prosseguimento da tradição. Neste sentido, a tradição consiste num repositório de ensinamentos morais, por norma, socialmente reguladores e apaziguadores, logo, um meio para atingir a ordem social.") *Salazarismo e Cultura Popular*, 48.

49 "Sabe-se que a indústria tem rentabilidade superior à agricultura e que só pela industrialização se pode decisivamente elevar o nível de vida [...]. Temos por outro lado que a agricultura, pela sua maior estabilidade, pelo seu enraizamento natural no solo e mais estreita ligação com a produção de alimentos, constitui a garantia por excelência da própria vida, e, devido à formação que imprime nas almas, manancial inesgotável de forças de resistência social. Aqueles que não se deixam obcecar pela miragem do enriquecimento indefinido, mas aspiram acima de tudo a uma vida que, embora modesta, seja suficiente, sã, presa à terra, não poderiam nunca [...] seguir por caminhos em que a agricultura cedesse à indústria [...]." Salazar, "Plano de Fomento," in *Discursos e Notas Políticas (1951-1958)*, 104.

50 For example, in the art of the Third Reich, paintings that depicted rural communities living in harmony with the rhythms of nature abounded, unlike in Soviet art, in which the rural world appeared populated by tractors and other symbols of technological progress. However, the images of idyllic rural life in Nazi Germany coexisted with the massive industrialization and militarization of the country immediately before and during the war (Clark, *Art and Propaganda in the Twentieth Century*, 55–8).

51 See Sapega, *Consensus and Debate in Salazar's Portugal*, 88.

52 "[...] a frescura, como a das fontes que brotam da terra, a simplicidade natural, a fraternidade humana e cristã do povo português, sem prejuízo de todas as conquistas do progresso, de todos os melhoramentos puramente materiais [...]." Salazar, "Portugal como Elemento," *Discursos e Notas Políticas (1951-1958)*, 157.

53 The first item of the *Ten Commandments of the New State* (*Decálogo do Estado Novo*) drafted by João Ameal, one of the regime's foremost ideologues, as a summary of the principles of Salazarism, refers precisely to the combination of modernity and tradition: "The New State represents the combination and the synthesis of all that is permanent and all that is new, of the living traditions of the Nation and its most advanced impulses." ("O Estado Novo representa o acordo e a síntese de tudo o que é permanente e de tudo o que é novo, das tradições vivas da Pátria e dos seus impulsos mais avançados.") 5.

54 "Não nos satisfaz a riqueza, nem o luxo da técnica [...], se a asa do espírito os não toca e submete ao serviço de uma vida cada vez mais bela, mais elevada e nobre. Sem nos distrair da actividade que a todos proporcione maior porção de bens e com eles mais conforto material, o ideal é fugir ao materialismo do tempo: levar a ser mais fecundo o campo, sem emudecer nele as canções das raparigas; tecer o algodão ou a lã no mais moderno tear, sem entrelaçar no fio o ódio de classe nem expulsar da oficina ou da fábrica o nosso velho espírito patriarcal." Salazar, "A Embaixada," in *Discursos e Notas Políticas (1935-1937)*, 276.

55 Rosas, *O Estado Novo nos Anos Trinta (1928-1938)*, 155. Fernando Rosas states

that, in the 1930s, one could distinguish two distinct and conflicting models of national development. One faction within the regime, composed mainly of the great landowners of the south of the country, sought to defend the interests of national agriculture, while the urban bourgeoisie called for investment in infrastructure that would allow for greater industrial development. Although the New State, in practical terms, tried to establish a precarious balance between the two groups, the rhetoric of Salazarism privileged rural Portugal. In a political context, this translated into the creation of the Ministry of Agriculture in 1933, which divorced agricultural policy from industrial policy, giving greater autonomy to the former. According to Rosas, the preference for a social model inspired in the rural world would be, in itself, an impediment to industrial development: "An ultra-conservative and rural ideology predominated and would largely remain the official image of the New State far beyond the real social weight of the classes that supported it, already forced to defend their threatened positions in the 1930s. This disproportionate ideological intransience is related, as we have seen, to the difficulties of the industrial development of Portuguese society, and it will become in itself a relatively autonomous economic and political barrier throughout the entire history of the regime." ("Uma ideologia ultra-conservadora e ruralista predomina e assim se manterá largamente como imagem oficial do Estado Novo muito para além do peso social real das classes que a suportam, já remetidas à defesa das suas posições ameaçadas nos anos trinta. Essa desmesurada permanência ideológica prende-se, como vimos, com as dificuldades do desenvolvimento industrial na sociedade portuguesa, e constituir-se-á, ela própria, num factor relativamente autónomo de bloqueamento económico e político ao longo de toda a história do regime.") *O Estado Novo nos Anos Trinta*, 155.

56 In films such as *Maria Papoila* and *The Village of White Clothes*, there is a valorization of the "rustic wit" ("esperteza saloia") typical of country women, who end up outdoing their city counterparts and marrying the male protagonists who oscillate between the love of both.

57 Granja, "A Comédia à Portuguesa," in *O Cinema sob o Olhar de Salazar*, 199. The only exception is perhaps *The May Revolution*, whose protagonist is a communist revolutionary. However, even in this film the worker is not really portrayed in his working environment (large factories) as the movie only briefly alludes to this space.

58 Salazar, *Como se Levanta*, 100–1. Salazar explained how he tried to integrate the proletariat into the society of the New State: "[…] since we do not want to privilege anyone, we cannot allow the workers to be a privileged class […]. In a regime with a strong authority, we only want their work to be orderly, honest, and aware

of the common good; the State will coordinate this work with other activities and integrate it into the whole of the national economy. [...] we will take care of their employment, their housing, their hygiene, their health, their disability, their salary, their education, their organization and defense, their social valorization, their dignity [...]." ("[...] como não queremos privilégios para ninguém, não podemos admitir que o operariado seja uma classe privilegiada [...]. Num regime de autoridade forte nós só queremos que o seu trabalho seja ordeiro, probo e consciente da utilidade comum; o Estado o coordenará com outras actividades e o integrará no conjunto da economia nacional. [...] nós trataremos do seu emprego, da sua habitação, da sua higiene, da sua saúde, da sua invalidez, do seu salário, da sua educação, da sua organização e defesa, da sua elevação social, da sua dignidade [...].") "Diferentes Forças," in *Discursos (1928–1934)*, 181–2.

59 "uma teoria *anti-natural* e profundamente anti-económica." Salazar, *Como se Levanta*, 179; emphasis added.

60 Salazar referred to the threat that communism posed to the regime in the following way: "Communism is cultivated and propagates as a phenomenon with religious characteristics, even though it is purely materialistic and avowedly atheist. [...] Because of this, it brought to the field of combat the virulence of religious wars, with the aggravating factor that, being essentially a totalitarian doctrine of life and the State, it must be intolerant as far as its principles go and a tyrannical master in relation to all power." ("O comunismo é cultivado e propaga-se como um fenómeno de características religiosas, ainda que puramente materialista e confessadamente ateu. [...] Porque o é, trouxe para o campo do combate a virulência das guerras de religião, com a agravante de que, sendo por essência doutrina totalitária de vida e de Estado, tem de ser intolerante quanto aos princípios e senhor tirano quanto a todo o poder.") "Breves Considerações," in *Discursos e Notas Políticas (1943–1950)*, 473. As Daniel Melo points out, the rhetoric of the New State establishes a Manichean dichotomy, according to which the regime's opposition—often organized by the Communist Party—is equated to absolute evil (*Salazarismo e Cultura Popular*, 60).

61 Salazar criticized the modern economic organization that breaks with the traditional ties binding the worker to his work: "We disconnected the worker from the natural context of his profession: free from associative ties, he remained alone; without the discipline of association, he was left free, but fragile." ("Desligámos o trabalhador do quadro natural da sua profissão: liberto dos laços associativos, ficou só; sem a disciplina da associação, ficou livre, mas frágil.") "Conceitos Económicos," in *Discursos (1928–1934)*, 193.

62 Paula Silveira conducted an analysis of primary school textbooks, from the first to the fourth grades, used during a period that stretches from the nineteenth-century

Liberalist governments to the New State. In this study, she concludes that the representation of relationships between employers and workers reproduces a family scheme, in which the employer takes the place of the father. Colleagues are portrayed as brothers who should help each other. The topic of labor relations is always referred to on a small scale, excluding factories of large dimensions ("Os Valores do Quotidiano," in *O Estado Novo*, 312). Silveira also argues that the New State simply consolidated values that were already present in nineteenth-century Liberalism (303). This continuity between Liberalism and the New State is symptomatic of the traditionalism of Salazar's government, in that more than a century after the beginning of the Liberal regime, the New State adopted the same social principles.

63 See Silveira, "Os Valores do Quotidiano," in *O Estado Novo*, 312. In the speech "Conceitos Económicos da Nova Constituição," Salazar supported what he called "adequate wage" ("salário suficiente"). This wage "is imposed by the demands of an adequate and dignified life" ("é imposto pelas exigências de uma vida suficiente e digna.") in *Discursos (1928–1934)*, 202. Salazar often presented this "adequate and dignified life" made of an honest poverty just a step above misery as an ideal to which the Portuguese people should aspire.

64 Rosas, *O Estado Novo nos Anos Trinta (1928–1938)*, 159.

65 Salazar condemned the desire of profit and wealth as the main purpose of the economy: "We should fight, more and more, the materialist idea that leads man to greediness of wealth in a dangerous and sickly sport, even when we see men distribute part of their fortune to institutions that benefit the poor, as sometimes happens in America. Rather it is more human and more Christian to seek a collective average in which neither misers nor archmillionaires can possibly exist." ("Devemos guerrear, cada vez mais, a concepção materialista que leva o homem à sofreguidão da riqueza, num desporto perigoso e doentio, ainda que o vejamos, por vezes, como na América, distribuir parte da sua fortuna por instituições de que beneficiam os pobres. É mais humano e mais cristão procurar antes aquela mediania colectiva em que não são possíveis nem os miseráveis nem os arquimilionários.") Ferro, *Entrevistas*, 172.

66 According to Salazar, all work should be valued, but that does not undermine the hierarchical structure of society, i.e. the existence of social classes whose members receive different salaries. He explains this paradox in the following way: "Work, all work, has the same nobility and the same dignity when it is the contribution provided by the abilities of each person to the collectivity to which he belongs. However, being equally dignified from the point of view of humanity does not mean that it has the same value in economic and social terms. Each work has a different usefulness and diverse yields, and because of this it cannot have equal

remuneration. For this reason, there is a differentiation in individuals, in their way of life, in social classes." ("O trabalho, todo o trabalho tem a mesma nobreza e a mesma dignidade, quando é a contribuição proporcionada às faculdades de cada um para a colectividade a que pertence. Mas, sendo igualmente digno sob o ponto de vista humano, não tem o mesmo valor sob o ponto de vista económico e social. Tem utilidades diferentes, tem rendimentos diversos e por isso não pode ter igual remuneração. Por este motivo há diferenciação nos indivíduos, nos géneros de vida, nas classes da sociedade.") "Conceitos Económicos," in *Discursos (1928–1934)*, 201.

67 Salazar described his political position in the following way: "[We affirm that we are] anti-communist on one hand and anti-democratic and anti-liberal on the other, authoritarian and interventionist, as openly social as the principle of equality of all in the face of the benefits of civilization demands that we are [...]" ("[Afirmamo-nos] por um lado anticomunistas e por outro anti-democratas e anti-liberais, autoritários e intervencionistas, tão rasgadamente sociais quanto de nós exige o princípio da igualdade de todos perante os benefícios da civilização [...].") "Problemas Político-Religiosos," in *Discursos e Notas Políticas (1938–1943)*, 236.

68 "economia liberal que nos deu o supercapitalismo, a concorrência desenfreada, a amoralidade económica, o trabalho-mercadoria, o desemprego de milhões de homens, morreu já." Salazar, "Estado Novo Português na Evolução," in *Discursos (1928–1934)*, 349.

69 "grande mal do nosso tempo." Salazar, "Governar Dirigindo," in *Discursos e Notas Políticas (1943–1950)*, 509.

70 "O liberalismo económico morreu e nós não somos portanto livres de ter ou não ter uma organização. Havemos de adoptar uma. Fomos para a organização corporativa, porquê? Porque nos pareceu que ela nos daria a síntese desejável dos interesses, o ponto de encontro dos representantes qualificados, a possibilidade de entendimento a substituir-se à luta de classes." Salazar, "Caminho do Futuro," in *Discursos e Notas Políticas (1951–1958)*, 495. In the speech "O Corporativismo e os Trabalhadores," Salazar once again described corporatism as a form of social organization that avoids the mistakes of both economic liberalism and socialism. (*Discursos e Notas Políticas (1938–1943)*, 358–61).

71 "despotismo do dinheiro." Salazar, *Como se Levanta*, 106–7; 122. Salazar criticized the excesses of capitalism, which he accused of promoting the exploitation of man by his fellow man: "As to the mass of true workers, we have nothing to fear. We are not responsible for nor involved in the abuses of capitalism or of private property; we want nothing to do with the excesses that work has been subjected to [...]." ("Quanto à massa dos verdadeiros trabalhadores, nada podemos recear. Nós não temos responsabilidades nem compromissos nos abusos do capitalismo ou da

propriedade; nada queremos ter com os excessos a que tenha sido sujeito o trabalho [...].") "Balanço," in *Discursos e Notas Políticas (1935–1937)*, 34.

72 Corporatism is a Christian, social-democratic doctrine put forth by the Catholic Church, more specifically by Leo XIII in the encyclical *Rerum Novarum*. It was later adapted to the Portuguese political situation with authoritarian undertones (Torgal, *Estados Novos*, vol. 1, 379–83).

73 "[...] *o corporativismo* [...] é como a consciência activa da nossa solidariedade na terra, no trabalho e na vida, isto é na Pátria—a nossa família que não more." Salazar, "Revolução Corporativa," in *Discursos e Notas Políticas (1938–1943)*, 131.

74 "Nós queremos caminhar para uma economia nova, *trabalhando em uníssono com a natureza humana*, sob a autoridade dum Estado forte que defenda os interesses superiores da Nação [...]." Salazar, "Conceitos Económicos," in *Discursos (1928–1934)*, 213; emphasis added.

75 "Na organização das corporações económicas [...] os interesses da produção têm de subordinar-se não só aos da economia nacional no seu conjunto, mas também à finalidade espiritual ou destino superior da Nação e dos indivíduos que a constituem." Salazar, "Estado Novo Português na Evolução," *Discursos (1928–1934)*, 345. Salazar considered corporatism to be the most "natural" form of organization and the most favorable to the life of the spirit: "Now, as in all critical moments, it is necessary to choose, know how to choose and know how to sacrifice—the accidental to the essential, matter to spirit, greatness to equilibrium, wealth to equity, waste to economy, struggle to cooperation." ("Agora, como em todos os momentos críticos, é preciso escolher, saber escolher e saber sacrificar—o acidental ao essencial, a matéria ao espírito, a grandeza ao equilíbrio, a riqueza à equidade, o desperdício à economia, a luta à cooperação.") "Conceitos Económicos," in *Discursos (1928–1934)*, 212.

76 Salazar stated that corporatism was not just an economic doctrine but a principle that should rule all aspects of Portuguese existence: "We seek to flee socialism and communism through corporations, applying the principle of corporatist organization not only to agriculture, commerce and industries, that is, to directly and purely lucrative activities, but also to spiritual and moral activities that coexist with the former and have as much importance in life, at least, as bread for the body." ("Nós procuramos fugir ao socialismo e ao comunismo por meio das corporações, aplicado [sic] o princípio da organização corporativa não só à agricultura, comércio e indústria, isto é, a actividades directa e puramente lucrativas, mas a actividades espirituais e morais que com elas coexistem e têm na vida tanta importância, pelo menos, como o pão do corpo.") "Princípios e a Obra," in *Discursos e Notas Políticas (1938–1943)*, 402.

77 Although it was filmed during a period outside of the scope of this project, *The Iron*

Cross is closer to New State films of the 1930s to 1950s than to the New Cinema of the 1960s. The movie displays both thematic and aesthetic continuities with the filmography of the first decades of Salazarism, which is why we included its analysis in this study.

78 The film begins by showing color images of the mountains, complemented by a voiceover. The narrator informs us in this initial sequence that the story of the iron cross—the inspiration for the film's title—took place years ago. There is then a temporal shift to the past and the movie switches to black and white.

79 "No dia em que as pessoas puderem viver umas sem as outras, acaba-se o mundo."

80 "princesas da cidade"; "bonequinhas de armar"; "só a nossa qualidade, é de lavar e durar."

4

The Miracle of Salazarism: *Fátima, Land of Faith (Fátima, Terra de Fé)*

Fátima in the New State

The consolidation of Fátima as the central religious phenomenon of Portuguese Catholicism, as well as the gradual international recognition of the sanctuary, coincided with the institutionalization of the New State and with Salazar's rise to power. Although the alleged apparitions that started the cult of Fátima took place between 13 May and 13 October 1917, the Portuguese Church did not grant an official blessing to the Marian devotion of the Cova da Iria until after the end of the First Republic. With the publication of the *Pastoral Letter on the Cult of Our Lady of Fátima* (*Carta Pastoral sobre o Culto de Nossa Senhora de Fátima*) in 1930, the Church declared that the visions of the three children Lúcia, Jacinta, and Francisco were credible and granted permission to worship the Virgin at Fátima.[1] Between the 1930s and the 1950s the number of believers visiting the sanctuary grew exponentially, quickly making Fátima the country's most visited pilgrimage site, a situation that prompted the state to draft an urban development plan for the area. This plan materialized in 1944 under the direction of Cottinelli Telmo, an architect who had previously headed other projects of the regime, such as the 1940 Exhibition of the Portuguese World. The internationalization of Fátima depended on the Vatican's recognition of the alleged miracles, a process that was initiated during the papacy of Pius XI (1922–39) and completed by Pius XII (1939–58), who was nicknamed "Fátima's Pope" for his support of the Portuguese sanctuary.[2]

The parallel development of the sanctuary of Our Lady of Fátima and of the New State was not just a historical accident. In fact, while the governments of the First Republic, with the exception of the Sidonist interregnum (1917–18), either implicitly or explicitly and militantly opposed the worship of the Virgin, Salazarism encouraged the expansion of the sanctuary. In the first decades of his rule, Salazar's position in relation to religion dovetailed with the essential principles of his regime, which was marked by a balance between positivist rationalism and a belief in unquestionable dogmas. The unending dispute between reason and faith, which had been at the root of the controversy that surrounded the apparitions of the Virgin during the First Republic, was one of the political paradoxes that Salazar sought to resolve both in his political practice and in his public speeches.

Significantly, the reason–faith duality lies at the core of the only fictional feature-length film about Fátima produced during the New State: *Fátima, Land of Faith*.[3] The movie, directed by Jorge Brum do Canto, was released on 2 July 1943 and premiered at the Éden cinema in Lisbon.[4] It was produced by the company Filmes Portugueses César de Sá and its plot was adapted to the screen by Catholic writer Mello e Alvim from his homonymous novel. *Fátima, Land of Faith* furnishes evidence for "certain key aspects of Salazarist Catholic political cinematography."[5] The movie received direct support from several official institutions,

Figure 4.1   Advertisement poster for *Fátima, Land of Faith*

including the Secretariat of Propaganda and the Ministry of Economics and Agriculture. The positive assessment of the film by the political elite of the regime was reflected in laudatory comments spun by newspapers at the time, which praised both the formal perfection of the movie and its edifying morals. For instance, the newspaper *Diário de Notícias* emphasized the quality of Brum do Canto's direction, which "reached its greatest height" during the last sequence of the film, and *Século* highlighted the movie's "moral and spiritual beauty."[6]

Since *Fátima, Land of Faith*'s portrayal of Catholicism reflects the position of the New State, the film can help us understand the religious ideology of Salazarism and the government's political response to the conflict between faith and reason. Furthermore, the reductive choice offered in the movie between adherence to scientific rationality and Catholic religious belief suggests that the New State aimed to avoid nihilism as a possible third path. This nihilistic approach, indifferent to pre-established values and associated with critical reason, would examine the premises of any religious or socio-political system, thereby putting into question the "great truths" of Salazarism.

Reason, faith and politics in cinema

The opposition of rationality and religious faith that we find in Brum do Canto's film marked the Fátima phenomenon since the first news of the Virgin's apparition to three children shepherding their flocks on 13 May 1917 reached the Portuguese media. The political elite of the militantly anti-clerical First Republic immediately denounced the alleged miracle as just another example of obscurantism orchestrated by reactionary religious leaders. The Catholic Church, on the other hand, took a position of cautious optimism. It initially refrained from unconditionally approving the phenomenon, but later came to support the worship of the Virgin. Some Catholic intellectuals viewed Fátima as a beacon of hope for a Catholic renaissance in the context of a hostile political atmosphere and the apparently relentless secularization of Portugal and Europe.[7] As early as 1917, the events of the Cova da Iria were compared to the apparition of the Virgin to a little girl in Lourdes, France, in 1858. Devout Catholics highlighted the similarities between the two incidents in order to associate the prestige of Lourdes with the Portuguese sanctuary, while skeptics accused the Church of trying to emulate the French success for financial gain and to increase its influence over a gullible population.[8]

The divergent positions of the two factions involved in the polemic surrounding Fátima during the First Republic were grounded on a fundamental disagreement not only about religion but also about the principles that ruled any socio-political community. The secular group, which inherited its ideals from the Enlightenment, believed that social and economic progress depended on a rational attitude and saw objective, impartial reason as the path to free an ignorant population from its atavistic beliefs. Conversely, the intellectuals close to the Catholic Church held that reason could not explain religious phenomena and criticized the reductive perspective of the rationalists. Underlying this philosophical debate about the Fátima miracles were two diametrically opposed conceptions of the state: for Republicans, the state should be secular and governed by a parliamentary system; the majority of the religious elite wanted a Catholic and Monarchical state.

The religious and political discord that marked the Republican debate about Fátima continued during the New State. Salazarism, which established a very close relationship with the Church, did not immediately succeed in dissolving the significant secular portion of the intellectual elite that espoused the ideals of the Republic. *Fátima, Land of Faith* may be seen as a response to the critics of the cult of Fátima and, more broadly, to the detractors of Salazar. The plot of the movie alludes to the divergent positions about religion and politics in Portugal, and emphasizes the mistakes of secular intellectuals. At the same time, it promotes the social structure advocated by Salazarism: a community based upon the values of Catholicism, united by a strong nationalism, and organized hierarchically, with the traditional family unit as its foundation.

Brum do Canto's film illustrates the errors of atheism through the character of Doctor Silveira (Barreto Poeira), a famous medical doctor, professor at the University of Coimbra, and fierce critic of religion. He lives in Coimbra, separated from his wife Maria Antónia (Maria Alvarez) and his two children, Madalena (Graça Maria) and young José Augusto (Armando Chagas), due to the incompatibility of his secular principles with his family's religiosity. His daughter, Friar Manuel (Manuel Correia), a family friend, and Bárbara (Teresa Gomes), the doctor's former wet nurse, seek in vain to convince the professor to reconcile with his wife and return to his home, an estate located just outside the city. Doctor Silveira's change of heart occurs only toward the end of the movie. It is triggered by a horseback riding accident that leaves his son José Augusto between life and death, in a situation where medicine is powerless. Desperate to save his son, Doctor Silveira ends up giving in to those who recommend that he take the boy to Fátima in order to place him under the Virgin's protection. During the blessing of the sick, José Augusto wakes up from his coma, which leads his father to reconsider his position on religion and return to his family.

At the beginning of *Fátima, Land of Faith*, the doctor embodies rationalist intellectual values. He only believes in facts that can be scientifically proven, and he opposes a religious worldview, as well as any interpretation of reality that would take miracles or the supernatural into account. In order to insert Doctor Silveira within the context of European anti-Catholic thought, his employee Bárbara says that he looks more and more like the bust of Voltaire he has in his office. The French writer—one of the most well-known philosophers of the Enlightenment and a thinker known for his ferocious criticism of the Catholic Church—is presented as an intellectual inspiration for the professor. Upon contemplating the statue of Voltaire, the doctor's daughter Madalena remarks that the philosopher died long ago, thereby suggesting that the thoughts of the French thinker are not relevant in the present. Bárbara repeats this idea in a comic aside: when she learns that the philosopher already died, she says that "he must not have been missed at all."[9]

Figure 4.2 Doctor Silveira (Barreto Poeira) in *Fátima, Land of Faith*

As in the case of Voltaire, Doctor Silveira's rationalist and atheistic stance corresponds to a political attitude affiliated with the ideas of the French Revolution. In the film, the doctor delivers a "Lecture of Wisdom" entitled "Reason and Faith" at the University of Coimbra, where he summarizes his convictions. In this speech, the professor states that the root of human problems is of a spiritual nature, in that people believe in myths that curtail their capacity to think rationally and therefore their ability to exercise their freedom. The doctor praises reason and condemns God, saying that, if he were to find Him, he "would scream in contempt expressing his free reason."[10] Furthermore, he underscores his adherence to the principles of 1789 and hence his opposition to the New State, something that is not openly mentioned in the movie but is implicit in his statements. Several people leave the room, shocked by the content of the talk. When his lecture ends, the professor is left alone in the enormous hall where he gave the speech, abandoned both by the public and his colleagues at the university. The film thus offers a visual representation of Doctor Silveira's social isolation, which suggests that the great majority of the Portuguese people, represented in the film by the audience, would vehemently repudiate his opinions.

The connection between Doctor Silveira's atheism and his political convictions suggested in the "Lecture of Wisdom" becomes even more obvious if we take into account Álvaro Garrido's argument that this character was modeled on Bissaya Barreto, a doctor and university professor from Coimbra. Bissaya Barreto, just like Doctor Silveira in the movie, spent a large part of his life helping the destitute, an activity that earned him considerable renown at the time.[11] Nevertheless, the most relevant aspect of Barreto's biography was the radical change in his political allegiances. He began his career as a Republican and a Freemason, became a deputy in the Constituent Assembly of the First Republic, and later turned into a militant supporter of Salazar.[12] The New State saw Bissaya Barreto's adherence to the values of the regime as a propagandistic opportunity and presented the doctor as an ideal to which all citizens should aspire. Bissaya Barreto's conversion to the principles of the New State and Doctor Silveira's conversion in Brum do Canto's film are even more significant because both were lecturers at the University of Coimbra, where Portugal's intellectual elite was educated and where Salazar himself had been a professor. Both doctors are used by the regime's propaganda as examples for Portuguese intellectuals to follow.

Given that the character of Doctor Silveira was modeled, at least in part, on Bissaya Barreto, his conversion to Catholicism is inevitably accompanied by a rejection of his former revolutionary mindset. Like Bissaya Barreto, the doctor in *Fátima, Land of Faith* espouses the political principles of the New State when he returns to his family's home at the end of the film. He accepts his wife's religion and, by taking up his role as the head of the family, he tacitly lends his support to the traditional family structure that played a fundamental role in the ideology of the regime. The case of Doctor Silveira is similar to the situation portrayed in *The May Revolution*, where the main character surrenders, albeit in a more explicit way, to the obvious advantages of Salazar's politics, and abandons the erroneous beliefs of his communist past. To better understand Doctor Silveira's transformation and the propagandistic message that underlies his conversion, it is necessary to examine the position of scientific rationalism—represented by the doctor—and that of religious faith—associated with Fátima—in the ideological discourse of Salazarism. In addition, we need to analyze the way in which Salazar appropriated these two ways of explaining reality to cement the values of the New State.

Balancing reason and religion

In *Fátima, Land of Faith*, Doctor Silveira is faced with the limitations of science when he is unable to help his son, and he surrenders to Catholicism, the domain of spirituality and of the ineffable. The film does not reject scientific reason, represented by medicine, but it shows that rationality does not invalidate faith, in that the two are complementary ways of understanding the world. The former explains natural phenomena, while the latter reigns were the first falters, in the transcendent realm, which remains unfathomable for the limited power of human knowledge. In an interview with *Cine-Jornal* in August 1938, Aurélio Rodrigues, who had been the first choice to direct the film, confirmed that the plot intended to illustrate the complementary relationship between reason and faith:

> [interviewer] Is it simply a religious film?
> [Rodrigues] It is in fact a religious film whose development encompasses all the grandeur of the epic of Fátima. [...] A film in which conflicts and passions are discussed, as a framework for the theory that inspires the entire film. A contemporary theory, one of the most interesting ideas of Thomist philosophy, with which the film deals with suppleness and elegance, and I can affirm that it will deserve the attention of Catholics as well as of positivists and determinists.

[interviewer] What is the theory?

[Rodrigues] That there is no conflict between faith and science: God [is] the fruit of all knowledge and science is a reflection of God.[13]

The argument that reason and faith are compatible goes back, as Rodrigues himself points out, to medieval Scholasticism, and it was systematized in the philosophy of Saint Thomas Aquinas. At the beginning of the twentieth century, it gained ground all over the West in the wake of the critique of Enlightenment rationality. Sociologists like Max Weber denounced the "disenchantment" (Entzauberung) of the world that resulted from the use of a rational and scientific model to understand reality, while philosophers like Edmund Husserl, Henri Bergson, and William James challenged the scientific rationalism of their time and called into question the nexus between reason and socio-political progress. These ideas led to a revival of Christian European thought, which sought to give new impulse to the spiritual message of Christianity in the face of a growing secularization of society.

Figure 4.3 Friar Manuel (Manuel Correia) and Doctor Silveira (Barreto Poeira) in *Fátima, Land of Faith*

We find echoes of these ideas among Portuguese Catholic intellectuals in the first decades of the twentieth century. The notion that faith and reason can peacefully coexist is used by the believers in the miracles of Fátima in response to the critics of the apparitions. In 1917, António Sardinha, a theorist of Portuguese Integralism, published an article called "Fátima's Miracle" ("O Milagre de Fátima") in the newspaper *A Monarquia*, in which he criticized an archaic conception of science that does not recognize the existence of suprasensible realities.[14] Likewise, Manuel Cerejeira, who was Salazar's close friend, Cardinal Patriarch of Lisbon after 1929, and defender of the cult of Fátima, criticized in his work *The Church and Contemporary Thought* (*A Igreja e o Pensamento Contemporâneo*) the "stupid" rational and scientific "materialism" of his time that rejected the possibility of miracles. He believed in the religious renewal of Portugal, offering as an intellectual example Sardinha himself, who abandoned anti-clerical and revolutionary positions to become a fervent believer in Catholicism, a path that resembles Doctor Silveira's conversion in the film.[15] It is thus understandable that Brum de Canto's movie counted on the support of the Church, which contributed several suggestions to the plot.[16]

As Rodrigues emphasizes in the quote reproduced above, the theory presented in the film is "contemporary" and relevant not only to Catholics but also to "positivists and determinists." He suggests that the subject matter developed in the plot transcends the religious sphere since it appeals to both believers and atheists and has nationwide repercussions. In another article published a few months later, also in *Cine-Jornal*, the film critic Afonso Lopes Vieira refers once again to the movie's potential impact on Portuguese society, not just in religious terms, but more broadly, in regard to the values upon which the nation was founded:

> [...] this film will be, above all, *national and patriotic*, not strictly religious propaganda, since the Christian topic of the Virgin is embedded in all the decisive moments of Portuguese history. Furthermore, Fátima is not the creation of the Church, but of the Portuguese People itself.[17]

According to Lopes Vieira, the topic depicted in the film relates to the very identity of Portugal, since Christianity, and accordingly the cult of the Virgin Mary at Fátima, are part of the country's history. These statements make it clear that the movie was thought of and received by critics as a commentary on both religion and politics. Aurélio Rodrigues's words suggest that the Catholic religion is linked to the existence of the Portuguese nation, meaning that an anti-clerical political regime like the First Republic was not appropriate for the country. The New State, which is presented as an alternative to Republicanism, is suited to the national situation, since it is the political expression of the harmony of reason and faith.

As early as 1922, when Salazar was a member of parliament for the Portuguese Catholic Center, he outlined a political theory based on the non-contradiction of reason and faith as expressed in Thomist philosophy. According to Salazar, the justification of political power is found in God, which excludes a democratic and contractual origin of society. The ultimate end of any social organization is the common good, to which freedom is secondary. Yet, even though he believed that all nations were grounded on morality and religion, Salazar stressed the need to separate religious matters from politics. In other words, the future Prime Minister rejected the idea of a Catholic state and opted instead for a harmonious coexistence of religion and political power.[18]

In general, Salazar remained faithful to these notions when he came to power years later. The Salazarist New State oscillated between a secular model of government (the reason why intellectuals like the modernist António Ferro were chosen to fill important positions) and a politics influenced by religion. This religious bent was especially noticeable in education: crucifixes were placed in schools and lessons were crafted to agree with Christian morals.[19] If religious leaders, on the one hand, complained about the scarcity of religious references in the 1933 Constitution, on the other, the Concordat of 1940 between Portugal and the Vatican gave back to the Catholic Church some of the privileges that had been taken away from it during the First Republic.[20] The ambiguous nature of the New State's relationship with the Church led Manuel Braga da Cruz to classify the regime as "Catholaicism" (Catolaicismo), in other words, a non-Catholic state that protects and favors the Church.[21]

The close relationship between religion and politics in the New State mirrors the political theory of the German jurist Carl Schmitt. According to Schmitt, modern political concepts were developed as a modification of theological notions: "[a]ll significant concepts of the modern theory of the state are secularized theological concepts."[22] For example, God's absolute power is the model for sovereignty, while the economy of the Christian trinity is transposed to the political domain in the division of power into the judicial, legislative, and executive branches. However, Schmitt is careful to point out that political concepts do not directly translate religious notions, since the theological dogma suffers transformations in the process of secularization, when it is applied to modern political life. Despite avoiding direct interference of the Church in the government, Salazar, in the wake of Schmitt, recognized the relevance of religion in the New State as the origin and source of all political power. The statesman considered God to be the corollary and ultimate guarantor of the regime's social and political hierarchy.

In the speech he gave before the National Assembly in favor of the approval of the Concordat and Missionary Agreement, Salazar explained his conception of the Church's role in the Portuguese New State:

> The first reality that the State has before it is the Catholic formation of the Portuguese people; the second is that the essence of this formation translates into a historical constant. / We emerged as an independent nation already from the heart of Catholicism; to request shelter under the Church's protection was without a doubt an act imbued with political significance, but it was rooted in popular sentiment. [… there] never [was] a rebellion of conscience against faith. […] we can display to the world […] the rare example of identity of religious conscience: an extraordinary benefit, in the attainment of which a far-sighted policy has been engaged.[23]

According to Salazar, Catholicism is the central pillar of the state because religion is a fundamental element in the formation of the Portuguese people as a nation. Despite reaffirming the separation of Church and State in another passage of this same speech, Salazar stressed that respect for Catholicism is built into the history of Portugal, and that his government's protection of the "freedom to believe in God" emanated from a desire to "re-Portugalize" the country.[24] In other words, being Portuguese means, above all, being Catholic. Rejecting religion, as Doctor Silveira does in Brum do Canto's film, is tantamount to the rejection of patriotic values in favor of foreign doctrines like the revolutionary ideals of 1789.

It is worth noting that Doctor Silveira, disappointed by his colleagues' and friends' lack of support when he proclaims his atheism, decides to leave Portugal to attend a scientific conference in Argentina. His return to the Church at the end of the movie entails his return to his family's home, located in a small village near Coimbra, at the heart of the nation. The film illustrates in this way the identification between religion, nationalism, and the regime. Through the association of his administration and the political project of the New State with the true Portugal—"[…] it was not the people who understood the spirit of the [1926] Revolution; it was the Revolution that knew how to interpret the sentiment of the people," as he pointed out[25]—Salazar suggested that those critical of his government were ultimately nothing more than traitors, incapable of understanding the nation's spirit. All Portuguese citizens were free to use their reason to reflect upon the details of Salazarist politics, but no one was allowed to question the central values of the New State and especially Catholic religion. Such disbelief, synonymous with infidelity to the nation, would lead to the exclusion of the nonbeliever from the national community.

In the famous speech "As Grandes Certezas da Revolução Nacional" given in Braga on 26 May 1936 for the commemorations of the 1926 Revolution, Salazar develops a distinction between political questions that can be rationally discussed and those that lie beyond any questioning:

> We do not question God or virtue; we do not question the Fatherland and its History; we do not question authority or its prestige; we do not question the family and its morals; we do not question the glory of work and its obligations. [...] Aside from the intrinsic value of religious truth, individually, socially we need the absolute, and we are not going to create with our hands from contingent and ephemeral things that which exists above and beyond us [...]. Convinced of the value, of human life's need of a superior spirituality [...], *We do not question God.*[26]

The "great truths" of Salazarism listed here are the social foundations of the Portuguese New State. Religion is presented as the cornerstone that precedes and undergirds all other values.[27] The task of the citizens was to believe in these ideas without questioning them. Salazar also mentioned that the Portuguese felt comforted by their unconditional fidelity to the great political truths, in the same manner that believers find comfort in their faith in God. Therefore, it makes sense that Doctor Silveira is portrayed as a disturbed and unhappy man in *Fátima, Land of Faith*. Hounded by doubts and disbelief, he only reaches peace when he gives in to religion.

By postulating the existence of "great truths" beyond the scrutiny of reason, the New State adapted to its political reality the epistemological distinction developed in Kantian philosophy between phenomena, which human beings can know and understand rationally, and noumena, or the things-in-themselves, which are beyond human reason. However, Salazarism altered Kant's emancipating and self-regulating vision of the Enlightenment, according to which each individual, free in the realm of noumena, is the source of his own beliefs and morals. Salazar placed a strong emphasis on authority, which defined the "truths" that should orient both the nation and the private lives of each citizen.[28]

In his interviews with António Ferro, he underlined the importance of authority in the political system he headed:

> Authority and freedom are two incompatible concepts ... [...] Let us then surrender freedom to authority, because only authority knows how to administer it ... and defend it. [...] The freedom guaranteed by the State, conditioned by authority, is the only possible freedom, the freedom which may lead to, I would not say man's happiness, but rather the happiness of all men.[29]

Individual freedom, subordinated to the collective good, should be controlled by authority, which limits it in order to guarantee national unity and the proper functioning of organized society.[30] The "great truths" of the New State—God, Nation, Family, and Work—materialized in authority figures to whom the Portuguese owed obedience: the Catholic Church (and its hierarchical structure, going from the Pope, through the Cardinals, Bishops, etc.), political representatives (The Head of State, the Head of Government, etc.), the Father, and the Boss. Salazarism thus created a hierarchical social chain similar to the medieval *scala naturae*, in which all citizens had a fixed place and God was the highest authority. Doctor Silveira's conversion in Brum do Canto's film represents his reintegration into the regime's socio-political structure: the doctor accepts the limits of reason, recognizes his error of disproportionate trust in science, and surrenders to the Church's authority in the moral sphere and to the New State in the political realm. However, the film leaves out the existence of a powerful repressive apparatus, essential for dealing with those who, unlike the doctor, insist on remaining unfaithful and do not comply with the great truths of the regime.

Beyond reason and faith: The danger of nihilism

One of the key sequences of *Fátima, Land of Faith* occurs near the end of the film, when Doctor Silveira goes to the hospital to visit his son, José Augusto, who is in a deep coma after a fall from a horse. The doctor, hopeless because of science's failure to help the boy, is for a short period of time in an ideological limbo: he has abandoned his trust in scientific reason, but does not yet believe in the salvation offered by religion. The film depicts the severity of the situation through the recreation of a gloomy scenario, inspired by the tradition of the ultra-Romantic literature of the 1800s: it is night-time, and the dingy room where the doctor is sitting near his son's bed is periodically illuminated by lightning from the storm raging outside, with the sound of pouring rain joining the ominous rumble of thunder. Yet, Doctor Silveira's moment of indecision does not last long. A nun, José Augusto's nurse, advises the professor to have faith and reminds him that the following day is the celebration of Our Lady of Fátima. As if to lend more weight to these words, the lightning that flashes outside the dark window projects the shadowy image of a cross on to the room's white wall. Influenced by these signs, the doctor decides to bring his son to the Fátima sanctuary, which leads to the child's cure and to the professor's conversion.

In Brum do Canto's film, the transformation that Doctor Silveira undergoes takes place seamlessly. The doctor transfers the faith that he had in scientific reason to religion, after a brief moment of disbelief that takes place in the aforementioned scene. The film does not involve a reassessment of scientific values or an awareness that universal "great truths" do not exist, but rather the replacement of unconditional belief in the power of reason for belief in religion. Catholicism is depicted as a panacea for all evils, working even in situations in which medicine is powerless.

Theodor Adorno and Max Horkheimer's central thesis in *The Dialectic of Enlightenment* provides a useful tool for interpreting this episode of the film. According to the German thinkers, the notion that enlightened reason is the salvation of humanity is a mere inversion of a mythological conception of existence, religion being another one of the manifestations of this worldview. Enlightened reason and mythology are, in the end, two sides of the same coin, and rationality can easily regress to the point of becoming myth once again, leading to the self-destruction of the Enlightenment as a socio-political project. In Adorno and Horkheimer's words, "Myth is already enlightenment, and enlightenment reverts to mythology."[31] Interpreted under this prism, Doctor Silveira's transformation is no more than a mutation that takes place in enlightened scientific rationality, which returns to the domain of religious mythology, a sphere from which it has never completely broken free.

By presenting belief in scientific reason and the adoption of Catholicism as Doctor Silveira's only two possible options, the film promotes a tendentious view of reality that is in line with the ideology disseminated by the New State. The doctor quickly overcomes the moment of doubt that he experiences in the hospital room, thereby avoiding the fall into a state of nihilism that would reject *both* the values of enlightened reason *and* religious dogma. In fact, nihilism, not loyalty to scientific rationality, is what Salazar considered to be the greatest threat to the stability of his government. He warned of this potential threat in *Como se Levanta um Estado*:

> But the philosophic mania has started to weaken in intellects their adherence to eternal certainties and undermine in [people's] souls the great truths. [...] God, certainty, truth, justice, morality were denied in the name of skepticism, pragmatism, Epicureanism, thousands of confused systems whose emptiness was filled with difficulty. But negation, indifference, doubt cannot be the source of action, and life is action.[32]

What destroys Salazar's "great truths" is not the belief in the unlimited power of human reason, but the "philosophic mania" that leads to nihilism—to negation, indifference, and doubt—and drives nihilists to question all moral, religious, and political values.[33] In this excerpt, Salazar's appeal for action, as opposed to reflection, echoes the ideology of other authoritarian governments—Nazism or Mussolini's fascism—which, with their bellicose rhetoric, underscored precisely the need to act, in order not to give their populations room to think. Adherence to the ideology of the New State, either through faith in reason, which as we saw transforms itself easily into religion, or through a desire for action, necessarily excludes nihilism. The nihilistic third path makes a brief appearance in *Fátima, Land of Faith* only to be immediately discarded by Doctor Silveira as a nonviable option and substituted by the adoption of Catholicism.

The struggle against the threat of nihilism and indifference to Salazarism's values pervaded the various sectors of the governing apparatus of the New State. One example is the directive issued by the National Institute of Labor and sent to the Ministry of the Interior in 1942, a year before the premiere of Brum do Canto's film. This document recommended the rejection of the statutes of the recently created Portuguese Federation of Educational and Recreational Organizations, which represented more than 400 groups from all regions of the country:

> Does [...] the Federation intend to exist in a *system of absolute political and religious indifference* (articles 27 and 125 of the statues), and *therefore at the margins of any concept of moral order* [...]? [...] it becomes necessary to establish firm and clear principles that express a certain understanding of life, something that goes against *the political and religious indifference of the Federation*. [...] the statutes should be meticulously revised [...] to agree with the ideas that, in a superior fashion, guide the action of the State. [...] Their *proclaimed political and religious indifference has served to pervert or reduce the nationalist sentiment*.[34]

This dispatch criticizes the statutes proposed by the Federation because they do not define religious or political directives, choosing instead a position of indifference in relation to the "great truths" of Salazarism. Such *indifference* is not in itself immoral, but worse, it is insidiously amoral. Therefore, it could potentially corrupt the nationalist feeling that sustained the ideological structure of the New State. For this reason, indifferent nihilism emerges as the great enemy of the regime, the source of what Salazar calls (significantly using a religious vocabulary) the "great heresies of our time," which include internationalism, communism, syndicalism, and class struggle.[35]

While Salazar identified communism as the political expression of moral indifference and as the principal threat to the values of the New State, the same occurred in the rhetoric of the Catholic Church, which accused communist materialism of destroying spirituality and religion. The ecclesiastic authorities interpreted the Fátima apparitions from early on as a reaction against the atheism of the Russian Revolution, partly because both events took place in the same year.[36] Cardinal Cerejeira declared that "Fátima—the World's altar—opposes Moscow, the capital of the kingdom of the Anti-Christ."[37] This statement was later supported by Sister Lúcia's 1941 memoirs. She revealed the "secrets" that Our Lady of Fátima communicated to the three children, one of which was the Virgin's petition for the conversion of Russia to her Immaculate Heart.[38] Communism, with its atheism, its internationalism, its dissolution of traditional hierarchies, and its desire for social equality, is the antithesis of the nationalism of the New State. It is therefore understandable that Salazar was militantly "against those without nation and without God."[39] The danger of religious apostasy resided not only in the negation of God and the spiritual power of the Church, but also in the rejection of all values that were adopted uncritically, including the "great truths" of Salazarism.

Nihilism, moral indifference, and their political incarnation—according to Salazar, atheist communism—are perceived as threats to the regime. Because of this, films close to the ideology of the New State, like *Fátima, Land of Faith*, seek to exorcize these notions. By limiting Doctor Silveira's choices to faith in enlightened reason and Republicanism, on the one hand, or acceptance of the Catholic religion and the New State, on the other hand, the film nullifies the possibility of a third option: of nihilism and a critical reason that would analyze its conditions of possibility. This is precisely the critical reason that Adorno and Horkheimer identify as a way of escaping the impasse of Western culture's perpetual vacillation between myth and Enlightenment. For these thinkers, reason needs to carry out a permanent analysis of its assumptions and decisions, as well as its socio-economic conditions and political context. Nihilism is thus the point of departure for critical thought that rejects pre-conceived ideas. However, the critique of reason does not mean a paralysis of the emancipatory desire of the Enlightenment, reduced to a radical nihilism that would prevent the creation of new values. Instead, it denotes the unfinished character of all emancipatory projects, both ethical and socio-political. In order to avoid their fossilization as myth, they should open a space for constant self-reflection. The New State's crusade against nihilism and the moral indifference that results from a "philosophical mania" is a way to safeguard the values upon which the regime was founded. Citizens should have faith in "great truths" because without this belief, the ideology of Salazarism would collapse along with its authoritarian and hierarchical structure.

The beginning of *Fátima, Land of Faith* offers a portrait of social and political stagnation—what Salazar euphemistically called "order and stability"—which would be jeopardized by a critical reflection in the manner recommended by Adorno and Horkheimer. Brum do Canto's film opens with a sequence that depicts a traditional Portuguese home on Christmas Eve: the family is gathered around the fireplace, and the camera focuses on the nativity scene in order to highlight the religiosity of those present. The movie signals the absence of the father of the family, Doctor Silveira, a situation resolved in the end of the film when the professor returns to his family.

This portrait of immutability contrasts with the depiction of high speed and modern technology in the movie. The film emphasizes movement by depicting various means of transportation, such as a horse, a car, and an airplane. Also, the sequence in which the doctor performs a surgery was, according to Brum do Canto, one of the most meticulously planned segments of the film.[40] However, speed, movement, and technical–scientific knowledge have nefarious consequences. Doctor Silveira's son suffers a riding accident after a sequence in which his horse goes out running at full speed, pursued by his riding teacher also on horseback. Another high-speed scene takes place when a taxi departs from the Lisbon hotel where the doctor was staying with a telegram to inform him of his son's accident. Despite its haste, the taxi arrives at the airport too late, as the professor's airplane had already taken off. When he finally receives the telegram on board, the doctor cannot persuade the crew to return to Lisbon and allow him to deplane.[41] Likewise, the surgery conducted by the doctor and filmed with great detail goes wrong, and the child undergoing the procedure dies shortly after. By associating velocity, change, and technology with negative effects, the film obliquely highlights the advantages of the New State. It suggests that resisting the seduction of these false idols is imperative for avoiding disaster. Doctor Silveira, who is led astray by the allure of modernity, coupled with technical–scientific rationality, can only be saved by the miracle that takes place in the Fátima sanctuary at the end of the movie.

José Augusto's miraculous cure gives way to another miracle: the doctor's religious and political conversion. The Fátima theophany is, in this sense, not only the materialization of the divine—made manifest to believers without intermediaries, first in the apparitions of the Virgin and, subsequently, in miraculous events like the boy's recovery—but also the materialization of the power of Catholicism itself, to which the doctor succumbs when he realizes its dimensions. Miracles, which happen in this world but are not exactly of this world, form the basis of the Church's sovereignty, as Carl Schmitt points out in his reflections on religion. According to Schmitt, the miracle in the theological realm corresponds to the state of exception (Ausnahmezustand) in political terms, i.e. to an extra-ordinary, anarchical situation in which the law that was previously in force no longer applies and the sovereign needs to take an extra-legal decision in order to create a new system of laws. The decision on the exception, upon which the new legality is built, is a secular form of the religious *creatio ex nihilo*—"The decision, considered in normative terms, has its origin in the void"[42]—the establishment of a solid foundation on the basis of nothing.

Schmitt's thoughts on the religious miracle and the decision on the state of exception as the translation of this event into political terms clarify the central role of the supernatural phenomenon witnessed by Doctor Silveira in *Fátima, Land of Faith*. Having abandoned his belief in reason and science, the Doctor is ready to surrender to nihilism. The nihilistic worldview, which does not recognize any laws or values, parallels in political terms the complete disorder and anarchy that precede the decision on the state of exception. The miracle is what justifies the doctor's religious faith and allows for his reintegration into the political, juridical, and social order of Salazarism. In a similar manner, the very event of Salazar's rise to power is described by the regime as the foundation of a new order—*nomos*, in Schmitt's words—arising from the disorder that reigned in the country during the First Republic.

The similarities signaled in Brum do Canto's film between the religious miracle of Fátima and the political "miracle" of the formation of the New State were underlined by the Church from very early on. The religious miracle that announced the spiritual rebirth of Portugal was followed by Salazarism's self-proclaimed moral, economic, and political regeneration of the country.[43] Salazar is therefore often described as a messianic savior of the nation.[44] In his personal correspondence with Salazar throughout the 1940s, Cardinal Cerejeira frequently referred to the statesman as the one chosen for carrying out the task of national regeneration.[45] Doctor Silveira's rejection of scientific and critical reason and his conversion to religion and to the principles of the New State correspond to his acceptance of Salazarism as a miraculous event and of Salazar as the messiah that would save Portugal. At the end of *Fátima, Land of Faith*, the Professor espouses the values that, according to the New State, should be adopted by all Portuguese intellectuals. Only such an intellectual elite would be able to lead the nation toward the miracle of national resurgence.

Notes

1 In 1922, the Catholic Church created a Canonical Commission that was responsible for investigating and giving an opinion on the Fátima apparitions. The miracles were finally declared to be credible by the *Pastoral Letter on the Cult of Our Lady of Fátima* (*Carta Pastoral sobre o Culto de Nossa Senhora de Fátima*) in 1930, and after this date the sanctuary saw rapid growth. For a detailed analysis of the development of the Fátima sanctuary, see Luís Filipe Torgal's *As "Aparições de Fátima"*, 67–87.
2 Vatican support of Fátima was confirmed during the papacy of Pius XII, who delivered a speech dedicated to the sanctuary in Portuguese. This speech was broadcast by the Portuguese National Radio (Emissora Nacional) on 31 October 1942 (Torgal, "*Aparições*," 119).
3 In 1928, Rino Lupo directed *Miraculous Fátima* (*Fátima Milagrosa*) about the apparitions of the Virgin. During the New State, António Lopes Ribeiro and Miguel Spiguel filmed the documentaries *Fátima, Hope of the World* (*Fátima, Esperança do Mundo*, 1967) and *Fátima in the Middle East* (*Fátima no Médio Oriente*, 1969). There were also other fiction films about religion produced during the New State, such as *The Heron and the Serpent* (*A Garça e a Serpente*, Arthur Duarte, 1952) and *Heroic Plain* (*Planície Heróica*, Perdigão Queiroga, 1953). In 1951 Spanish filmmaker Rafael Gil directed *The Lady of Fátima* (*La Señora de Fátima*). After the end of the New State in 1974, several other films about Fátima were produced, including the historical feature *Fátima* (Fabrizio Costa, 1997) and a number of documentaries.
4 According to the 29 August 1938 edition of *Cine-Jornal*, Aurélio Rodrigues was

initially chosen to direct *Fátima, Terra de Fé* (Matos-Cruz, *Brum do Canto*, 105). Later, the direction was offered to Brum to Canto (Ribeiro, *Filmes, Figuras*, 460–2).

5 "certos aspectos angulares da política cinematográfica católica salazarista." Garrido, "Coimbra nas Imagens do Cinema," in *O Cinema sob o Olhar de Salazar*, 280. According to Álvaro Garrido, "[w]e are therefore in the presence of a film that unites a group of elements of Catholic ideology, deliberately or subconsciously combined with the ideology of the New State." ("[e]stamos, assim, na presença de um filme que reúne todo um conjunto de elementos da ideologia católica, conjugada, de forma deliberada ou inconsciente, com a ideologia do Estado Novo.") "Coimbra nas Imagens do Cinema," in *O Cinema sob o Olhar de Salazar*, 281.

6 "atinge a maior altura"; "beleza moral e espiritual." Cited in Ribeiro, *Filmes, Figuras*, 463.

7 For a description of the controversy that surrounded the phenomenon of Fátima during the First Republic see António Teixeira Fernandes, *O Confronto de Ideologias na Segunda Década do Século XX: À volta de Fátima*. For the role of Fátima in the Catholic revival in Portugal, see Luís Filipe Torgal, "*Aparições*," 147–75.

8 Torgal, "*Aparições*," 74–5.

9 "não deve ter feito falta nenhuma."

10 "gritaria o desprezo da sua razão libertada."

11 Garrido, "Coimbra nas Imagens do Cinema," in *O Cinema sob o Olhar de Salazar*, 282–4. For an exhaustive analysis of the similarities and differences between Bissaya Barreto and the character of Doctor Silveira in *Fátima, Land of Faith*, see Álvaro Garrido, "Coimbra nas Imagens do Cinema no Estado Novo," in *O Cinema sob o Olhar de Salazar*, 282–8.

12 In addition to being a supporter of the New State, Bissaya Barreto was a personal friend of Salazar, who had been one of his colleagues at the University of Coimbra (Garrido, "Coimbra nas Imagens do Cinema," in *O Cinema sob o Olhar de Salazar*, 286).

13 "— [entrevistador] É um filme simplesmente religioso?
    — [Rodrigues] É de facto um filme religioso em cujo desenrolar se enquadra toda a grandeza da epopeia de Fátima. [...] Um filme em que se debatem conflitos e paixões, como caixilho para a tese que anima todo o filme. Uma tese actual, uma das mais interessantes da filosofia tomista, tratada com uma leveza e elegância, que poderei afirmar que merecerá o interesse de católicos e de positivistas e deterministas.
    — [entrevistador] A enunciação da tese?
    — [Rodrigues] Não há conflito entre a fé e ciência: Deus, fruto de todo o saber e a ciência reflexo da divindade."
    Cited in Matos-Cruz, *Brum do Canto*, 105.

14 Torgal, "*Aparições*," 35–6.
15 For a description of the role of Cardinal Cerejeira in the official recognition of the Fátima sanctuary, see Luís Filipe Torgal's As*"Aparições de Fátima*," 164–8.
16 In the same interview published in *Cine-Jornal* in August 1938, Aurélio Rodrigues reports that the Catholic Church offered several suggestions for the plot of *Fátima, Terra de Fé*. Garrido points out that the Church realized from early on the potential of cinema for spreading Catholicism. In Pope Pius XI's encyclical *Vigilanti Cura*, the prelate called for the production of films inspired by Christian ideas. This idea was taken up by Cruz Neves, author of *Cinema and the Christian Sense of Love and of Family* (*O Cinema e o Sentido Cristão do Amor e da Familia*), in which he states that cinema, being the modern substitute of literature, models the habits and the morality of the people and, because of this, it should be guided by Catholic morality (Garrido, "Coimbra nas Imagens do Cinema," in *O Cinema sob o Olhar de Salazar*, 274–5). According to Garrido, the New State aimed to "[…] bring film production closer to a set of unquestionable spiritual values, subordinating them to the concept that the Church itself had of film and sought to instill in their believers" ("[...] aproximar a produção cinematográfica de um conjunto de valores espirituais inquestionáveis, subordinando-os ao conceito que a própria Igreja fazia do cinema e pretendia incutir nos seus crentes") 276.
17 "[...] este filme será, antes de mais nada, *nacional e patriótico*, não propriamente de propaganda religiosa, visto que o tema cristão da Virgem se acha enquadrado em todos os lances decisivos da história de Portugal. De mais, Fátima é a criação, não da Igreja, mas do próprio Povo Português." Cited in Matos-Cruz, *Brum do Canto*, 107.
18 Salazar expounded his views on the relationship between Church and State during the Second Congress of the Portuguese Catholic Center in 1922. For a detailed description of Salazar's speech at this event, see Luís Reis Torgal, *Estados Novos, Estado Novo*, vol. 1, 432–5.
19 Paulo, *Estado Novo e Propaganda*, 54–5.
20 Cardinal Cerejeira protested the non-confessional nature of the 1933 Constitution in a letter to the President of the Republic (Torgal, *Estados Novos*, vol. 1, 438). Also, Salazar frequently stated that the State would not interfere in Church matters, in the same way that the Church should not seek to influence the country's government: "I have observed that political intervention in religion and the confusion of the spiritual interests with the material interests of a people, of the Church with any organization that, acting in the political terrain, could be taken as a party, aspiring or not aspiring to govern, are not convenient for the development and purity of religious life. Especially in a country like ours, with old Catholic traditions, but with a generally poorly educated religiosity and a narrow mindedness in partisan fights,

the strictly political activity of the Church brings to it and its clergy serious frictions and distrust that threaten its purely spiritual action." ("Tenho observado como é inconveniente ao desenvolvimento e pureza da vida religiosa a intromissão da política na religião, a confusão dos interesses espirituais com os interesses materiais dos povos, da Igreja com qualquer organização que, actuando no terreno político, possa ser tomada como um partido, aspirando ou não ao governo. Sobretudo num país como o nosso, de velhas tradições católicas mas duma religiosidade geralmente pouco esclarecida, e de um estreito feitio de espírito nas lutas partidárias, a actividade propriamente política da Igreja levanta-lhe e ao seu clero atritos e desconfianças graves que a prejudicam na acção puramente espiritual.") "Diferentes Forças," in *Discursos (1928-1934)*, 173. In a later speech, Salazar reiterated this idea: "[...] The State will abstain from playing politics with the Church, with the certainty that the Church will abstain from playing politics with the State." ("O Estado vai abster-se de fazer política com a Igreja, na certeza de que a Igreja se abstém de fazer política com o Estado.") "Problemas Político-Religiosos," in *Discursos e Notas Políticas (1938-1943)*, 239. In the 1949 speech "O Meu Depoimento," Salazar summarizes his position in relation to the Catholic Church, pointing out the importance of this institution in the formation of Portuguese culture but emphasizing the need of maintaining a separation between religion and politics. *Discursos e Notas Políticas (1943-1950)*, 370-3.

21 Cruz, *O Estado Novo e a Igreja Católica*, 15. For more information about the terms of the Concordat and Missionary Agreement see Bruno Cardoso Reis, *Salazar e o Vaticano*, 139-92.

22 "[a]lle prägnanten Begriffe der modernen Staatslehre sind säkularisierte theologische Begriffe." Schmitt, *Politische Theologie*, 43.

23 "A primeira realidade que o Estado tem diante de si é a formação católica do povo português; a segunda é que a essência desta formação se traduz numa constante da história. / Nascemos já, como nação independente, no seio do catolicismo; acolher-se à protecção da Igreja foi sem dúvida acto de alcance político, mas alicerçado no sentimento popular. [...] nunca [houve] rebelião da consciência contra a fé. [...] podemos apresentar perante o mundo [...] o exemplo raro da identidade de consciência religiosa: benefício extraordinário em cuja consecução se empenhou uma política previdente." Salazar, "Problemas Político-Religiosos," in *Discursos e Notas Políticas (1938-1943)*, 232-3.

24 "liberdade de crer em Deus"; "reaportuguesamento." Salazar, *Para a Compreensão*, 7. Although the Church cannot interfere in the details of governing the country, this limitation does not invalidate its spiritual power. Thus, Salazar claimed that the Church played a fundamental role as the spiritual leader of the nation: "[...] Church, whose spirituality that is always alive and whose teaching that is always

certain must continue to be the peoples' guide in the uncertain times in which we live [...]." ("[...] Igreja, cuja espiritualidade sempre viva e cujo magistério sempre seguro têm de continuar a ser guia dos povos nas horas incertas que vivemos [...].") *Para a Compreensão*, 14.

25 "[...] não foi o povo que compreendeu o espírito da Revolução [de 1926]; foi a Revolução que soube interpretar o sentimento do povo." Salazar, "Grandes Certezas," in *Discursos e Notas Políticas (1935-1937)*, 138-9.

26 "Não discutimos Deus e a virtude; não discutimos a Pátria e a sua História; não discutimos a autoridade e o seu prestígio; não discutimos a família e a sua moral; não discutimos a glória do trabalho e o seu dever. [...] Àparte o valor intrínseco da verdade religiosa, individualmente, socialmente temos necessidade de absoluto, e não vamos criar por nossas mãos de entre as coisas contingentes e efémeras o que existe fora e acima de nós [...]. Compenetrados do valor, da necessidade na vida duma espiritualidade superior [...] -*Não discutimos Deus.*" Salazar, "As Grandes Certezas," in *Discursos e Notas Políticas (1935-1937)*, 130-1. Another version of this passage can be found in *Como se Levanta um Estado*: "[...] we are not asking for much: a notion and sense of the Fatherland and national solidarity; family, the building block of society par excellence; authority and hierarchy; [...] the obligation of work; the superiority of virtue; the sacred character of religious sentiments [...]." ("[...] não pedimos grande coisa: noção e sentido da Pátria e da solidariedade nacional; família, célula social por excelência; autoridade e hierarquia; [...] obrigação do trabalho; superioridade da virtude; carácter sagrado dos sentimentos religiosos [...].") 51. Salazar also states in the same text: "If faith is not a lie, it is an inexhaustible source of spiritual life; but, if faith as a virtue is a gift from God, we do not understand why it should be imposed by force, nor why there would be any advantage in countering its action." ("Se a fé não é uma mentira, é uma inexaurível fonte de vida espiritual; mas, se como virtude ela é um dom de Deus, nós não compreendemos nem que se a imponha pela força, nem que exista vantagem em contrariar a sua acção.") 127.

27 These "great truths" were the origin of the New State's motto, "God, Fatherland, Family." The maxim was inspired by Brazilian politician and President Afonso Pena's expression "God, Fatherland, Freedom, and Family" that was on the cover of the newspaper of the school where Salazar was prefect in Viseu: *Echos da Via Sacra* (Torgal, *Estados Novos*, vol. 1, 426).

28 On the surface, one might think that Salazar would have agreed with Kant when he states in "Answering the Question: What is Enlightenment?" that we can disagree with our leaders' decisions but we have to obey their orders. However, Salazarism overturned the famous Kantian distinction between the private use of reason—in other words, our use of reason while holding a political office—and the public use

of reason—our use of reason as members of a socio-political community, which should be free. For Salazar, reason is always subordinated to authority, which excludes the public and free use of reason under any circumstances.

29 "Autoridade e liberdade são dois conceitos incompatíveis ... [...] Entreguemos, pois, a liberdade à autoridade, porque só ela a sabe administrar ... e defender. [...] A liberdade guarantida pelo Estado, condicionada pela autoridade, é a única possível, aquela que pode conduzir, não digo à felicidade do homem, mas à felicidade dos homens." Ferro, *Entrevistas*, 34.

30 Salazar had already formulated the idea that individual freedom should be subordinated to the collective good in 1922 at the Second Congress of the Portuguese Catholic Center mentioned above. Salazar repeated this idea in his speech "Political–Religious Problems of the Portuguese Nation" ("Problemas Político-Religiosos da Nação Portuguesa"): "The State has been forced more and more to subordinate the freedom of individuals to collective needs and objectives." ("O Estado tem-se visto forçado a condicionar cada vez mais a liberdade dos individuos a necesidades e escopos colectivos.") *Discursos e Notas Políticas (1938–1943)*, 235.

31 Horkheimer and Adorno, *Dialectic of Enlightenment: Philosophical Fragments*, xviii.

32 "Mas a mania filosófica tinha começado a enfraquecer nas inteligências a adesão às verdades eternas e a minar nos espíritos as grandes certezas. [...] Negara-se Deus, a certeza, a verdade, a justiça, a moral, em nome do cepticismo, do pragmatismo, do epicurismo, de mil sistemas confusos cujo vazio fora preenchido com dificuldade. Mas a negação, a indiferença, a dúvida não podem ser fontes de acção, e a vida é acção." Salazar, *Como se Levanta*, 84–5.

33 In his speech *Politics of the Spirit and the Literary Prizes of the SPN (Política do Espírito e os Prémios Literários do SPN)* from 21 February 1935, António Ferro condemned nihilistic anxiety: "But there is anxiety and there is anxiety, that is, the one that instinctively searches for order and the one that delights in disorder, constructive anxiety and diabolic, nihilistic anxiety." ("Mas há inquietação e inquietação, isto é, aquela que procura instintivamente a ordem e a que se compraz na desordem, a inquietação construtiva e a inquietação diabólica, niilista.") 9.

34 "Será [...] que a Federação pretende viver em *sistema de absoluta indiferença política e religiosa* (artigos 27 e 125 dos estatutos), *à margem portanto de qualquer concepção de ordem moral* [...]? [...] torna[-se] necessário estabelecer princípios firmes e claros que exprimem uma determinada compreensão da vida, o que briga com o *indiferentismo político e religioso da Federação.* [...] os estatutos devem ser minuciosamente revistos [...] de acordo com as ideias que superiormente orientam a acção do Estado [...]. O *apregoado indiferentismo político ou religioso tem servido para desvirtuar, ou atenuar o sentimento nacionalista.*" Cited in Melo, *Salazarismo*

e Cultura Popular (1933–1958), 342; emphasis added. The Portuguese Federation of Educational and Recreational Organizations was increasingly viewed with distrust by the New State due to its openness to any national collective, regardless of its political orientation, and because it was based upon democratic practices. For an analysis of the government's response to the creation of the Portuguese Federation of Educational and Recreational Organizations and its statutes, see Melo, *Salazarismo e Cultura Popular*, 332–44.

35 "as grandes heresias do nosso tempo." Salazar, *Como se Levanta*, 51.
36 For example, on 13 May 1930, the Church organized prayers for the salvation of communist Russia in Fátima (Torgal, "*Aparições*," 204).
37 "Fátima—Altar do Mundo—opõe-se a Moscovo capital do reino do Anti-Cristo." Cited in Ameal and Reis-Santos, *Fátima, Altar do Mundo*, 15.
38 Sister Lúcia began writing her memoirs in 1935 at the request of the Bishop of Leiria. Her texts were progressively revealed to the public in the following decades. These documents describe the "secrets" of Fátima, one of which refers to the conversion of communist Russia to the Immaculate Heart of Mary.
39 "contra os sem-Pátria e os sem-Deus." Salazar, *Como se Levanta*, 51.
40 Brum do Canto says about *Fátima, Land of Faith* in the December 1959 edition of the magazine *Filme*: "In this film I left my mark mainly in two sequences: the surgery scene, staged with such care that I attended many operations in a white robe, and the scene in which doubt assails the Doctor's conscience and leads him to carry his son in his arms to Fátima." ("Neste filme reconheço-me principalmente em duas sequências: a cena da operação, encenada com um cuidado que me levou a assistir de bata branca a muitas operações, e a cena em que a dúvida assalta a consciência do médico e o faz levar o filho nos braços para Fátima.") Cited in Matos-Cruz, *Brum do Canto*, 105. It is significant that Brum do Canto links these two scenes because it is the doctor's rejection of medicine, represented in the first, that leads to his faith in the Virgin of Fátima, illustrated in the second.
41 These film sequences seem to be somewhat superfluous, since they do not advance the plot. The filmmaker perhaps kept these high-speed scenes in order to criticize the notion of modernity, progress, and technical–scientific rationality to which they allude.
42 "Die Entscheidung ist, normativ betrachtet, aus einem Nichts geboren." Schmitt, *Politische Theologie*, 37–8.
43 Moisés de Lemos Martins shows the parallels between the religious discourse of faith and conversion, and the political discourse of the New State in his work *O Olho de Deus no Discurso Salazarista*. For example, the rather vague term "regeneration" had been used in Portugal since the nineteenth century in order to mobilize the population around a political project. In the ideological discourse of

the New State this expression has religious undertones and denotes the regime's desire to generate a spiritual, economic, and socio-political resurgence in the country (Proença, "O Conceito de Regeneração," in *O Estado Novo*, 257–8).

44 In the speech "As Grandes Certezas da Revolução Nacional," Salazar stated that he had faith in the resurgence of Portugal. However, he stressed that sacrifice and above all the dedication of the Portuguese people are necessary for this renewal to continue: "Today, ten years that built merely an era of *restoration* in national History come to an end; now another ten will commence that will create an era of *aggrandizement*, to be erected on more difficult sacrifices, higher heroisms and surer dedications." ("Findam hoje dez anos que construíram na História pátria apenas uma era de *restauração;* vão começar outros dez que hão-de constituir uma era de *engrandecimento,* a erguer sobre mais duros sacrifícios, mais altos heroísmos e mais seguras dedicações.") *Discursos e Notas Políticas (1935–1937)*, 141.

45 Barreto, *Religião e Sociedade*, 41. The association between Fátima and the resurgence of Portugal comes through in the titles of books about the sanctuary, such as Father José Maria Félix's *Fátima e a Redenção de Portugal* (*Fátima and the Redemption of Portugal*, 1939).

5

Gender Stereotypes in New State Cinema

Women in New State films

Portuguese cinema from the 1930s to the 1950s bequeathed us a variety of female characters who paint a portrait of the roles played by women during the New State. From the shrewd villager Gracinda (Beatriz Costa) in *The Village of White Clothes* (*Aldeia da Roupa Branca*, Chianca de Garcia, 1939) to the sophisticated fado singer Maria da Graça, played by Amália Rodrigues in *Bullfighting Blood* (*Sangue Toureiro*, Augusto Fraga, 1958), from Luisinha (Milú), a bank clerk and representative of the Lisbon petit bourgeoisie in *Costa of the Castle* (*O Costa do Castelo*, Arthur Duarte, 1943), to the two wealthy aunts from Trás-os-Montes (Teresa Gomes and Sofia Santos) in *A Song of Lisbon* (*A Canção de Lisboa*, Cottinelli Telmo, 1933), cinema during the first decades of the Salazar regime featured characters not only from diverse social classes but also from various geographic origins, even including foreigners such as Nina (Olly Gebauer), the protagonist of *Wild Cattle* (*Gado Bravo*, António Lopes Ribeiro, 1934). However, this showcase of female roles has significant gaps. Peasant women are typically from Northern or Central Portugal, thereby excluding the poorer rural workers from the vast plains of the Alentejo; women employed in factories are usually not portrayed in film; and marginalized groups, such as beggars, prostitutes, etc., are also absent from the movies of this period.

In general, there is a tacit agreement between the representation of women in Salazarist cinema and the idealized model of femininity advocated by the regime. Female characters took on particular relevance in the dissemination of the values of the New State because of the importance that Salazar attributed to the traditional family. For Salazar, the family—not the individual or the citizen—is the core of society and one of the unquestionable "great truths" that served as the pillars of his government.[1] A harmonious family life leads to social peace, a necessary condition for the country's stability and development.[2]

Salazar's conception of the family is inspired by a Catholic conservative morality, according to which the relationship between women and men teleologically moves toward its purpose of marriage, child bearing and child rearing. The different members of the household have pre-defined masculine and feminine roles. With the ratification of the 1933 Constitution, the husband legally became the head of the family, and his function was to work and provide sustenance for his dependents. In this social hierarchy, the role of housewife and mother is reserved for the woman, who is subordinate to her husband. Despite proclaiming the equality of all citizens before the law, the Constitution added, with regard to women, that "the differences resulting from her nature and the good of the family" must be taken into account.[3] Some of the restrictions imposed on women in order to guarantee the "good of the family" included limited suffrage, discrimination in the labor market, and a Civil Code that required women to obtain their husbands' prior authorization to travel outside of the country, sign contracts, and administer their assets, to list only a few examples.[4]

In his interviews with António Ferro, Salazar recognized that the woman's function as mother and educator of children "is not inferior to man['s function]" and added: "I do not know, in the end, which of the two [man or woman] has the most beautiful, highest, and most useful role…"[5] In his speeches, the statesman went even further and compared his activity as manager of the country's finances with the feminine task of household administration: "I always advocated for an administrative policy that is so clear and so simple that any good housewife could perform it […]."[6] Certainly, Salazar cultivated a public persona with some feminine traits—modest, shy when speaking in public, polite—distancing himself from the virility of political leaders like Hitler, Mussolini, and Franco.[7] However, the politician's alleged proximity to a Portuguese housewife is nothing more than a discursive ruse. Such rhetoric evinced the New State's desire to make the public domain reflect the private sphere, thus reducing political activity to the mere administration of resources. The cited passages are representative of the comments that Salazar would repeatedly make about femininity. On the one hand, he praised women and recognized the importance of their social role as mothers, household administrators, and educators. On the other hand, women were, in concrete terms, placed in a position of inferiority and relegated to the private realm, with the vast majority of Portuguese women banned from participation in the public life of the nation.

The New State's treatment of women was no different from that of other European totalitarian regimes of the 1930s and 1940s. Paradoxically, these regimes mobilized women for their political projects by glorifying maternity and family management as central elements of a national renaissance, while simultaneously excluding women from the political arena.[8] The New State, like Italian and German fascism, accomplished a notable feat: it counted on the enthusiastic support of many women and at the same time sacrificed the rights of the female population in the name of abstract concepts such as "the good of the family."[9] Christine Garnier mentions this contradiction in her book about Salazar:

> The majority of Portuguese women are "in favor of the Situation:" they find Salazar so seductive! He never stopped battling against women's liberation. He has the austere reputation of a misogynist. Yet, the most beautiful faces surround him when he happens to preside at a party.[10]

Even though the vast majority of women let themselves be seduced by Salazar's rhetoric, it was still necessary to encourage the female population's support of the regime in order to guarantee that they would continue to yield happily to the limitations that were imposed on them. This was the goal of organizations such as the Mothers' Work for National Education (*Obra das Mães para a Educação Nacional*, OMEN), created in 1936, and the Female Portuguese Youth (*Mocidade Portuguesa Feminina*, MPF), which appeared a year later, both under the auspices of the Ministry for National Education of the New State. Inspired by similar groups developed under Italian and German fascism, these organizations promoted traditional family values. However, unlike what happened in Germany, for instance, in Portugal they also emphasized Christian morals. The OMEN operated mostly in rural regions and included a significant component of social assistance to poor families. The MPF worked mainly with schoolgirls, who were concentrated in urban areas, and membership was usually mandatory until the age of fourteen.[11] One of the goals of OMEN was to propagate the image of the happy, albeit poor, Portuguese peasant woman. As we read in a publication from the Secretariat of Propaganda entitled *Domestic Economy* (*Economia Doméstica*), it fell especially to women to live a life of "pleasant destitution."[12] The priority of the MPF, on the other hand, was to teach home economics to its young members, preparing them for their future task as mothers. Classes in culinary arts, childcare, hygiene, and sports were some of the activities organized by the institution.

The OMEN and the MPF outlined standards of feminine behavior and disseminated them through interventions in the fields of education and social assistance. Such notions of womanhood permeated the cultural production of the New State, including cinema. The model of femininity promoted by the OMEN—a rural woman who is Catholic, honest, and hardworking—appears in numerous films. This ideal was embodied by characters that became icons of Portuguese culture at the time: the previously mentioned Gracinda, a young girl from the countryside who is diligent and astute (played by the famous Beatriz Costa in *The Village of White Clothes*); and Maria Papoila, the protagonist of a 1937 Leitão de Barros film (played by the equally acclaimed Mirita Casimiro), a young village girl who rejects the hypocrisy of the big city. There is also Bastiana (Elsa Rumina) from *The Song of the Earth* (*Canção da Terra*, Jorge Brum do Canto, 1938), who flees from her mother's home to live with Gonçalves (Barreto Poeira), but quickly repents her rash decision and normalizes her situation through marriage in the Church at the end of the film. In *Wolves of the Mountain* (*Lobos da Serra*, Jorge Brum do Canto, 1942) we find the example of Margarida (Maria Domingas), a dedicated wife who, faced with her husband's despair when a flood destroys their crops, persists in agricultural work and rejects the easy but dishonest solution of smuggling. And in *Maria of the Sea* (*Maria do Mar*, Leitão de Barros, 1930), as well as

Figure 5.1 Gracinda (Beatriz Costa) in *The Village of White Clothes*

in *Up and Away!* (*Ala-Arriba!*, Leitão de Barros, 1942), we encounter village women who are faithful to their husbands and loyal to ancestral traditions. In general, the countrywomen represented in New State cinema are repositories of the principles of integrity, fidelity, honesty, and hard work. They frequently stand in contrast to masculine characters, who are depicted as insecure, fickle, capricious, and even lazy.[13]

The filmography of this period echoes not only the ideal of the hard-working peasant woman preached by OMEN but also the image of womanhood put forth by the MPF. This other model of femininity was that of the educated, intelligent woman who feels at ease both in conversations about current events and in domestic tasks such as sewing and cooking.[14] The popular Portuguese-style comedies (comédias à portuguesa), with plots essentially focusing on unexpected events in the lives of members of the Lisbon bourgeoisie, offer several examples of this other vision of how a woman should behave. This new conception of female conduct became more relevant as the country urbanized and literacy increased among women.[15] As Paulo Granja describes in his article about this film genre, Portuguese-style comedies are permeated by a deeply conservative morality that censures women who put the traditional family structure at risk and condemns any attitudes that deviate from the social patterns established by the regime.[16]

Branca (Maria Eugénia) from the comedy *The Lion of Estrela* (*O Leão da Estrela*, Arthur Duarte, 1947), a simple, domestic young woman who wants nothing more than an honorable husband, exemplifies what urban women should be like. Her conduct contrasts sharply with that of her sister Jujú (Milú), a frivolous girl who is critical of her social position and longs for a rich boyfriend.[17] At the end of the film, both sisters marry members of the wealthy upper bourgeoisie. Given her moral rectitude, Branca is deserving of her new, more socially advantageous position. Jujú's marriage, arranged in the last minutes of the movie by a *deus ex machina* in the form of the Commandant (Tony D'Algy), results from the propensity of Portuguese-style comedies for ending with the happy marriage of the female leading characters.

Marriage looms in New State comedies as the *terminus ad quem* of the story. All conflicts, whether between members of different social classes as in *Costa of the Castle* or between rivals belonging to the same class as in *The Radio Girl* (*A Menina da Rádio*, Arthur Duarte, 1944), are resolved through marriage. Furthermore, marriage is the main purpose of the female characters' lives, a goal that becomes clear in an oneiric sequence of *A Song of Lisbon*, in which flirtatious Alice (Beatriz Costa) dreams of marrying Vasco (Vasco Santana). It is also expected that women give up their jobs before their wedding. Alice will certainly not continue working as a seamstress once she is Doctor Vasco's wife, while the banker Luisinha (Milú) abandons her job to live in the home of her future husband in *Costa of the Castle*. As if illustrating the New State's ideology about the social function of women, the comedies portray marriage as the center around which women's lives revolve. Marriage represents not only a harmonious solution to all disputes, but also the culmination of the female characters' ambitions.

Despite their tendency towards conformity, some comedies allude to the profound changes that were transforming the lives of Portuguese women. A striking example is a dialogue between Chico (Francisco Ribeiro, the "Ribeirinho") and Tatão (Leonor Maia) in *The Tyrannical Father* (*O Pai Tirano*, António Lopes Ribeiro, 1941). Tatão says that "we young women are no longer the same […] now we want a different life"[18] and praises the active and independent modern woman, with whom she identifies. Meanwhile, Chico would like his girlfriend to be an "old-fashioned Portuguese" girl.[19] Significantly, the film ends with the marriage of the two. Tatão gets together with a conservative husband, whose ideas she had previously ridiculed, and she accepts the position of traditional wife and future mother that she once scorned.[20] The happy ending of Portuguese-style comedies implies the domestication of characters like Jujú and Tatão and their drive to modernize social relations. Their desire to distance themselves from the established patterns of femininity is portrayed as an adolescent whim that will be overcome through marriage. The denouement of the comedies involves normalizing the behavior of the more rebellious women, who resign themselves to their role as wives and mothers.

If the female protagonists of the majority of movies from the 1930s to 1950s represent the model of feminine behavior idealized by the New State, how were the women who refused to adopt a traditional lifestyle depicted in film? Cinema was ambivalent toward women who did not fit into the Salazarist family structure and lived at the margins of New State society. This is clear in films about artists, particularly fado singers, whose portrayal combines fascination and condemnation, magnetism and repulsion. Despite leading a glamorous life, female singers are forced to choose between the independence that their status as artists grants them and their reinsertion into Salazarist society as wives and mothers.

Singing as a transgression

Films about singers, especially fado singers, enjoyed great popularity in the first decades of the New State. The movies took advantage of the public's fascination with fado and often selected famous singers as protagonists. The plot of these films draws on the idea that the artistic milieu leads to permissive social behavior, and it juxtaposes this environment to the traditional structure of society. Specifically, the movies establish a contrast between female artists and women who embody the values of femininity defended by Salazarism. This contrast can be found in comedies like *The Courtyard of the Ballads* (*O Pátio das Cantigas*, Francisco Ribeiro, 1942), which highlights the differences between Amália (Maria Paula), an indiscreet, flirtatious, amateur fado singer, and her industrious and circumspect sister Susana (Graça Maria). While these issues are resolved through marriage in the comedies, the plot of other films about female artists exacerbates the distance between the singers' conduct and that of women who accept the norms imposed on them by the prevailing morality.

Female singers radicalize the discontent expressed by some women in the comedies and therefore overstep the ideological boundaries that restrict their movements. They endanger the so-called "normal" family, since they attract men to a bohemian lifestyle that leads them to abandon their social responsibilities. Consequently, the *chanteuses* and fado singers are often punished for their abnormal behavior at the end of the films. Significantly, male singers do not suffer the same fate, as they succeed in transitioning between the artistic realm and traditional Salazarist society. This is what happens to Vasco Leitão (Vasco Santana), a character who metamorphoses from a fado singer into a respected doctor and head of family in *A Song of Lisbon*. José Duarte (the fado singer Alberto Ribeiro) from *Black Mantels* (*Capas Negras*, Armando de Miranda, 1947) also combines his career as a famous fado singer with his work as a lawyer. If men were allowed some mobility within the social organization of the New State, female artists were summarily classified as "lost women" without hope of redemption.

The prototype of films about female singers is perhaps *Severa* (*A Severa*), a 1931[21] production of the Sociedade Universal de Superfilmes directed by Leitão de Barros, and the first Portuguese sound film.[22] The movie, based on Júlio Dantas's homonymous theatrical play from 1901, tells of the tumultuous relationship between Severa (Dina Teresa),[23] a legendary, mid-nineteenth-century fado singer from Mouraria, and the Count of Marialva (António Luís

Figure 5.2 Severa (Dina Teresa) and the Count of Marialva (António Luís Lopes) in *Severa*

Lopes, a famous bullfighter at the time), whose name became synonymous with a noble gentleman bullfighter leading a bohemian life.[24]

Severa is a gypsy woman from the Alentejo, where she meets the Count, who owns vast properties in the region. She is brought "by her fado/fate to Mouraria," a poor neighborhood of Lisbon, as we read in one of the title cards.[25] Her talent carries her fame beyond the Lisbon *bas-fonds*, earning her the attention of the nobility in the capital, and the Marquises of Seide invite her to sing at a party in their palace. Yet, Severa rejects the niche offered to her as a mere fortuitous entertainer of the powerful and occasional submissive lover of the Count of Marialva. She proves to be an independent, proto-feminist woman who endangers established morality: she lives alone; she seduces potential lovers that hover about her door; she rejects a wealthy man's offer of riches because she believes they are not worth more than her greater wealth, her "freedom"; and she criticizes men as the "worst cattle there is."[26] It is patently impossible to chain Severa's libertarian drive and force her to accept an innocuous social position as the domesticated and silent lover of an influential man. The only solution is the death of the protagonist, which happens at the end of the film.

Severa was an enormous box office success, and it also received enthusiastic praise from film critics at the time.[27] It is therefore understandable that several elements of the film's plot were repeated in movies featuring *chanteuses* and fado singers in the first decades of the New State. For instance, the artists belong, as a rule, to marginal social groups, which explains their refusal to adjust to the prevailing social order. As we have seen, Severa was of gypsy descent, and according to legend she was not just a fado singer but also a prostitute. In *Wild*

Figure 5.3 Nina (Olly Gebauer) and Manuel Garrido (Raul de Carvalho) in *Wild Cattle*

Cattle, a 1934 film directed by António Lopes Ribeiro, we also find a singer, Nina (Olly Gebauer). She is a foreigner hailing from Austria and therefore unfamiliar with the more conservative norms that govern the relationships between men and women in Portugal. Nina, whose dubious morality becomes apparent to the viewers in a scene that involves an old lover, seduces the famous bullfighter and landowner from Ribatejo, Manuel Garrido (Raul de Carvalho), just like Severa seduced the Count of Marialva. This distances Manuel from his girlfriend Branca (Nita Brandão), a young Portuguese woman from his social class, and therefore endangers the social codes of the New State, which will be reestablished at the end of the narrative.

In the Portuguese fictional films about fado starring the famous singer Amália Rodrigues[28]—*Black Mantels*[29]; *Fado, Story of a Songstress* (*Fado, História de uma Cantadeira*, Perdigão Queiroga, 1948); *Bullfighting Blood* (*Sangue Toureiro*, Augusto Fraga, 1958), the first Portuguese film in color; and *Fado Corrido* (Jorge Brum do Canto, 1964)[30]—the singer does not belong to a marginalized social group but is invariably from the lower classes. By contrast, the male protagonists generally belong to the bourgeoisie or the nobility. For example, in *Black Mantels* Maria de Lisboa (Amália Rodrigues), a poor young woman from Lisbon who works in a tavern in Coimbra, falls in love with a student from Porto, future lawyer José Duarte. This inequality, already present in Severa's liaison with the Count of Marialva, leads to the portrayal of female singers as disturbing elements in the lifestyle of the upper classes. In the stratified society of the early decades of the New State, where the social position of each individual was still predominantly determined by family ties, female singers were regarded with suspicion and forced to adapt to implicit rules or else face social exclusion. In *Bullfighting Blood*, the class difference separating Eduardo (played by the bullfighter Diamantino Viseu), the only son of a landowning Ribatejo family, from his lover, the fado singer Maria da Graça (Amália Rodrigues), is identified by his family as the greatest impediment to their union.

Still, the transgression of female artists who establish relationships with men of higher social classes does not fully explain the unfortunate end they meet in the majority of New State films. As we have seen in comedies from the period, marriage was considered an acceptable means to resolve class conflict, particularly when it involved a man offering his higher social position to a poorer woman. What inevitably condemns the artists is their independence, which becomes possible because they have a well-paid profession. The plot of *Fado, Story of a Songstress*, for instance, revolves around a set of misunderstandings between the fado singer Ana Maria (Amália Rodrigues) and her beloved Júlio (Virgílio Teixeira), which result from Júlio not accepting the fact that his girlfriend can be professionally successful.

Fado, Story of a Songstress is a tragic version of the comedy *The Radio Girl*, in which Geninha (Maria Eugénia) becomes a famous radio singer alongside the composer Óscar (Óscar de Lemos), who marries her at the end of the film. Geninha, unlike Ana Maria in *Fado*, does not consider herself to be primarily an artist. The film emphasizes the difference between the behavior of Geninha and the frivolous habits of Teresa (Teresa Casal), a professional singer who is portrayed in a rather negative light. The independent spirit of Ana Maria contrasts with the docility of Geninha, who arrives at the radio station hand-in-hand with her fiancé Óscar and whose career is nothing more than a complement to her future husband's work. In *Bullfighting Blood*, Eduardo succinctly sums up the male view of what the feminine essence should be when he defines woman as "a marvelous defect, a well-domesticated little animal."[31] Still, his infatuation with the singer Maria de Graça results precisely from the fact that she refuses to "be domesticated," challenging conventions and rejecting the position that was destined to her as a woman.[32]

Female economic independence and the emancipation of women from masculine tutelage by entering the workforce were discouraged by the New State, similarly to what happened in Italian and German fascism and Spanish Francoism. According to Salazar, women working outside of the home would trigger the dissolution of the family: "[…] we advocate that married women, and generally even single women, integrated in the family and not responsible for it, should not be encouraged to work: there was never a good housewife who did not have a great deal of work to do."[33]

Salazarist policy of encouraging women to return to the home was partly a response to the high unemployment rate in some sectors of the economy. There was a fear that women would replace men in some industries because they accepted lower wages, leading to an increase in male unemployment that could cause social instability. The New State thus adopted several measures to prevent the feminization of the industrial workforce, including a ban on female employment in certain industrial activities, the prohibition of hiring women during periods of high male unemployment, and the definition of limited timeframes when women could work.[34] In addition to these more practical considerations, the Constitution of 1933 mentioned ideological reasons for preventing women's employment that were tied to female "nature." Certain professions, such as diplomacy and being a judge, were considered to be incompatible with the feminine condition and women were therefore prohibited from pursuing them, while other occupations, like being a nurse or a flight attendant, were barred to married women.[35]

The New State's conception of femininity implied that women were predetermined to pursue certain activities and should be excluded from others. In a text published by the Female Portuguese Youth we read: "It is not a serious flaw when a woman does not know how to draft the plan for a bridge, manage a company, defend an action in court—someone wrote; but it would be extremely serious if she were incapable of caring for a child or managing a household."[36] The artists portrayed in the films commit an "extremely serious" transgression, in that they engage in professional activities that give them financial independence. As a consequence, they subvert traditional family values and jeopardize the attempts at eliminating women from public and political spaces, thereby destabilizing the traditional relations between the sexes.

Furthermore, by seducing men from higher social classes, the singers prevent their partners from marrying other women who are their equals. Fado singers are therefore "lost women" from the perspective of the New State. Not only are they "lost" in the most common sense of the phrase that connotes a sexual freedom only allowed to men, but they also disregard other social rules imposed on women. They become lost to the New State since they do not participate in the reproduction of the patriarchal society upon which Salazarism was based and reject the family model that, according to Salazar, would be the foundation of national regeneration.

The audacity of those women who dare to challenge the status quo is invariably punished in the films. In *Severa*, the fado singer dies from cardiac disease, which is the physical correlative of her metaphoric heartbreak for the Count of Marialva. In *Wild Cattle*, Nina's punishment is even more obvious: she is assassinated by an old lover. The film thus establishes a direct causal link between her lifestyle and her tragic end. In *Black Mantels*, the condemnation of feminine transgression culminates in the last scene, in which Maria de Lisboa is literally tried in court, where she stands accused of abandoning her newborn son.[37] This film differs from the other movies about singers because the protagonist is not a professional artist and she does not long for financial independence or social emancipation. She merely transgresses the unwritten laws of Salazarist morality. The modesty of Maria de Lisboa, who only wants to find the father of her illegitimate son, allows for the happy ending of the film. She will marry her lover and become a faithful wife and mother, thereby reestablishing social order.

The rest of the films about fado starring Amália Rodrigues—*Fado, Story of a Songstress* and *Bullfighting Blood*—also stigmatize the character played by the fado singer. Yet her condemnation in these movies is subtler than the one suffered by Maria de Lisboa in *Black Mantels*. The New State approved of Amália as a national symbol and made use of her reputation within and outside of the country to project a positive image of Salazarism. She was, for instance, the only actress to receive three SNI awards for best actress in the films *Fado, Story of a Songstress*, *Fado Corrido*, and *Marvelous Gale*. However, the singer's lifestyle did not conform to the regime's ideology, a situation reflected in the films in which she plays the leading role.

As Tiago Baptista points out in his study of the cinematographic representations of Amália, the films in which she starred were based on a metonymic exchange of identities: the character played by Amália became entangled with the star that she was in real life.[38] The division between fiction and reality was blurred, in that the public tended to interpret the narrative unfolding on screen as reflecting moments in the life of the leading actress. Amália was already well known in the 1940s through her performances in fado houses, in theaters, and on the radio, as well as through the publication of articles about the details of her daily life in newspapers and magazines.[39] Both films explicitly play on this ambiguity, since their plots are loosely based on the artist's biography, as the title of *Fado* indicates.[40]

Because of her dual role as actress and fado singer, the punishment of Amália for the challenge that her life as a famous artist implicitly posed to the moral code of the New State would have to be different in these last two films. It could not entail her transformation into a devoted wife and mother like in *Black Mantels*, nor could it be achieved through the singer's death, repeating Severa's fate or the denouement of *Wild Cattle*. Amália's fame, as well as the similarities between the films' protagonists and the fado singer herself, made both of these resolutions unrealistic and unpopular. Instead, the singer's punishment for her violation of the social code that governed feminine behavior in the New State entails a metaphorical death in both films. The character played by Amália is forced to leave Portugal for Brazil or for the United States.

In *Fado, Story of a Songstress*, the singer's departure is temporary, since Ana Maria rejects a wealthy suitor and returns to Lisbon to marry her old sweetheart Júlio. Júlio tells Ana Maria that she is only valued in Alfama, in the place where she was born. According to him, she would lose her true self if she were

Figure 5.4 Ana Maria (Amália Rodrigues) and Júlio (Virgílio Teixeira) in an Alfama street in *Fado, Story of a Songstress*

to leave her community to sing professionally. Ana Maria's return represents her symbolic reinsertion into the group to which she belongs, abandoning the career of professional fado singer so as to continue singing in her old neighborhood. The artist herself acknowledges her mistake in leaving. In a sequence with hints of misogynistic auto-flagellation, she confesses her desire to submit to Júlio, who, in her opinion, should have exercised his masculine authority over her: "What he [Júlio] should have done [...was] to boss me around, force me to obey. I was his, he should have kept hold of me. That is what being a man would have been, that is what it would have meant to love."[41]

Conversely, in *Bullfighting Blood*, Maria da Graça's departure separates her from her lover Eduardo for good. He marries a woman from his social class, the heiress of a family from Ribatejo. As the voiceover at the end of the film says, "[h]e [Eduardo] followed the path of tradition, she [Maria da Graça] followed her path as an artist,"[42] the two routes being presented as clearly incompatible. Maria da Graça's departure from her homeland suggests that there is no place in Salazarist society for autonomous women, an interpretation that leads, in turn, to two distinct readings. On the one hand, we could see in the film a veiled critique of Salazarism, whose oppressive treatment of women forces the country's most promising female artists to abandon their homeland. On the other hand, the end of the movie could be seen as a warning to Portuguese women, showing them that, *in extremis*, the price of nonconformity is exile. In any case, both films clearly portray the options that stand before female artists, and by implication, before any Portuguese woman who dares to defy national customs: the reintegration into tradition and the abandonment of their independence, like Ana Maria; or, following the example of Maria da Graça, exile and the severance of all affective ties that bind them to Portugal.

Fado, fatalism and the Portuguese *femme fatale*

In the filmography of the New State, artistic calling is presented as a curse from which women cannot escape. The destiny of the artists is to sing, almost always fado, and it is fado/fate that inevitably leads them to live on the margins of social rules and to be punished for their transgression. The films' plots invoke the various connotations of the word "fado" mentioned in the lyrics of several famous fado songs. For example, at the end of *Bullfighting Blood*, when Maria da Graça sings in front of an audience in New York, she says that "Fate [fado] wanted our love/To be unfortunate/To be unable to live,"[43] in an obvious reference to her romantic setback with Eduardo. The roaring ovation that the singer receives at the end of her performance makes her heartache, expressed by a tear on her sad face, even more poignant.

The link between an unhappy life and artistic success is reaffirmed on screen, as is the connection between fado and sorrow. Emotional suffering, heartache and longing have been the main themes of fado ever since the time of Severa, with whom Amália Rodrigues seeks to identify in several moments of her career.[44] Portuguese cinema from this period broadened the Romantic notion of the cursed artist and applied it to female singers. These artists sacrifice happiness for art, or better yet, they fulfill their desires only in the artistic realm, choosing an unhappy life, a sort of death in life, as the condition for being able to cultivate their talent. The distinctive elements of fado—the plaintive tone, the drawling voice, the fatalism of the lyrics—are particularly suitable to the situation of these female singers, who are social pariahs precisely because of their status as stars.[45]

The New State struggled with the popularity of fado from early on.[46] The celebration of this musical genre as the national song began as a reluctant

Figure 5.5 Ana Maria (Amália Rodrigues) sings the fado in *Fado, Story of Songstress*

concession to popular taste, only to be consolidated after the late 1940s with Amália's national and international success.[47] Indeed, the *amor fati*, accompanied by a certain masochist pleasure in suffering, that lies at the core of so many fado songs, is not consistent with the virtues of hard work, moderation, and perseverance that the regime wanted to instill in the Portuguese people. Also called the "song of the defeated," fado was not well accepted by intellectuals from both the Left and the Right,[48] who resisted recognizing it as a symbol of Portuguese culture. Salazar himself confessed to Christine Garnier that he did not like fado because he thought that this musical genre was depressing: "He [Salazar] usually says that fados soften the Portuguese character, drain the soul of all energy, and incite inaction. He prefers the vigorous songs from the North, the *viras* from Minho or the the *chulas* from Beira."[49] According to Salazar, fado would lead to languor, apathy, and inertia. Predictably, he favored songs with rural origins in Minho and Beira over the fado, whose legendary roots were in bohemian Lisbon. This preference is consistent with Salazarist ideology that, at least on a rhetorical level, upheld the values of rural Portugal as the cornerstone of the regime.

The role of fado in the city–countryside dichotomy is depicted explicitly in *The Village of White Clothes*. The male protagonist, Chico (José Amaro), nearly abandons the family business and calls off his wedding with Gracinda because he falls in love with a renowned fado singer from Lisbon, played by the actual singer Hermínia Silva. In *Bullfighting Blood* we find a similar plotline. Eduardo leaves his family home on the plains of Ribatejo to live with the fado singer Maria da Graça in Lisbon. The story is repeated in *Wild Cattle*, though here it is not a fado singer but the cabaret artist Nina who leads the male protagonist astray. In other words, the singers represent city life and an incipient cosmopolitanism—Nina comes to Portugal from Vienna, while Ana Maria in *Fado* and Maria da Graça in *Bullfighting Blood* tour Brazil and the United States—that threaten the values of religion, nationalism, authority, and hierarchy associated with rural Portugal. It is thus not surprising that the films generally take the side of tradition, representing fado itself and fado singers as simultaneously attractive and dangerous, a vortex into which men are inevitably drawn.

The attraction of fado also derives from the sensuality of the women who sing it, depicted in many of these films despite the censorship prevalent during the New State. Severa, who chooses from among several candidates which lover she wants to spend the night with; Nina, the protagonist of *Wild Cattle*, who clearly tells Manuel that she wants to become his lover; and Maria da Graça in *Bullfighting Blood*, who enjoys a freedom barred to the majority of women, all openly embrace their sexuality and play an active role in the relationships with their partners. The behavior of these singers was particularly striking at a time when women were usually infantilized in Portuguese cinema, with the physical expression of desire reduced to short hugs and innocent kisses.[50]

It is not surprising that the male protagonists of these films are not prepared to resist the passion of the singers. Men let themselves be seduced by the artists' voluptuousness and quickly abandon their more chaste girlfriends. Even though at the end of some movies the male characters separate from the singers, the reincorporation of the former into the conventions of the New State depends once again on the resolve of their partners. Artists often choose to sacrifice their love and abandon their lovers, so that men can find happiness in the fold of the traditional social structure. The films thus unwittingly show the reverse of the Salazarist ideal of masculinity. Men are depicted as the obverse of the all-powerful head of the family and source of all decisions. In these movies, male characters find themselves at the mercy of women, who decide upon the lives of their lovers.

On the one hand, the relationship between the male protagonists and the female artists, who stand for a life without responsibility or duties, could be seen as an escape valve for men from the rigid morals of the New State. Men were charged with the burden of supporting their families and representing them in the public sphere. The Salazarist paradigm of masculinity, predicated on physical courage, virility, robustness, and even violence, was almost as oppressive as the regime's ideal of femininity. In a society where the behavior of both sexes was determined by a rigid script, female singers, who live at the margins of the normative model of womanhood, irresistibly attract men. For the male protagonists, their relationships with female artists are ways—if not socially acceptable, at least socially tolerated ones—of attenuating the pressure created by social expectations. Their romantic escapades postponed the moment when they would take up their position in the hierarchy of the New State as heads of powerful families, wealthy men, famous bullfighters, and so on.

On the other hand, the male protagonists' vulnerability goes back to a conception of man according to which he is, by definition, sexually available for a relationship with the opposite sex. Men seek to conquer almost indiscriminately any woman, leaving to the ladies the responsibility of repelling the advances of their suitors. This traditional masculine ontology is destabilized in films like *Severa*, *Wild Cattle*, and *Bullfighting Blood* by the dynamism of women. The artists are the ones who seduce their gullible lovers and reveal men as surprisingly immature when compared to the sentimental complexity and determination of the singers.

The attraction of the fado singers and the concomitant masculine inability to resist them echoes the role of other marginalized female characters in cinema. A case-in-point is the *femme fatale*, popularized in American *films noir* from the 1940s and 1950s. Just like the fado singer, the *femme fatale* is a woman with ambiguous morals who fascinates men, leading in some movies to the imprisonment or death of the male protagonists. In the context of a generalized repression of feminine desire, the *femme fatale* is often interpreted as the incarnation of this hidden sexuality, which would reemerge in cinema as threatening and potentially lethal from a masculine perspective.

A marked difference between the *femmes fatales* and their Portuguese counterparts lies in the former's connection to illicit activities and in the immolation of their lovers at the end of the narrative. Both elements are absent from the plots of Portuguese movies. In the case of the fado singers, their crime is their desire—of sexual equality, of political independence, of financial autonomy, etc.—prohibited by a traditionalist society. As Salazar tells Christine Garnier, many women do not understand that happiness is not reached through pleasure (*jouissance*) but through resignation.[51] Therefore, it becomes necessary to neutralize the risk presented by such women, which in the films about artists entails the real or symbolic death of the singers. Having the Salazarist patriarchy as a backdrop, the cinema of the New State does not entertain the possibility of either feminine desire, much less its fulfillment (*jouissance*), or of masculine sacrifice. Singers must take the blame for their putative transgressions and, uniting fado and fatalism, embrace resignation and follow their destiny as "lost women."

Notes

1 See Salazar, "Grandes Certezas," in *Discursos e Notas Políticas (1935–1937)*.
2 Salazar defined the family as an "irreducible social building block, original nucleus of the parish, the commune, and therefore, of the Nation" ("célula social irredutível, núcleo originário da paróquia, da comuna e, portanto, da Nação"). *Como se Levanta*, 70.
3 "as diferenças resultantes da sua natureza e do bem da família." Art. 5.° of the 1933 Constitution. Anne Cova and António Costa Pinto stress that Salazarism strictly followed the Catholic Church's doctrine in its conceptualization of a feminine "nature" that predisposed women for performing domestic tasks. This idea was explained by the Church in encyclicals like *Rerum Novarum* and *Quadragesimo Anno* ("Salazarismo e as Mulheres," *Penélope*, 72).
4 Although Salazarism gave women limited voting rights for the first time in Portugal, the New State represented a setback for the female legal situation, with the abolition of several of the civil rights acquired by women during the First Republic.
5 "não é inferior à do homem"; "Não sei, afinal, qual dos dois [homem ou mulher] terá o papel mais belo, mais alto e mais útil ..." Ferro, *Entrevistas*, 90.
6 "Advoguei sempre uma política de administração tão clara e tão simples como a pode fazer qualquer boa dona de casa [...]." Salazar, "Problemas Nacionais," in *Discursos (1928–1934)*, 11. During the 1958 presidential campaign, a pamphlet

signed by "A Commission of Mothers" (Uma Comissão de Mães) repeats this idea: "Salazar wanted to govern Portugal like you want to govern your home: with a united and strong family." ("Salazar quis governar Portugal como vós quereis governar a vossa casa: com a família unida e forte.") Cited in Belo, Alão, and Cabral, "O Estado Novo e as Mulheres," in *O Estado Novo. Das Origens ao Fim da Autarcia (1926–1959)*, 270. Maria Belo, Ana Paula Alão, and Iolanda Neves Cabral list several other New State publications that spin a comparison between the government of the country and home economics (270–1).

7 Belo, Alão, and Cabral, "O Estado Novo e as Mulheres," in *O Estado Novo. Das Origens ao Fim da Autarcia (1926–1959)*, 273.

8 See Anne Cova and António Costa Pinto, "O Salazarismo e as Mulheres: Uma Abordagem Comparativa," *Penélope*, 89–91, and Maria Belo, Ana Paula Alão, and Iolanda Neves Cabral, "O Estado Novo e as Mulheres," in *O Estado Novo. Das Origens ao Fim da Autarcia (1926–1959)*, 272–3 for a comparison of the various approaches to women's issues in the Portuguese New State and Hitler's and Mussolini's Fascism.

9 "bem de família." Belo, Alão, and Cabral, "O Estado Novo e as Mulheres," in *O Estado Novo. Das Origens ao Fim da Autarcia (1926–1959)*, 272; Clark, *Art and Propaganda in the Twentieth Century*, 68. Toby Clark points out that there was a profound misogyny in Hitler's Germany, even though many women supported the Nazi movement. This contradiction was partially resolved by limiting the role of women to motherhood: "Party ideology aimed to reconcile the contradictory messages about the strength of the German woman and her natural subservience by channeling notions of strength and service back to the domestic sphere and child-bearing. Child-bearing was explicitly cast as the means to propagate the nation and to provide the future manpower required for warfare and labour" (70).

10 "La plupart des Portugaises sont "pour la Situation": elles trouvent Salazar tellement séduisant! Il n'a cessé de lutter contre l'indépendance des femmes. Il a la réputation austère d'un misogyne. Et cependant les plus jolis visages s'assemblent autour de lui quand, par hasard, il préside une fête." Garnier, *Vacances*, 49.

11 For an in-depth discussion of these institutions and a comparison between them and their sister organizations in other European totalitarian regimes, see Irene Flunster Pimentel, *História das Organizações Femininas no Estado Novo*, 93–end.

12 "penúria agradável." Cited in Belo, Alão, and Cabral, "O Estado Novo e as Mulheres," in *O Estado Novo: Das Origens ao Fim da Autarcia (1926–1959)*, 266. The motif of happy poverty was developed in the song "Uma Casa Portuguesa," based on a poem by Reinaldo Ferreira and set to music by V. M. Sequeira and Artur Fonseca. Made famous by Amália Rodrigues's rendition, this was one of the National Radio Broadcast's most aired songs (Torgal, *Estados Novos*, vol. 2, 173).

13 A paradigmatic example of this conception of men is António (António de Sousa) in *Wolves of the Mountain* (*Lobos da Serra*), who lets himself be allured to contraband by other smugglers, while his wife Margarida persists with the arduous work of the land.

14 Graciete Branco's lecture, transcribed by Luís Reis Torgal in *Estados Novos, Estado Novo*, is particularly insightful in this regard: "I also go to the casino, to the beach [...] but in my heart, I always have lit, and very upright, the sacred flame that represents love and devotion to my home [...] She can be informed about national and international politics; she can be familiar with Laval's political positions and Mussolini's domineering gestures, but she should always be a woman, who knows to give her intelligent opinion with a sweetly feminine smile, that treats her knitting with the same love that she treats her books [...]. All happiness depends on the home, and the divorce of the woman from the home inevitably results in the divorce between woman and man." ("Eu também vou ao casino, à praia [...] mas dento do meu coração, tenho sempre acesa, e muito bem direitinha, a chama sagrada que representa o amor e o culto pela minha casa [...] que ande a par do dia a dia da política nacional e internacional; que conheça as posições de Laval e o gesto dominador de Mussolini, mas que seja sempre mulher, que saiba dar a sua opinião inteligente, com um sorriso docemente feminino, que trate das suas rendas com o mesmo amor com que trata dos seus livros [...]. Do nosso lar depende toda a felicidade e do divórcio da mulher do lar resulta, fatalmente, o divórcio entre a mulher e o homem.") Vol. 2, 170–71.

15 Irene Flunster Pimentel summarizes the main points of the educational policy of the New State with respect to women and presents statistics about the literacy rates among women from the 1930s to the 1960s (*História das Organizações Femininas*, 73–92).

16 "A Comédia à Portuguesa," in *O Cinema sob o Olhar de Salazar*, 220.

17 One of the signs of Jujú's frivolity is her critical position towards her condition, in a society that values cohesion and where the hope of social mobility is usually condemned. When her father does not manage to buy train tickets to go to Porto to see the Sporting–Porto soccer match, Jujú says: "So father was convinced that we, the same old paupers, also had the right to have a life? We are condemned to watch the others enjoy themselves and have fun, always the others" ("Então o pai estava convencido de que nós, os pelintras de sempre, também tínhamos direito à vida? Nós estamos condenados a ver gozar e divertir os outros, sempre os outros"), to which her mother, incarnating the voice of authority, responds: "Stop speaking nonsense, young lady!" ("Não digas disparates, rapariga!")

18 "nós as raparigas já não somos as mesmas [...] nós hoje queremos a vida doutra maneira."

19 "à antiga portuguesa."
20 For an analysis of the ways in which the comedies reflect the values of the New State, see Paulo Granja, "A Comédia à Portuguesa, ou a Máquina de Sonhos a Preto e Branco do Estado Novo," in *O Cinema sob o Olhar de Salazar*.
21 As João Bénard da Costa notes, Leitão de Barros had been planning to film *Severa* since 1918, when he had contacted actress Ângela Pinto to play the leading role (*Histórias*, 50).
22 Fado appeared for the first time on film in French filmmaker Maurice Mariaud's *Fado* (*O Fado*, 1923), but it was not until *Severa* that this musical genre established itself as a central theme in cinema.
23 The casting of the protagonist was done by means of a competition that searched for a "Portuguese-type" actress. Dina Teresa was a relatively unknown chorus girl who was catapulted into fame by her participation in the film (Costa, *Histórias*, 50).
24 The fado singer Maria Severa's romance was with the Count of Vimioso. However, in his play Júlio Dantas replaced him with the Count of Marialva, probably due to the stereotype of the Marialvan: a nobleman who loves bullfighting and a bohemian lifestyle. In the film, Leitão de Barros, faithful to Dantas, keeps the character of the Count of Marialva. For more regarding Marialvismo, see Miguel Valle de Almeida's article, "Marialvismo. Fado, Touros e Saudade como Discursos de Masculinidade, da Hierarquia Social e da Identidade Nacional."
25 "pelo seu fado à Mouraria." In Portuguese, the word "fado" literally means "fate."
26 "pior gado que há."
27 João Bénard da Costa estimates that the film was seen by more than two hundred thousand spectators over the course of its six months of screening in movie theaters (*Histórias*, 52).
28 I am excluding from this list the fictional films *Marvelous Gale* (*Vendaval Maravilhoso*, Leitão de Barros, 1949), *The Lovers from the Tagus* (*Os Amantes do Tejo*, Henri Verneuil, 1954), and *Enchanted Isles* (*As Ilhas Encantadas*, Carlos Villardebó, 1965) in which Amália also stars as the leading female protagonist. The first is a historic film that takes place in Brazil, and Amália does not play a fado singer but rather the character of Eugénia da Câmara, nineteenth-century Brazilian poet Castro Alves's lover. Directed by a Frenchman, the film *The Lovers from the Tagus* adopts an external perspective on fado since it seeks to showcase this music genre for a foreign public, and therefore does not reproduce the gender stereotypes of the New State. In *Enchanted Isles*, Amália plays the role of a woman shipwrecked on a desert island, and the film has no connection to fado.
29 In *Black Mantels*, unlike what happens in *Fado, Story of a Songstress* and *Bullfighting Blood*, the main character is not a professional singer. Maria de Lisboa sings fado but she is not an artist. Despite this difference, we included *Black Mantels* in our

analysis of movies portraying female singers, given that it shares several elements with this kind of films: the class difference that separates the male and female protagonists; the fatalism that pervades the plot; the importance of fado in the development of the story; and Amália Rodrigues as the leading female actress.

30 *Fado Corrido* will not be analyzed in this book, since it premiered in 1964 and is thus part of a socio-political period of the New State different from the one that we propose to study.

31 "um defeito maravilhoso, um animalzinho bem amestrado."

32 Tiago Baptista argues that Maria do Amparo's desire for independence in *Bullfighting Blood* reflects the biography of Amália Rodrigues, who enjoyed an exceptional degree of freedom for a woman at that time. Baptista stresses that Amália's situation was the exception that confirmed the more traditional norm: "Accepting the exceptionality of Amália's condition because she herself was an exceptional woman—like all public figures—was accepting that the same freedom was from the outset out of reach of 'normal' people." ("Aceitar a excepcionalidade da condição de Amália porque ela própria era excepcional—como o são todas as figuras públicas – era aceitar que a mesma liberdade estava à partida fora do alcance das pessoas 'normais'.") *Filmes de Amália*, 112. Notwithstanding the freedom granted to Amália, Maria do Amparo still pays her toll to the New State morality, as she is forced to abandon her lover and leave Portugal.

33 "[…] defendemos que o trabalho da mulher casada e geralmente até o da mulher solteira, integrada na família e sem responsabilidade da mesma, não deve ser fomentado: nunca houve nenhuma boa dona de casa que não tivesse imenso que fazer." Salazar, "Conceitos Económicos," in *Discursos (1928-1934)*, 204. In the same speech, Salazar also said: "Women' work outside of the home disintegrates the home, separates family members and turns them a bit into strangers. Communal life disappears, the education of children suffers, the number of children diminishes; and the poor or impossible functioning of the domestic economy, [reflected upon] the arrangement of the house, the preparation of food and clothing, becomes an important loss, hardly offset by the salary received." ("O trabalho da mulher fora do lar desagrega este, separa os membros da família, torna-os um pouco estranhos uns aos outros. Desaparece a vida em comum, sofre a obra educativa das crianças, diminui o número destas; e com o mau ou impossível funcionamento da economia doméstica, no arranjo da casa, no preparo da alimentação e do vestuário, verifica-se uma perda importante, raro materialmente compensada pelo salário percebido [sic].") "Conceitos Econónimos," in *Discursos (1928-1934)*, 203–4.

34 Despite the regime's rhetoric discouraging female labor outside of the home, several members of the government during the New State recognized that the minimum

wage was not sufficient to cover the basic nutritional needs of a family. This was one of the reasons why women, and sometimes children, were forced to work (Pimentel, *História das Organizações Femininas*, 46–7).

35 In his interviews with Christine Garnier, Salazar remarked about female labor: "The great nations should set an example and keep women at home. But these great nations seem to ignore that the solid constitution of the family cannot exist if the wife lives outside of her house. I am convinced that a wife who has her mind on the care of her home cannot do a good job outside of it, and I will therefore always fight against the independence of married women." ("Les grandes nations devraient donner l'exemple, en retenant les femmes à leur foyer. Mais ces grandes nations semblent ignorer que la constitution solide de la famille ne peut exister si l'épouse vit hors de chez elle. Persuadé qu'une épouse qui a en tête le souci de son foyer ne peut faire un bon travail au dehors, je lutterai toujours contre l'indépendance des femmes mariées.") *Vacances*, 15–16.

36 "Não é grave que uma mulher não saiba traçar o projeto de uma ponte, gerir uma empresa, defender uma causa nos tribunais—escreveu alguém; mas é gravíssimo que não esteja em condições de cuidar de uma criança ou de governar uma casa." Cited in Granja, "A Comédia à Portuguesa, ou a Máquina de Sonhos a Preto e Branco do Estado Novo," in *O Cinema sob o Olhar de Salazar*, 225.

37 The last scene of *Black Mantels* was altered due to the intervention of censors. Censorship would not allow the film to end with the two protagonists singing in the courtroom, possibly because such behavior could be considered a sign of disrespect of authority (Baptista, *Filmes de Amália*, 38–9). Therefore fado is played by a group of former students from Coimbra on the steps of the Palace of Justice, while inside the court a verdict is read declaring that Maria de Lisboa is not guilty.

38 Baptista, *Filmes de Amália*, 16–18. Baptista points out that beginning in the late 1940s, when Amália became a public figure, she adopted a standardized image that comes through in cinema. This image included the use of a black dress or shawl, her placement in front and not behind the guitar players, as was then usual, and characteristic gestures (49–50, 58).

39 Amália's fame brought crowds of fans to the premieres of films in which she played the leading role in hopes of seeing the singer (Baptista, *Filmes de Amália*, 13). Films starring Amália, especially *Black Mantels* and *Fado, Story of a Songstress*, were huge box office successes, remaining in theaters for nearly six months in Lisbon alone (Costa, *Histórias*, 84).

40 João Bénard da Costa states that one of the reasons for *Fado, Story of a Songstress*'s success was the "reality effect" that resulted from its plot being based on a "mythical biopic of Amália, from her poor origins to her great success" ("biopic mítico de Amália, desde os pobres inícios à grande fama") (*Histórias*, 84).

41 "O que ele [Júlio] deveria ter feito [… era] mandar em mim, obrigar-me a obedecer. Eu era dele, guardasse-me. Isso sim era ser homem, isso sim era gostar."
42 "Ele [Eduardo] seguiu o caminho da tradição ela [Maria da Graça] seguiu o seu caminho de artista."
43 "O nosso amor quis o fado/ Que fosse desventurado/ Que não pudesse viver."
44 Baptista, *Filmes de Amália*, 90–100. Tiago Baptista also points out that the plot of *Bullfighting Blood*, in which Amália plays the leading role, is similar to the 1946 operetta *Mouraria*, also starring Amália. The storyline of the operetta includes several elements of Júlio Dantas's play *A Severa*.
45 Leitão de Barros had already emphasized the fatalistic undertones of the film *Severa*: "[the film] reveals a human type that accepts fatality and misery without revolt, and it derives its dramatic force from this inertia or this abandonment" ("[o filme] vai desencantar uma tipologia humana, que aceita sem revolta a fatalidade e a miséria e dessa inércia ou desse abandono retira a sua força dramática") (Barros, cited in Costa, *Histórias*, 84).
46 Brito, "A Cidade do Fado," in *Penélope*, 188. For a comparison of the ways in which fado was portrayed in the first Portuguese sound films, namely *Severa* and *A Song of Lisbon*, see Michael Colvin, "Early Fado Films and the Estado Novo's Notion of Progress."
47 As Joaquim Pais de Brito states: "During the New State, fado was an emerging problem; no one knew what to do with it. Only afterwards, with the possibility of presenting a model of excellence—Amália—and an orderly performance, contained in typical houses, would things become easier." ("O fado foi, em pleno Estado Novo, um problema emergente, não se soube bem como dar-lhe a volta. Só depois, com aquela possibilidade de apresentar um paradigma de excelência – Amália – e de espectáculo ordenado, contido na casas típicas, as coisas se facilitaram.") "A Cidade do Fado," *Penélope*, 188.
48 Torgal, *Estados Novos*, vol.2, 168.
49 "Il [Salazar] a coutume de dire que les fados amollissent le caractère portugais, vident l'âme de toute énergie et incitent à l'inaction. Il préfère les vigoureux chants du Nord, *viras* du Minho ou *chulas* de la Beira." Garnier, *Vacances*, 215.
50 Paulo Granja points out that in Portuguese-style comedies, women were almost always presented as asexual and love usually resulted in marriage ("A Comédia à Portuguesa," in *O Cinema sob o Olhar de Salazar*, 224).
51 Garnier, *Vacances*, 14–15.

6

The Empire as Fetish:
Spell of the Empire (Feitiço do Império)[1]

Portugal and its colonies

According to the concept of nationality disseminated by the Portuguese New State, mainland Portugal was inextricably linked to its overseas territories. At several public appearances, Salazar stressed that "[...] Portugal, with its colonies, forms a whole [...],"[2] and insisted that the country would never give up its sovereignty over its overseas territories: "Despite all conspiracies, we will not sell, cede, rent, or share our colonies [...]. Our constitutional laws do not allow it, and even if these texts did not exist, the national conscience would not allow it."[3] According to Salazar, the colonial impulse did not stop at the laws that united Portugal to its empire. On the contrary, sovereignty over the colonies emanated from the "national conscience," in other words, from the essence of the nation as an organic entity.

For Salazar, the laws that governed colonial administration—especially the legislation included in the Colonial Act of 1930, the legal foundation of Portuguese colonization during the first decades of Salazarism—merely reflected the "colonizing nature of the Portuguese people."[4] As stated in the 1942 text *A Obra Colonial do Estado Novo*, a joint publication of the Secretariat National Propaganda (SPN) and the General Agency of the Colonies (Agência Geral das Colónias), "[i]t [the Colonial Act] is based [...] on the same organic force that led the Nation to expand and create an Empire, to carry out the civilizing and nationalizing work that will transform the colonial territories into countries within the greater unity of an Empire and of a Nation."[5] More than an economic, political, or administrative issue, Portuguese colonialism was linked to the ontology of Portugal: for the New State, the Portuguese nation was, by definition, a colonizing nation.

In the public discourse of Salazarist leaders, the colonies are presented as the inheritance of an honorable past, which was endangered by the First Republic but later consolidated by the New State. As António de Almeida, member of parliament and professor at the Colonial University (*Escola Superior Colonial*), put it in a 1942 lecture: "It is perhaps in the colonial effort that we can most confidently see how the New State is the heir of the past, of the best parts of our history, and also a government that corrects past errors and finally accomplishes past goals, which once only resulted in disorder."[6] For example, the Colonial Act was an effort toward ordering and unifying colonial legislation and strengthening the relations between the colonies and Portugal. The colonies became a measure of the achievements of the New State, as the country's destiny was considered to be dependent on the success of the colonial project.

The ideological construction of the role ascribed to the overseas territories in the New State and the ways in which the regime appropriated its colonial heritage in its definition of the nation's future require further analysis. What was the status of the empire in the ontology of the New State? How was the instrumentalization of the colonies carried out in order to justify the need for an authoritarian form of government such as Salazarism? Which of Portugal's inadequacies were compensated for by the emphasis on the colonies? In order to answer these questions, we will analyze the regime's representation of the empire in its colonial propaganda. We will focus here on cinematographic

Figure 6.1 Advertisement poster for *Spell of the Empire*

propaganda created in defense of the colonial project, more specifically on the movie *Spell of the Empire* (*Feitiço do Império*, 1940), directed by António Lopes Ribeiro and financed by the General Agency of the Colonies. In the following chapter we will turn to *Chaimite* (Brum do Canto, 1953), another film that praises Portuguese colonialism in Africa.

The magic of Africa

The empire was unequivocally considered by the New State as a legacy that had to be preserved. Yet, its position in relation to metropolitan Portugal remained ambiguous. On the one hand, the idea that Portugal was the center of a constellation in which the overseas territories occupied a clearly subaltern position was common currency. In a speech given for the First Economic Conference of the Portuguese Colonial Empire in 1936, Salazar declared that the main function of the overseas territories was to balance the Portuguese economy: "Well, in such circumstances [i.e., given the economic problems of Portugal] this solution is logical—let the Colonies sell raw material to the Metropolis, and with the profits acquire manufactured goods."[7] The empire's economic dependence was accompanied by political dependency. The administration of the colonial territories fell under the Colonial Ministry, which was part of the Portuguese government. In the social sphere, Salazar referred to the "decadent or backwards" "inferior races" that inhabited the empire, "races" which the Portuguese would civilize and evangelize.[8]

Concurrent with this notion of the colonies' subalternity, the regime developed an egalitarian rhetoric, according to which there were no differences between European Portugal and its territories overseas: "Our policies were not always made from Lisbon or from the continent, but also from other areas. This is due to the idea that our colonies are not like those of other nations, but rather integral parts of the same national whole."[9] This egalitarian discourse was intensified after the late 1940s, when Portugal began to feel international pressure to grant independence to its colonies. For instance, in his interviews with Christine Garnier published in 1952, Salazar said: "[…] the Portuguese from Timor and Macau enjoy the same rights as the Portuguese from the Algarve or Estremadura."[10] The parity between the various parts of the whole formed by Portugal—understood as a multi-continental nation that extended from Europe to Asia, passing through Africa—corresponded to the equality among all

Portuguese people, regardless of the territory they inhabited. Salazar went even further and denied the existence of racism not only among Portuguese citizens but also in relation to any inhabitant of the colonies: "[…] if anyone preaches and implements the principles of racial equality, independence, and moral and material elevation of the [colonized] people to the limit of their greatest possibilities, it is us."[11] The statesman emphasized that no sort of discrimination, racial or otherwise, was practiced within the borders of the empire.

The New State rhetoric about the Portuguese colonial empire, which oscillated between a discourse of domination and one of equality, revealed a duplicity that evokes what Jacques Derrida defined as the "logic of the supplement." For Derrida, this logic underlies any relationship between binary opposites involving power relationships, such as center/periphery, necessary/accessory, inside/outside, etc. Derrida indicates that even though the supplement is usually viewed as an accessory, it forms the core of that which it supplements. The supplement covers up an original absence, i.e., the inexistence of an origin that would function simultaneously as a source and guarantor of a given system.

In the discourse of the New State, the colonial empire functions as a supplement. It is hierarchically dependent on European Portugal, from where political and economic directives, as well as social orientations, emanate. The regime described Portugal as a mother that nourishes its colonial offspring. The latter are like "[…] a tree that, feeding on the vigorous Lusitanian sap, spreads long branches to different suns, and with its shade it shelters the most diverse populations, all equally Portuguese […]."[12] The metaphor used here by Salazar leaves no doubt about the derivative nature of the colonies fed by the vital Portuguese sap. However, he does not fail to emphasize once again the equality of all under Portuguese rule, which puts into question the supplementary character of the empire.

Although the colonies were *de facto* a supplement within the New State, the regime sought to conceal this. Not only did it openly recognize the importance of these territories in the self-definition of the nation, but it also made it appear that they occupied a position of equality *vis-à-vis* European Portugal. The dissimulation of colonial subalternity—a cornerstone of New State discourse—cannot simply be interpreted as a response to international pressure for decolonization. Salazarism presented the empire as the complement and not the supplement of Portugal in an effort to disguise the "logic of the supplement" and the shortcomings that, according to Derrida, the supplement always reveals. What was the ontological deficiency of continental Portugal that the colonies supplemented? Was there a dark core within the New State that they concealed?

We already saw that, for Salazar, the colonial empire should help balance the country's economy. However, the national deficiency supplemented by the overseas territories was not limited to the economic sphere. This becomes clear as one analyzes political speeches about the colonies. At the closing ceremony of the First Conference of Colonial Governors in 1933, Armindo Monteiro, Minister of the Colonies, stated the following:

> You [the colonial governors] will show the nation, which despite everything still considers itself small, the immensity and the variety of the territories that belong to it and the races that are linked to it. You will prove to it that it is not an Iberian country, squeezed into a nook of European land, but a nation that dilates in the World so extensively that its interests still span nearly all seas and continents. You will show the nation that, at this time of noisy ambitions, its responsibilities are spread over an immense area, which places it in the category of one of the vastest countries on earth.[13]

In this excerpt, Monteiro highlights that Portugal, with its colonies, was a country of considerable dimensions. The small metropolitan territory was amplified to encompass all seas and continents, thereby forming a large nation. The hyperbolic choice of vocabulary is noteworthy—"immensity," "span," "immense area," "one of the vastest countries," and in particular, the use of the word "dilate," which in Portuguese evokes an image of the empire as one of the nation's limbs in permanent expansion. This emphasis on the size of colonial Portugal pervaded the entire ideological edifice of the regime, and was repeated countless times by its leaders. Along these lines, Salazar referred to the nation as "this sweet country that is Portugal—small in Europe, *great and dilated* on the other continents [...],"[14] accentuating once more Portugal's enlargement.

The most elaborate expression of the prominence that the regime attributed to the size of the country is perhaps found in a famous map, significantly titled "Portugal is not a Small Country." The map represented the borders of the various European countries, superimposing onto them, in red, the maps of the Portuguese colonies in order to show the colonies' dimensions compared to the size of other European nations. It also included information on the extension of the Portuguese imperial territory, which was greater than the combined size of some of the major European countries like Spain, France, England, Italy, and Germany.

The colonies gave Portugal a dimension that allowed it to compete, in terms of territorial area, with other European states. The country had an important geo-strategic position since, as Armindo Monteiro argued, it spanned "nearly all seas and continents." Through the empire, a magic trick is performed over the course of which a small, peripheral nation is transformed, as if by alchemy, into a vast European power. The overseas territories are therefore a supplement that is central to the Salazarist conception of Portugal's importance. The patriotism of the regime and its valorization of nationalism, to which individual freedom was subordinated, were only justifiable if they referred to a great nation. Salazar's position was accepted in that he was presented as the savior of such a nation, whose dignity had been jeopardized by Republican democracy.

The empire is the supplement that covers, just like a magician's handkerchief, a feeling of Portuguese inferiority, a negative self-perception of the country with deep roots in the national psyche. Its genealogy dates back at least to the eighteenth-century Portuguese intellectuals known as the "Foreigners" (Estrangeirados), who compared Portugal to other more developed European nations. This sense of Portuguese inferiority culminated in the intellectual sphere in Antero de Quental's 1871 pamphlet "Causes of the Decadence of Peninsular Peoples" (Causas da Decadência dos Povos Peninsulares) and in the political realm in the British Ultimatum at the end of the nineteenth century.[15] Along this line of dysphoric interpretations of the national situation, Portugal was consistently seen as a country in decline.

Far from being a source from which the vital force that nourishes the empire would spring, European Portugal is a black hole that unproductively absorbs all efforts of regeneration. This is the abyss that the New State sought to conceal. The regime developed a rhetoric of progress that instrumentalized the colonies as a means of overcoming the country's deficiencies. It then masked this move with a discourse of equality, in order to hide the logic of the supplement at work in its conception of the empire. According to Salazarism, Portugal was not a small country—neither in geographic terms nor in economic and political relevance—because vast areas in Africa and Asia were added, as if drawn from a magic hat, to its reduced European territory. However, what happened was in fact the opposite: it was the empire that held the magic hat and pulled from it a dependent, ontologically incomplete Portugal that sought at all costs to hide its shortcomings.

The empire as a fetish

In the political interventions of the leaders of the New State, the fear of losing the colonies surfaced very often.[16] For example, Armindo Monteiro criticized the principle of colonial autonomy, which would lead the colonies to progressively distance themselves from the mainland.[17] Salazar himself alluded to the fear of losing the empire on several occasions in order to dispel any doubts about Portuguese control of its overseas territories:

> We must do away with the constant fear that is typical of decadent nations, and as such incompatible with our renaissance and with our will to work. We cannot be made uncomfortable by the clichés of dubious critics about our lack of men and capital for colonization. [...] Our sovereignty is our life, and only we can decide on our life. The criticism that is usually leveled at our colonial administration seems to me to be biased, made in bad faith. [...] As a matter of fact, our overseas territories were not conquered from any other nation. We were the ones who discovered them, they were always ours. [...] What country can pride itself on having more colonial experience than we do?[18]

The obsession with Portugal's unquestionable sovereignty over its colonies reveals a latent fear of losing the empire. According to Salazar, this was an unfounded fear that the New State sought to dispel. He stressed that Portuguese sovereignty over its colonies was incontestable, and that these domains had always belonged to the Portuguese people, who discovered them and, in a certain way, molded them in their own image.

What is at stake here is Portugal itself, whose aspiration of becoming a powerful nation in economic and political terms depended, as we have seen, on the colonies. Losing the overseas empire would mean losing the country itself, i.e., renouncing the conception of the nation that the New State disseminated. The overseas territories supplemented the mainland and sustained an image of a country that did not really exist. Using Freudian terminology, the colonial empire functioned as a fetish. The colonies simultaneously hid and revealed the regime's inability to produce a nation that corresponded to the magnificent idea of Portugal created in its leaders' speeches. The angst associated with the loss of the overseas possessions can therefore be explained by a fetishist fear of ruining this vision of the country and, consequently, the national project outlined by the New State.

Freud developed the notion of the fetish as a way to explain a psychological phenomenon that entails the repression and concurrent negation of a traumatic event. In Freudian psychoanalysis, the repressed event is the male child's realization that his mother does not have a penis.[19] This reality unleashes in the child the terror that his own penis might be cut off. Such castration anxiety leads him to develop a fetish as a way of replacing the lost maternal organ. However, the absence of the mother's penis is not completely repressed. Freud observed that, in the fetishists' psyche, the negation of female "castration" coexists with the reality that women do not have penises. Thus, the fetishist finds himself in a state of suspension between two alternatives. This allows him to fantasize a penis that takes the form of a fetish and, at the same time, to function in a world where women do not in fact have penises.[20]

If we extrapolate from the Freudian theory of fetishism to analyze Salazarist discourse about Portugal, we can see that, on the one hand, the leaders of the New State were conscious of the true political, economic, and geo-strategic dimensions of the country as a peripheral European nation. On the other hand, they aggrandized Portugal by drawing attention to the size of its territory and through the use of sexually charged terms like "dilation" and "sap." The empire thus functioned as a fetish that helped keep the illusion that the country was a great European power. In other words, the empire was the nation's lost phallus. The destruction of the empire-fetish would lay bare the fantasy of national greatness constructed by the regime. It would reveal the traumatic reality of Portugal's smallness, which translates in Freudian terms into the realization that there is no maternal penis. Without the empire-fetish, the New State would be forced to acknowledge the reverse side of its nationalism and face a suddenly emasculated Portugal, which would not have a penis, the attribute of other bigger and stronger countries. Salazarism's phallogocentric discourse, inherited from centuries of imperialism, could not survive this reduction of Portugal to its true dimensions. Therefore, the colonial war and the dismemberment of the empire inevitably brought about the fall of the New State and prompted a profound reflection on the self-definition of the Portuguese nation.

Freud claimed that the complex web of repression and acceptance of reality that occurs in the fetishist's psyche contributes to an idealization of the fetish: "The fetish comes about as follows: it is the result of a special kind of repression that could be described as partial; part of the complex is repressed, and in compensation for that another part pertaining to it becomes idealized."[21] This psychic mechanism is illustrated through a historical parallel with female inferiority during the Middle Ages, which coexisted with the idealization and exaltation of the Virgin Mary.[22] The fetishist fantasy simultaneously implies the denigration of the real object. This mechanism was incorporated into the New State discourse on the colonies. Salazarism presented the overseas territories as regions that were dependent on European Portugal, which undertook the civilization and evangelization of the "inferior races." Yet, at the same time, the regime idealized the empire-fetish as a central element for the national ontology.[23]

The description of the fetish as an idealized object is not only found in Freudian psychoanalysis but also appears as a central premise in psychoanalyst Donald Winnicott's description of child development. According to Winnicott, children create illusive "transitional objects" and "transitional phenomena" that are at the base of human experience. These fantasies are possible to the extent that the mother adapts to the baby's needs and allows her or him to keep the illusion that the objects that she or he imagines truly exist. Although these fictions are a part of the normal psychic maturation of a human being and enable the development of areas such as imagination, art, and religion, they are normally recognized as illusory as the child grows up. The fetish is created when the adult is incapable of perceiving that the "transitional objects" are not real, or, in Winnicott's words, "[t]he transitional object may eventually develop into a fetish object and so persist as a characteristic of the adult sexual life."[24] For Winnicott, the creation of fantasies is part of a healthy psyche, but after a certain point in the child's life, it becomes necessary to differentiate between the illusory and the real.[25] The creation of the fetish results from the inability to establish a distinction between illusory "transitional objects" and reality.

The Portuguese colonies were often presented as an illusory object upon which the fantasies of the colonizer were projected. For instance, Salazar referred not only to the vastness of the empire but also to the fact that he never visited these territories. He only thought about them from afar:

> To lead a battle, Salazar replied, must the general be present at the battlefield? I would go further and say: the atmosphere and the environment influence men's judgment and can lead them to make mistaken decisions because they are biased. Our empire is very large: only from afar can one grasp a vision of the whole.[26]

Salazar pointed out here that it was only possible to envision the whole of the overseas territories by observing them from a distance, and asserted that his separation from the empire allowed him objectively to legislate on colonial matters. He recognized that he was unfamiliar with the local characteristics of the various Portuguese colonies—"the atmosphere and the environment"— which are absent from his idealization of the territory as a homogenous whole. Therefore, his decisions about these regions were based upon a virtual empire, an illusory object conceived as a caricature of reality. In other words, what was at stake was not something concrete and palpable, but rather a fetish created by the fetishist's fantasy as a replacement for the lost object.

This fetishized image of the empire, which reduced the vast territories under Portugal's control to a series of stereotyped representations, was conveyed to the Portuguese public through the regime's propaganda. The glorification of the colonial empire was not specific to the New State propaganda apparatus. It was part of propaganda efforts both in dictatorial governments such as Mussolini's fascist state and in countries like England and France. For example, in England large-scale imperial propaganda developed over the course of the nineteenth century, and cinema was used, starting in the Boer Wars, as a propagandistic tool that sought to forge a positive image of the British colonies.[27] In the New State, one of the roles of the SPN, as defined by Article 5 of Ordinance 23054, was to encourage the support of the Portuguese people and the international community for the government's imperial policies. The SPN's international section should "enlighten international opinion about our civilizing action and especially the action undertaken in the colonies and the progress of the Overseas Empire [...]."[28] This purpose became more urgent from the late 1940s onwards, when the process of decolonization started in a number of European nations.

In the face of increasing international pressure to give autonomy to the colonies, which were referred to as "overseas provinces" after 1951, the New State sought to convey an image of Portugal as a multi-continental country.[29] To achieve this goal, the SPN/SNI carried out several activities, including incorporating a colonial section into the Exhibition of the Portuguese World and a Triumph of Colonialism Float in the Historical Pageant of the Portuguese World. Here, the colonies were depicted as the culmination of the period of overseas expansion, which was considered to be Portugal's golden age.

Beyond the foregrounding of its colonies at exhibitions and other cultural events, the most efficient means for Portugal to create a positive image of its empire was through cinema. The SPN/SNI funded the production of various films about the colonized territories, frequently in collaboration with the

General Agency of the Colonies. The majority of these productions consisted of short films such as documentaries about presidential trips to the overseas provinces that emphasized the local population's enthusiasm for the Portuguese leaders' visits. Imperial propaganda also included some feature-length films, like *Chaimite* (Jorge Brum do Canto, 1953), which we will analyze in the following chapter, and António Lopes Ribeiro's *Spell of the Empire*. *Spell* premiered in Éden Theater on 23 May 1940. The event was attended by both president Óscar Carmona and Salazar himself, as well as by a number of other intellectuals affiliated with the regime.[30] The film offered a stylized portrait of the empire by representing the African population through stereotypical images. The New State thus infantilized the Portuguese spectators, who were unable to distinguish between the real overseas territories and the illusory, fetishized construction of Africa created by Salazarist propaganda.

Spell of the Empire and colonial propaganda

The narrative of *Spell of the Empire* depicts the spell (feitiço) that the Portuguese overseas territories cast on Luís Morais (Luís de Campos), a young Portuguese–American man whose family lives in Boston.[31] Luís is getting ready to marry an American woman, Fay Gordon (Madalena Sotto), and become a United States citizen. However, his father Francisco Morais (Alves da Cunha), a wealthy Portuguese emigrant, persuades him to visit Portugal and its African colonies before he finalizes these decisions. Attracted mostly by the possibility of hunting in Africa, Luís is not impressed by the first stop of his journey in Lisbon. While there, taxi driver Chico do Austin (Francisco Ribeiro, the "Ribeirinho") takes him to several entertainment venues, but Luís gets bored in the capital and does not enjoy listening to fado. Yet, once in Africa, the protagonist cannot resist the allure of the Portuguese overseas territories, where his "conversion" to New State values takes place.[32]

The script of *Spell of the Empire* was adapted by the film's director António Lopes Ribeiro from a homonymous novel. This narrative by journalist Joaquim Pereira Mota Júnior had won the General Agency of the Colonies' competition for the best movie plot. Despite this, the cinematographic version of the story is substantially different from the book, especially with regard to the description of the United States. In Mota Júnior's text, the main character never rejects his American side, but instead combines it with his Portuguese heritage, which is symbolized by his marriage to an American woman at the end of the story. Conversely, Luís's transformation in the film is accompanied by his rejection of American values, a change that corresponds on the affective level to his decision to abandon his American girlfriend and marry Mariazinha (Isabel Tovar), a young Portuguese woman he meets in Africa.[33] In the film, Luís explains to his American girlfriend Fay his recently acquired admiration for the Portuguese empire:

> You can't even imagine, Fay, the new world that I discovered in Africa! What fascinated me the most about your country was precisely that expansive force of a half dozen men who, through their courage, through their perseverance, built a great nation by themselves. It's true that they were unscrupulous, and compensated for this by their resourcefulness. But what did that matter? Think about what it meant for me to find out that the nation to which I belong *scrupulously* erected a great Empire, defying all greed, and that, for its greater glory, it built and kept the Empire *without any sort of resources*![34]

Luís's fascination with the United States, which fueled his desire to become a citizen and marry Fay, was linked to the American vitality that made the

Figure 6.2 Luís (Luís de Campos) and Mariazinha (Isabel Tovar) in the jungle in *Spell of the Empire*

creation of a powerful nation possible. American expansion and the settlers' progressive conquest of the continent's Western territories are compared here with Portuguese rule in Africa. However, Luís states that the expansion of the American "frontier" was often achieved through unscrupulous means. In contrast, the Portuguese empire was *scrupulously* built. This suggests that the Portuguese succeeded in uniting the American impetus to conquer with respect for moral values. Confronted by this reality, Luís embraces his Portuguese heritage. The United States becomes "your [Fay's] country" in opposition to "the nation to which I belong,"[35] with which the protagonist identifies at the end of the story. The film is thus a defense of the empire, and it strives to promote Portuguese immigration to these territories—and not to the United States—by implying that not only Luís but any Portuguese citizen will be seduced by the colonies. Furthermore, the criticism of American imperialism goes hand-in-hand with a rejection of capitalism and liberalism, which Salazar considered to be outdated socio-political doctrines that should be replaced in Portugal by corporatism.

When he returns to Lisbon after spending some time in Africa, Luís finally acknowledges the positive aspects of the city, which he had overlooked during his first visit. Upon arriving at the capital by boat for the second time, he says: "I went up to the ship's deck; Lisbon stood before me, prettier than ever. Now that I know our Africa, the city seemed greater, more important."[36] At this moment, Luís unlocks a small box, a gift from his father, who had recommended that he only open it when he was impressed or moved by something Portuguese. The box contained a copy of *The Lusiads*, a sixteenth-century epic poem about the Portuguese discoveries. This text, along with its author Luís de Camões, had been instrumentalized by the regime's propaganda in order to justify the Portuguese colonial project. Luís's appreciation for European Portugal, metonymically represented by Lisbon, is confirmed by his reading of Camões's work. It is only through the mediation of his experiences in the colonies that Luís learns to admire his fatherland. Here we find once again the fetishist logic of the supplement, according to which the colonial possessions compensate for Portugal's lackluster. The protagonist avoids the trauma of recognizing that he is a citizen of a peripheral country, which lacks the territorial size and economic development of the United States, by focusing his attention on the vastness of the empire.

This interpretation of *Spell* is corroborated by reviews of the film from the time of its release. Afonso Lopes Vieira commented on the movie in a letter to the director of the magazine *Animatógrafo* in December 1940, in which he wrote: "The first Portuguese who called Portugal a *small country* was a traitorous dog."[37] Another article published in *Correio Português* in Rio de Janeiro in 1942 read: "[The Portuguese man] will balloon with pride upon seeing how great, and worthy of an epic, is his Portugal, often considered small. *Spell of the Empire* is not just a film. It is a world, a race, a living portrait of an entire civilization."[38] These film critics realized that the size and prestige of Portugal and its empire were the real subject of *Spell*. It is through the empire that Luís reconciles himself with his fatherland and, consequently, with his father, who is a patriot despite being an emigrant.[39] Which characteristics of Portuguese Africa enchant Luís, so that he changes his opinion about continental Portugal? How does the protagonist come to the conclusion that the Portuguese "scrupulously" colonized a vast overseas territory that compensates for the colonizers' insignificance? What leads him to form an image of an empire-fetish that transforms his admiration for the United States into a fascination with Portugal?

One of the main differences between the American nation and the Portuguese empire mentioned in *Spell* concerns the coexistence of blacks and whites. According to the film, while a politics of integration that results in the westernization of Africans is practiced in the United States, the Portuguese prefer to let the African population keep their ancestral customs. When the characters observe a black ritual in Marracuene, the following dialogue takes place:

> *Fay* – I don't understand how you can allow these people to remain in this state of savagery!
> *Administrator* – It has always been a Portuguese rule to respect other people's customs so that they will respect ours […].
> *Luís* – Mr Administrator, the collaboration between two so very different races that I have seen in all of our colonies is truly admirable. And it is during these barbaric festivals that one can best assess the distance separating the one from the other, and therefore how difficult and far-reaching this collaboration is.
> *Fay* – I definitely prefer the blacks from Harlem.[40]

In this exchange, Fay represents the American perspective. It shocks her to see that the Portuguese make no effort to integrate the African population in their society, and to realize that Africans still live in accordance with old traditions, unlike the African-Americans from Harlem. Luís and the administrator counter Fay's opinion by explaining that Portuguese behavior toward Africans stems from their respect for different cultures. Luís recognizes that the native festivals are "barbaric," but he believes that they should be tolerated in order to ensure the peaceful coexistence of colonizers and colonized.

Beyond revealing a blatant ignorance of the differences between the African-Americans in the United States and the African population of the Portuguese colonies, this dialogue showcases the contradictions within the regime's racial discourse. On the one hand, the New State operated, as President Carmona himself affirmed, "without discrimination of race, beliefs, or social conditions,"[41] which should have led to the respect for African cultural practices that Luís and the administrator applaud. On the other hand, this rhetoric of equality merely masked a paternalistic attitude towards the Africans. Their culture was tolerated in the same way that childish games are permitted, but the need for a strong authority to administer the territory, guide the colonized, and civilize them remained. In the film, the reading lessons that Mariazinha gives to a group of African children are an example of the benevolent colonizer's role purportedly taken by the Portuguese. The regime's discourse alludes to the acceptance of foreign culture as an insidious way of justifying both the black colonial population's poverty and the need for Portuguese colonization. Such discourse implies that the Africans, being so distant from Western civilization, are not capable of self-governance.

Spell of the Empire underlines the gap that separates the Africans from the Portuguese through the use of documentary images inserted into the film's fictional plot. The movie was made in the context of the First Cinematographic Mission to the Colonies, a delegation that also produced several documentaries. The Mission was headed by Carlos Selvagem, and *Spell*'s director António Lopes Ribeiro served as its artistic director.[42] *Spell* was the first fictional Portuguese film made in Africa,[43] and it includes much documentary footage recorded by the Cinematographic Mission.[44] One of the purposes of these sequences is to highlight the achievements of Portuguese colonization. Therefore, as the protagonist passes through various regions of the empire, he comes across bridges, factories, schools, and administrative buildings, all of which function as symbols for the economic advantages of Portuguese imperial rule and for the progress made in civilizing the overseas territories.

But the vast majority of documentary footage in the film focuses on the daily lives of African people, their different customs and traditions. The movie depicts local dances, war simulations, native markets, and so on, which convey the image of an exotic Africa, completely different from European Portugal. Even the Africans working in factories or on Portuguese plantations and wearing European clothes, are represented as foreign to Western civilization. This is the case of one of the men working for Luís's uncle, who appears incongruently dressed in Portuguese countryside garb in the middle of Angola. Towards the end of the film, documentary images and the fictional plot merge when Luís, Mariazinha, and her father appear in a crowd gathered to witness President Carmona's visit to Luanda.[45] This technique, previously employed by Lopes Ribeiro in *The May Revolution* (1937), of interspersing fictional and documentary footage contributes to the blurring of the boundaries between fiction and reality.

The film's documentary footage conjures up an exotic portrait of the colonies, which cements the fetish function attributed to the empire. The African colonies can only serve as a fetishized supplement to European Portugal if they represent a space that is completely different from the colonizing country. Although the fetish covers up the absence of something very close to the fetishist—the penis—this object becomes extraordinary, since it is made of a material component and an affective element that is transferred to the fetishized object, thereby idealizing it. Therefore, the empire is necessarily fantasized in order to fulfill its role as a fetish in New State discourse. Portuguese tolerance for the culture of its African colonies' inhabitants does not derive from respect for foreign customs, but from the need to imagine the empire as something that is completely other, mysterious, and exceptional.

The documentary images of *Spell of the Empire* paint a picture of the Africans as a primitive people who engage in pagan dances and tribal rituals. Unlike the European characters, the representatives of the native population are not individualized in the film. According to Homi Bhabha, this stereotyping of the colonized is another kind of fetish. Bhabha states that fetishism is located at the intersection of similarity (everyone has a penis) and difference (only some have a penis), and thus is comparable to colonialism, which preaches racial equality but practices discrimination. The creation of the stereotype, according to Bhabha, is the colonizers' response to the anxiety caused by difference. The colonizer claims that he possesses a cohesive self and his stereotype of the other is a way of keeping this self intact by transferring to the colonized any type of dissonance lurking in the colonizer's identity.[46] The fetishist described by Freud is characterized by his capacity to hold two contradictory beliefs, since he knows that the mother never had a penis, while at the same time believing that she had possessed one, represented by the fetish. Similarly, the image of the fetish-stereotype of the colonized generates a kind of ambiguity in relation to the status of the native population that we can observe in *Spell*: the coexistence of the idea that the Africans are equal to the Portuguese and can be "civilized" with the belief that the native population of the colonies is fundamentally different and will remain forever exotic.

The documentary images in *Spell of the Empire* set in motion a circular logic that reveals a skillful distortion of reality. The "real" Africa represented in the documentary footage is a stereotyped continent, but this vision of the colonies is a fetish, an idealization that aims to compensate for Portugal's deficiencies. Consequently, the documentary "reality" coincides with the highest degree of fictionalization because it is just a subtle form of idealization. However, if the fetish is always a replacement for something that the subject possesses and fears being deprived of—the penis, in Freud's theory—Africa stands not only for what Portugal is lacking, be it size or vitality, but also for something that the country created by the New State has and is afraid of losing. This object that the regime wants to keep is the image of its greatness mediated by Africa itself, not as the fictionalized territory that appears in documentary images, but as a real space that made Salazarism's economic and social policies possible. The fear of losing Africa and the knowledge that this loss is imminent is what leads the regime to imagine Africa as a fetish.

During his first moments overseas, the protagonist of *Spell of the Empire* incessantly photographs the autochthonous cultural practices, as a way of distancing himself from the territory where he behaves as a tourist. Yet, as his stay in Africa progresses, Luís lets himself be bewitched by the region, a process that accompanies his fetishization of the empire. This development is metonymically represented by the hunting sequence, which begins with the protagonist watching the animals from a car. He later switches to horseback to pursue a herd of wild boars, and further on in the film continues on foot. This moment of proximity to the African wilderness is when the hero decides to chase a lion, ignoring the recommendations of his African companion who is clearly afraid of the animal. This scene highlights the contrast between the native attitude of respect for nature and the Western desire to conquer it through technology, represented by the protagonist's rifle. Luís manages to kill the lion, but he is wounded in the process and must be transported on his companion's shoulders to the house of the Portuguese settler Vitorino da Umbala (Estêvão Amarante) and his daughter Mariazinha, who treats his injuries.

Despite Luís's apparent victory over the African wilderness, symbolized by the lion's death, the protagonist leaves this encounter a changed man. Vitorino

Figure 6.3 Luís (Luís de Campos) prepares to kill a lion in *Spell of the Empire*

places the sick Luís on a bed below an image of the Virgin Mary with Jesus. When he awakens, Luís is out of danger, and the camera moves in a traveling shot that goes from the protagonist to the statuette of the Virgin, suggesting that Luís owes his recovery to her. However, in his delirium during the first night after being injured, Luís enters the heart of darkness and dreams not of Christian figures but of pagan deities. The film uses unfocused and shaded expressionist images to convey the hero's oneiric and feverish state. He sees a succession of black faces, statuettes, and idols: the African fetishes.[47] It is in the course of this delirium that Luís, marked by Africa's power, allows himself to be bewitched and simultaneously begins to fetishize the colonies, recognizing in them the strength and size that Portugal lacks. The spell and the fetish remain trapped in the protagonist's subconscious. In daylight, only the image of the Virgin Mary appears, but Africa ends up dominating Luís's life. It makes him fall in love with Mariazinha (who prefers the African countryside to the city), leave his American girlfriend, and recognize Portugal's prestige as head of a vast colonial empire. Luís's metamorphosis thus occurs by means of a transformation of Africa from a space observed through the lens of a camera to a fetish that forms an integral part of both the protagonist's psyche and of the imaginary of the New State.

Spell of the Empire operates as a vehicle for propaganda that disseminates the Salazarist vision of the colonies as a space of infinite possibilities, where the fantasies of the Portuguese people can come true. The film suggests that anyone who travels to Africa will succumb, like Luís, to the spell of the empire. However, the movie also reveals that being seduced by the overseas territories carries with it serious consequences. The affective investment in the colonies is associated with the fear of their loss. Giving up the empire would entail renouncing a larger-than-life image of Portugal, which is why the attraction to the overseas territories is necessarily accompanied by its imaginary elaboration as an exotic and stereotyped fetish. Lopes Ribeiro's film reveals that, as the etymology of the word itself indicates, the spell (feitiço) that emanates from Africa prompts the fetishization of the continent. This process unfolds in the movie through the use of documentary images, which present a primitivist version of the African population, the same primitivism that Luís will later revisit in his delirium. The empire-fetish appears in the film, as well as in the New State's colonial discourse, as a supplement to European Portugal's shortcomings. The regime thus justifies its own existence as the guardian of the country's overseas possessions, without which the Salazarist vision of the Portuguese nation would become unviable.

Notes

1 An earlier version of this chapter was published in Portuguese in the academic journal *P—Portuguese Cultural Studies* (no. 3: 126–44) under the title "O Império como Fetiche no Estado Novo: *Feitiço do Império* e o Sortilégio Colonial," 126–44 (http://www2.let.uu.nl/solis/PSC/P/VolumeTHREE.htm). We thank the editors of *P—Portuguese Cultural Studies* for their permission to reproduce here a longer, revised version of this essay.

2 "[...] Portugal constitui, com as suas colónias, um todo [...]." Salazar, "O Momento Político," in *Discursos e Notas Políticas (1935–1937)*, 82.

3 "Alheios a todos os conluios, não vendemos, não cedemos, não arrendamos, não partilhamos as nossas colónias [...]. Não no-lo permitem as nossas leis constitucionais; e, na ausência desses textos, não no-lo permitiria a consciência nacional." Salazar, "Suposto Arrendamento," in *Discursos e Notas Políticas*

(1935–1937), 264. In this speech, Salazar was discrediting the rumor that Portugal was going to rent the territory of Angola to Germany.

4   "temperamento colonizador dos portugueses." Salazar, "A Nação na Política Colonial," in *Discursos (1928–1934)*, 235. President Óscar Carmona also emphasized that the link between Portugal and its colonies was not only legal but also emotional: "[…] today the colonial mission is, as it has been for centuries, the natural calling of the Portuguese people, and because of this it should be emphatically and decisively reaffirmed as soon as the circumstances permit." ("[…] a missão colonizadora constitui hoje, como há séculos, a vocação natural dos portugueses, e por isso deveria ser afirmada com relevo e com decisão logo que as circunstâncias o permitissem.") "A Mensagem do Chefe de Estado," in *A Política Imperial*, 34.

5   "[e]le [o Acto Colonial] baseia-se […] na própria força orgânica que levou a Nação a expandir-se e a criar o Império, a realizar a obra civilizadora e nacionalizadora que dos territórios coloniais fará países dentro da grande unidade de um Império e de uma Nação." *Obra Colonial do Estado Novo*, 32. The Colonial Act defined the status of the colonies within the New State. The Act was drafted by Salazar himself in 1930 and published again with the 1933 Constitution.

6   "É talvez na obra colonial que com mais segurança podemos ver o Estado Novo como herdeiro do passado, no que tem de melhor, como reparador também dos seus erros, e único realizador finalmente das suas aspirações que antes só eram motivo de desordem." Almeida, *Política Colonial*, 17. In the same text, António de Almeida stressed that the First Republic put the integrity of the colonial empire at risk and claimed that the authoritarian politics of the New State contributed to the consolidation of the Portuguese presence in the colonies (17–20).

7   "Pois bem, em tais circunstâncias [i.e., em vista dos problemas económicos de Portugal] é lógica esta solução—que as Colónias vendam à Metrópole as matérias-primas e com o preço destas lhe adquiram os produtos manufacturados." Salazar, "Império Colonial na Economia," in *Discursos e Notas Políticas (1935–1937)*, 159.

8   "decadentes ou atrasadas"; "raças inferiores". Salazar, "A Nação na Política Colonial," in *Discursos (1928–1934)*, 241; Salazar, "Atmosfera Mundial," in *Discursos e Notas Políticas (1951–1958)*, 427. Salazar described the Portuguese nation's civilizing mission in the following way: "We believe that there are races that are decadent or backwards, however you would like to describe them. We espoused the duty of calling them to civilization—a labor of human education to be carried out humanely." ("Nós cremos que há raças, decadents ou atrasadas, como se queira, em relação às quais perfilhámos o dever de chamá-las à civilização—trabalho de formação humana a desempenhar humanamente.") "Atmosfera Mundial," in *Discursos e Notas Políticas (1951–1958)*, 427. The statesman also frequently referred

to the Portuguese efforts aimed at "civilizing" the African peoples: "[We] have spilled blood and spent riches to bring to the poor African peoples order, work, health, and along with faith, a little civilization." ("[Nós] havemos derramado sangue e despendido fazenda para levar às pobres gentes africanas a ordem, o trabalho, a saúde e, com a fé, um pouco de civilização.") *Para a Compreensão*, 13.

9 "Nem sempre a nossa política se fez de Lisboa ou da parte continental, mas de outros pontos, tal a ideia de que as colónias não o foram à maneira corrente mas partes integrantes do mesmo todo nacional." Salazar, "O Momento Político," in *Discursos e Notas Políticas (1935–1937)*, 80. The Colonial Act also emphasized the unity of Portugal and its colonies: "The Portuguese Colonial Empire stands in solidarity with its component parts and with the Metropolis." ("O Império Colonial Português é solidário nas suas partes components e com a Metrópole.") Article 5.

10 "[…] le Portugais de Timor ou de Macao jouit les mêmes droits que le Portugais de l'Algarve ou de l'Estremadure." Garnier, *Vacances*, 157.

11 "[…] os princípios de igualdade racial, de independência, de elevação moral e material dos povos [colonizados], se alguém os pregou e executa na medida das máximas possibilidades, somos nós." Salazar, "Nação Portuguesa Irmandade," in *Discursos e Notas Políticas (1943–1950)*, 283.

12 "[…] como árvore que, alimentando-se da seiva lusitana, espalhasse longos ramos a sóis diferentes e à sua sombra abrigasse as populações mais diversas, todas igualmente portuguesas […]." Salazar, "O Meu Depoimento," in *Discursos e Notas Políticas (1943–1950)*, 356.

13 "A um povo que, apesar de tudo, ainda se julga pequeno, mostrarão a imensidade e a variedade dos territórios que lhe pertencem e das raças que lhe andam ligadas. Provar-lhe-ão que ele forma não um país ibérico, comprimido numa nesga de terra europeia, mas uma nação que se dilata pelo Mundo tão largamente que os seus interesses abarcam ainda quasi todos os mares e continentes. Indicar-lhe-ão que as suas responsabilidades se dividem, nesta hora de ruidosas ambições, por uma área imensa, que o coloca na categoria de um dos mais vastos países do globo." Monteiro, "Trabalhos da Conferência," in *Conferência do Império Colonial*, 40. Armindo Monteiro also mentioned the idea that Portugal, along with its colonies, was a considerably large country in his speech "Directrizes duma Política Ultramarina:" "A country like ours, *small in Europe, yet so big in the World* and so scattered, can only find the necessary strength to overcome the difficulties of the present and build a better future through strong governmental unity." ("Um país como o nosso, *pequeno na Europa, tão grande no Mundo* e tão disperso, só numa forte unidade governativa pode encontrar a força precisa para vencer as dificuldades do presente e construir um futuro melhor.") *Conferência do Império Colonial*, 12; emphasis added.

14 "Este doce país que é Portugal – pequeno na Europa, *grande e dilatado* nos outros Continentes [...]." Salazar, "O Meu Depoimento," in *Discursos e Notas Políticas (1943–1950)*, 356; emphasis added.
15 This appraisal of the national situation continued into the first half of the twentieth century with thinkers like António Sérgio. Sérgio claimed that the irrationality dominating Portugal transformed the country into a "cadaverous kingdom" and that only culture and education could lead it back to reason.
16 This concern went back to the aforementioned 1890 British Ultimatum, when the United Kingdom forced Portugal to withdraw its troops from the African territories between Angola and Mozambique.
17 Monteiro, "Directrizes," in *Conferência do Império Colonial*, 11–13.
18 "É preciso acabar com o eterno receio próprio de povos decadentes, incompatível, porém, com o nosso renascimento e com a nossa vontade de trabalhar. Não podem incomodar-nos os lugares-comuns de críticos suspeitos sobre a nossa falta de homens e de capitais para colonizar. [...] A nossa soberania é a nossa vida, e da nossa vida, só nós podemos dispor. As críticas geralmente feitas à nossa administração ultramarina afiguram-se-me tendenciosas, de má fé. [...] Aliás, os nossos domínios ultramarinos não foram conquistados a qualquer outra nação. Fomos nós que os descobrimos, foram sempre nossos. [...] Qual o país que pode orgulhar-se de possuir maior experiência colonial do que o nosso?" Ferro, *Entrevistas*, 181–2.
19 Freud, "Fetishism," *International Journal of Psycho-Analysis*, 161–2.
20 Freud, "Fetishism," *International Journal of Psycho-Analysis*, 165.
21 Freud, "Letter to Karl Abraham," in *The Complete Correspondence of Sigmund Freud and Karl Abraham 1907–1925*, 83.
22 Freud, "Letter to Karl Abraham," in *The Complete Correspondence of Sigmund Freud and Karl Abraham 1907–1925*, 83.
23 The logic of the fetish pervaded the entire ideological edifice of the New State. Not only the empire but also other symbols of the country's greatness were often fetishized. We see an example of this process of fetishization in the way the regime appropriated the figure of Camões, which compensated for the country's lack of international cultural projection.
24 Winnicott, "Through Paediatrics," *International Psycho-Analytic Library*, 236.
25 Winnicott described the creation of illusory objects as a universal and healthy phenomenon, as long as it is restricted to childhood: "I would then go further and say that we must keep a place for the illusion of a maternal phallus, that is to say, an idea that is universal and not pathological. If we shift the accent now from the object onto the word illusion we get near to the infant's transitional object; the importance lies in the concept of illusion, a universal in the field of experience." "Transitional Objects," *International Journal of Psycho-Anaysis*, 96.

26 "Pour diriger un combat, répond Salazar, un général a-t-il besoin de se trouver sur les lieux mêmes de la bataille? Je dirai plus: l'ambiance et le milieu exercent une influence sur le jugement des hommes et peuvent les amener à prendre des décisions entachées de partialité. Notre empire est très vaste: on ne peut en avoir une vue d'ensemble que de loin." Garnier, *Vacances*, 151. Salazar's statement is a reply to Christine Garnier, who mentioned she was surprised to hear that Salazar had never visited Portugal's colonies.

27 MacKenzie, *Propaganda and Empire*, 70. MacKenzie points out that the British imperial propaganda permeated the educational system, the army, the Church, missionary societies, and several forms of entertainment like exhibitions and variety shows (*Propaganda and Empire*, 2–3). Cinema was used from early on as a way to disseminate colonial propaganda. The War Office Cinematograph Committee was created in 1916 and produced both documentaries—about royal visits to the colonies, technical progress in the colonized regions, etc.—as well as fictional films. In these movies it was prohibited, for example, to portray "white men in a state of degradation amidst native surroundings" and "equivocal situations between white girls and men of other races," in order to promote an image of the colonizer as morally superior to the colonized (cited in MacKenzie, *Propaganda and Empire*, 78–9). Imperial propaganda continued in England until after the Second World War, and decolonization led to a surge of films about imperial nostalgia.

28 "elucidar a opinião internacional sobre a nossa acção civilizadora e, de modo especial, sobre a acção exercida nas colónias e o progresso do Império Ultramarino [...]." Cited in Paulo, *Estado Novo e Propaganda em Portugal e no Brasil*, 75.

29 In order to underscore the fact that the colonies were an inalienable part of Portugal, the New State created the administrative division of "overseas province" (província ultramarina). The first region to receive this designation was the Portuguese State of India in 1946; all the other colonies were renamed "overseas provinces" in 1951. The concept of "colonial empire" was therefore abolished and replaced by that of the "overseas" (ultramar).

30 Ribeiro, *Filmes, Figuras*, 413. The version of *Spell of the Empire* we have today consists only of the visual track, since the soundtrack was lost. The first fifteen minutes of the film were also lost. The lost footage included the opening credits and the beginning of the story (Matos-Cruz, *Lopes Ribeiro*, 184).

31 The English term "fetish" originated in the Portuguese word for "spell," *feitiço*. The Portuguese used "feitiço" to refer to African magic. It is telling that in the film *Spell of the Empire* (*Feitiço do Império*), the Portuguese colonies function both as the source of a spell and of a fetish.

32 This "conversion" is similar to the conversion of the protagonist of *The May Revolution* (*A Revolução de Maio*, 1937), as Luís Reis Torgal has pointed out (see

"Propaganda, Ideologia e Cinema," in *O Cinema sob o Olhar de Salazar*). Luís de Pina also stressed the similarities between the two films: "[…] a Portuguese-American visiting Portugal and its Empire gives in to the spell of our lifestyle and no longer wants to become a citizen of the United States, just like the revolutionary in that film [*Revolution*] gives in when confronted with modern Portugal." ("[…] um luso-americano em visita a Portugal e ao seu Império rende-se ao feitiço do nosso viver e não quer naturalizar-se cidadão dos Estados Unidos, tal como o revolucionário daquele filme [*Revolução*] se rende à evidência do Portugal moderno.") *História*, 100.

33 For an analysis of the differences between Mota Júnior's book and Lopes Ribeiro's film, specifically with regard to the way the United States is portrayed in both movies, see Luís Reis Torgal's article "Propaganda, Ideologia e Cinema no Estado Novo: a Conversão dos Descrentes," in *O Cinema sob o Olhar de Salazar*, 87–91.

34 "Nem tu imaginas, Fay, o mundo novo que descobri em África! O que mais me deslumbrava no teu país era, exactamente, aquela força expansiva de meia dúzia de homens que, pela sua coragem, pela sua perseverança, haviam construído sozinhos uma grande nação. É verdade que lhes faltava em escrúpulos o que lhes sobejava em recursos. Mas que importava isso? Calcula o que foi para mim verificar que o povo a que pertenço erguera *escrupulosamente* um grande Império, desafiando todas as cobiças, e que, para sua maior glória, o construíra e conservara *sem qualquer espécie de recursos*!" Ribeiro, "Planificação," in *António Lopes Ribeiro*, 388.

35 "o teu país [de Fay]"; "povo a que pertenço".

36 "Subi ao convés, diante de mim estava Lisboa, bonita como nunca. Agora que conheço a nossa África, parecia-me maior, mais importante." Ribeiro, "Planificação," in *António Lopes Ribeiro*, 391.

37 "O primeiro português que chamou a Portugal *país piqueno* foi um perro traidor." Vieira, "Carta ao Realizador," in *António Lopes Ribeiro*, 140.

38 "[O português] irá encher-se de orgulho ao verificar como é grande, e digno de epopeia, o seu Portugal considerado pequenino. *Feitiço do Império* não é um filme. É um mundo, uma raça, o retrato vivo de toda uma civilização." Cited in Matos-Cruz, Lopes Ribeiro, *António Lopes Ribeiro*, 141.

39 According to Freud, the son sees the father as responsible for the castration of the mother. By covering up this imaginary castration, the fetish allows for reconciliation with the father.

40 "*Fay*—Não percebo como consentem que essa gente se mantenha neste estado de selvajaria!
Administrador—Sempre foi norma de portugueses respeitar os costumes alheios para que respeitem os nossos. [...]
Luís—É verdadeiramente admirável, senhor Administrador, a colaboração entre

duas raças tão diferentes que tenho verificado em todas as nossas colónias. E é nestas festas bárbaras que melhor se pode avaliar a distância que as separa uma da outra e, portanto, a dificuldade e o alcance dessa colaboração.
Fay—Decididamente, prefiro os negros do Harlem."
Ribeiro, "Planificação," in *António Lopes Ribeiro*, 388–9.

41 "sem distinções de raças, de crenças ou de condições sociais." Salazar, "Mensagem do Chefe," in *A Política Imperial e a Crise Europeia*, 35.

42 The Cinematographic Mission departed from Lisbon in April 1938. At the time, the press lauded the initiative of sending a cinematographic mission to the overseas territories and noted that for the first time an expedition of this nature was accompanied by devices to record sound: "Well, this time, we are going to have the opportunity to hear the actual 'natural' voice of the jungle itself without artifice." ("Pois, desta vez, vamos ter ensejo de ouvir a própria voz da selva, sem artifícios, ao 'natural'") R. F., cited in Matos-Cruz, *Lopes Ribeiro*, 139.

43 Horta e Costa, *Subsídios para a História*, 62.

44 The exterior shots of *Spell* were also filmed in Africa, while the interiors were created by the painter António Soares and filmed in Tobis's studios in Portugal (Ribeiro, *Filmes, Figuras*, 412). The filming in the studio was rather costly. More settings were created for this than for any other Portuguese film made at the time (Matos-Cruz, *Lopes-Ribeiro*, 139).

45 Ribeiro, "Planificação," in *António Lopes Ribeiro*, 187.

46 Bhabha, *The Location of Culture*, 74–5.

47 Freud explicitly mentioned the relationship between the notion of the fetish developed by psychoanalysis and African idols: "What is substituted for the sexual object is some part of the body [...] or some inanimate object which bears an assignable relation to the person whom it replaces and preferably to that person's sexuality (e.g. a piece of clothing or underlinen). Such substitutes are with some justice likened to the fetishes in which savages believe their gods are embodied" ("Three Essays," in *The Standard Edition of the Complete Psychological Works of Sigmund Freud*, 153). The Africans believed that divinities incarnated in certain objects, in the same way that the Freudian fetishist sees the lost sexual object in a material body. This connection between African idols and fetishes is found in the etymological origin of the word "fetish."

7

The Spirit of the Empire in *Chaimite*[1]

Spirituality and materiality in Salazarism

A key foundation of the ideological edifice erected by the Portuguese New State was an emphasis on spirituality. In his public appearances, Salazar often referred to the spiritual crisis of Europe, which in Portugal had its political expression in the First Republic. In a 1933 speech he declared that the "world is most of all sick in its spirit,"[2] and that Europe, the source of Western values and the head of an imperial Leviathan, bore most of the responsibility for this situation of decadence: "European crisis, spiritual crisis; spiritual crisis, crisis of civilization."[3]

The leaders of the New State saw the expansion of communism's sphere of influence, the outbreak of the Second World War, and the ensuing process of decolonization as symptoms of European decadence, and they believed that Portugal distanced itself from this decline with the 1926 Revolution. In a lecture given in 1942, António de Almeida claimed that "[…] with the Revolution of May 28, 1926—*a purely spiritual movement*, not a shot fired—an aura of confident expectation touches upon and awakens all law-abiding Portuguese."[4] What stands out in this statement is the intention of attributing the armed revolt that ended the democratic Liberalism of the First Republic to a spiritual design, as well as the use of vocabulary associated with the ineffable—aura, expectation—to stress the *coup d'état*'s immaterial side. It is also noteworthy that the spiritual revolution mentioned by the author is not universal, but instead is limited to "law-abiding Portuguese" citizens, which suggests that, despite government efforts, not everyone had subscribed to the spirituality preached by the new regime. Contaminated by the European crisis, the skeptics of Salazarism were laboring under misconceptions. It was the task of politicians to persuade them of the advantages of the government since, according to Salazar, a "world that is falling apart due to the force of errors or of arms […] must be remade 'in spirit and in truth.'"[5]

Given the significance of spirituality in the New State, it behooves us to identify the semantic core of this term so often employed by the ideologues of the regime. What was understood by "spirit'? Were there historical or geographical variations in the definition of this concept? What was the relationship between Salazar's idea of spirituality and similar expressions developed by New State leaders, such as António Ferro's notion of a "politics of the spirit"? And finally, what was the role of spirituality in the administration of the Portuguese colonial empire and how was the spirit of the empire portrayed in cinema?

Salazar's version of spirituality was born, counter-intuitively, out of a confrontation with the spirit of the age:

> [...] Europe had experienced the greatest intellectual crisis of recent centuries. [...] Philosophism began by disrupting in minds the adherence to eternal truths, and corrupting in spirits the great certainties. [...] God, certainty, truth, justice, and morality were disavowed in the name of materialism, skepticism, pragmatism, Epicureanism, a thousand confused systems, in which the vacuum was filled with difficulties.[6]

Here, Salazar allied himself with thinkers like Paul Valéry and Edmund Husserl when he identified the moral and spiritual crisis that devastated Europe, a region dominated by materialism since the beginning of the twentieth century. However, the Portuguese politician scorned the philosophical reflections on the crisis that marked European thought, given that they questioned an immutable worldview and revealed the precariousness of Western values that up until that point were considered universal.[7] Salazar denied that these values could be relative, and he believed that the detractors of the "great truths" were victims of confused systems. In the wake of a tradition with roots in medieval Scholasticism, Salazarism stood for a society in which certain premises were not up for discussion, given that they were considered to be eternal and therefore trans-historical. God emerged both as one of these undisputable truths, similar to morality or justice, and as the guarantor of the entire system. Following the Christian tradition, Salazar delineated an opposition between spirit and matter: in the same way that the eternal nature of the soul contrasts with the vicissitudes and contingencies of an ephemeral body, so everlasting spiritual values shine above and beyond material constraints.[8] In the context of this conceptual structure, spirituality is considered to be the bedrock of the New State, determining all political and economic decisions of the regime.

The contrast between spirit and matter was also the basis for the politics of the spirit designed by António Ferro to bring "joy" to the New State:⁹

> Politics of the Spirit [...] is the one that is fundamentally and structurally opposed to the politics of matter. [...] it is the establishment and organization of the fight against everything that soils the spirit [...] everything that is ugly, rude, animalistic, everything that is evil, sickly, because of mere voluptuousness or Satanism. The Politics of the Spirit is the one that proclaims precisely the independence of Spirit, freeing it from the slavery of that tyrannical, insinuating materialism that constantly tries to bribe it, to intoxicate it. [...] That which is called the spirit of Evil is Satanism, materialism. The Spirit of Good is really Spirit itself.¹⁰

The concept of "matter" sketched by Ferro comprises all that endangers the patriarchal, hierarchical society envisioned by Salazar. Opposition to the New State is depicted as diabolic in Ferro's formulation, as he uses religious terminology when he describes materialism as satanic—a word that has communist connotations in both his and Salazar's speeches. The triumph of spirituality thus coincides with liberation from materialism or, in other words, with adherence to the values of the regime. Here, in a perversion of Kantian moral philosophy, Ferro draws an implicit parallel between the Salazarist version of spirituality and Kant's moral law: any rational person should acknowledge spiritual values by her- or himself and adopt them as her or his own. Individuals would become freer the more they conform to these norms.

Despite the abyss separating spirit and matter, the politics of the spirit delineated by Ferro is not without practical consequences. Ferro himself, in an article published in *Diário de Notícias* in 1932, stresses the material side of spirituality:

> Let there be a Politics of the Spirit, intelligent and constant, that consolidates the discovery, gives it height, significance and eternity. Don't consider spirit to be a fantasy, a vague, imponderable idea, but rather a defined, concrete idea, like a necessary presence, like an indispensable weapon for our resurgence. The Spirit, after all, is also matter, precious matter, the raw material of men's souls and the souls of nations ...¹¹

This passage emphasizes that the spirit is embodied in the material life of nations. In the Portuguese case, this translated into the politics of the spirit carried out by the Secretariat of National Propaganda (SPN) and later the National Secretariat of Information, Popular Culture and Tourism (SNI), which disseminated the notion of spirituality espoused by the New State.

This propagandistic effort also extended to the colonies as a defense of the Portuguese imperial project. For this purpose, it became necessary to mobilize a slightly modified version of the "spirit" adapted to the colonial context.

The spirit of Portuguese colonization

The ideology of the New State conferred a prominent position to the overseas colonies, which were understood as the material result of the action of the Portuguese spirit. As the then Minister of the Colonies, Armindo Monteiro, stated in 1933: "The essential element of colonization is a human one—that is, it has a *spiritual nature*."[12] The same conviction is repeated in a joint publication by the SPN and the General Agency of the Colonies (Agência Geral das Colónias): "The New State [...], as though it were dealing with a previous plan to be fulfilled, imposed with utmost continuity the moral politics and the politics of the spirit that would lead and did lead to a strong consciousness of the work of the Empire [...]."[13] In 1942, António de Almeida also associated Portuguese maritime expansion during the Renaissance with "manifestations of the spirit" that included the "development of science and culture," the "refinement of language" and an "artistic boom."[14]

Despite the efforts to highlight the incorporeal elements of the overseas colonization, these spiritual values were undeniably linked to material interests. In the 1936 speech "O Império Colonial na Economia da Nação," Salazar recognized that the colonies were essential to the country's economy as suppliers of raw materials, markets for the export of domestic production, and an immigration destination for the surplus population that European Portugal did not manage to absorb.[15] However, the material side of colonization is invariably subordinated to spirituality, and economic prosperity is considered to be dependent on morality: "We grew both in material power [...] and in spiritual force [...]."[16] Spirituality is a *sine qua non* condition of Portuguese action, which will always relegate material interests to the background: "If, for example, we feel indissolubly linked to the Portuguese State of India, it is not because of material interests [...] but because it, along with Macau, marks the Western spirit, which we had the glory, the audacity, let us say the sacrifice, of rooting there."[17] Salazar states that spiritual principles will always trample material interests, whenever there is tension between the two.

The alleged Portuguese spiritual superiority and the ensuing material development of the nation and its colonies were considered to depend upon a strong government: "While we were spiritually and materially superior and while we were guided by authoritarian governments and sought only to spread our Faith and the Empire, the country's leadership was honest and its will was beneficially manifested in all areas of national life."[18] The New State used the colonies to weave a discourse of self-justification: the leaders of the regime argued that Portuguese spirit, guided by the driving force of authoritarianism, was materialized in the tangible progress of the empire.

The regime makes use of the Hegelian notion of Spirit (Geist) in the construction of its ideology, as we already saw in the analysis of Leitão de Barros's films *Bocage* (1936) and *Camões* (1946). According to the German philosopher, Spirit is precisely that which is opposed to matter: "its [**Spirit's**] direct opposite [is] **Matter**. The essence of matter is gravity, **the essence of Spirit [...] is Freedom**."[19] Human activity and the succession of historical eras are the way in which abstract Spirit becomes concrete, gains self-consciousness, and reaches freedom. Spirit, identified with God as the highest principle of rationality, fulfills itself in historical becoming, a process that culminates in the complete materialization of Spirit, which coincides with the full spiritualization of the world and the end of human history. Salazar's *hybris*, supported by Sebastianist Millenarianism, consisted in suggesting that the Portuguese nation overcame European decadence by becoming the last bastion and the *telos* of Spirit. More pointedly, the New State *was* Spirit that encompassed both European Portugal and its colonies.

The primacy of spirituality in the Portuguese colonial project is associated with two other interdependent notions: civilization and christianization. These ideas were outlined in the Colonial Act, which stated in its Article 2: "It is of the organic essence of the Portuguese Nation to fulfill the historical role of possessing and colonizing overseas territories, and of civilizing the indigenous populations that inhabit them, exercising also the moral influence that is ascribed to it through the Priesthood of the Orient."[20] According to this document, Portugal's right to govern its colonies is justified by a civilizing mission of religious nature.[21] The Portuguese nation conquered and colonized vast areas outside of Europe with the intention of bringing the benefits of Western civilization and evangelization to other peoples: "[...] we should organize always better and more efficiently the protection of the inferior races; calling them to our Christian civilization is one of the boldest ideas and the highest works of Portuguese colonization."[22] This notion was repeated in a speech given by Salazar in 1940, when the Concordat and the Missionary Agreement with the Vatican were signed. On this occasion, Salazar highlighted that Christian doctrine played a fundamental role in the morality adopted by the New State, and asserted that the humane way in which the Portuguese have dealt with the colonized stemmed from the religious belief of the colonizers.[23]

Film was part of the SPN/SNI's efforts to promote the acceptance of Portugal's status as a colonizing country committed to civilizing and evangelizing the populations under its rule and thereby promoting spiritual and material progress in the colonized regions. The activities of the propaganda services involved, among others, support for fictional feature-length films such as *Feitiço do Império* (António Lopes Ribeiro, 1940), which we discussed in the previous chapter, and *Chaimite: The Fall of the Gaza Empire* (*Chaimite. A Queda do Império Vátua*), a movie directed by Jorge Brum do Canto that premiered in 1953. *Chaimite* exemplified the principles of the "politics of the spirit" that served as a guideline for artistic production in Portugal, in that it instrumentalized the concept of spirituality to glorify Portuguese military feats in Africa.

The politics of the spirit in *Chaimite*

Chaimite's plot chronicles events that took place during the course of the war between the Portuguese and the Gaza Empire in Mozambique at the end of the nineteenth century. The movie underlines the regime's colonizing ideals and seeks to impart them to the Portuguese citizens, in order to achieve what Armindo Monteiro, the Minister of the Colonies, called the "imperialization" of the nation: "[…] thus we will continue getting closer to that which I would dare call the imperialization of Portuguese life—I mean to say, the understanding that Portugal, as a world power, at all times has to behave, to conduct itself with the feeling and the responsibility that correspond to this fact."[24] This imperialization of the country means the internalization of its colonizing role, an attitude that should become second-nature and inform all activities of the Portuguese at home and overseas. *Chaimite* depicts the spiritual and civilizing aspects of the colonial project, as well as its material and warlike counterpoint, thereby contributing to the imperialization of Portugal.

In his exhaustive study of *Chaimite*, the history of its screening, and its reception in the media at the time of its release, Jorge Seabra provides information that allows us to situate the film in relation to the regime's propaganda and to the official discourse about the empire. Seabra mentions that, in an interview, Jorge Brum do Canto said he had neither an institutional nor a political involvement with Salazarism.[25] The film was produced by Cinal—Cinematografia Nacional—and not by the state. Furthermore, some scenes originally planned for the movie were removed from the script by censors and therefore could not be filmed.[26] For these reasons, *Chaimite* cannot be called, *stricto sensu*, a propaganda film. Yet, despite this fact, the vision of the empire conveyed by the movie closely follows the colonial ideology disseminated by the New State, which incidentally Brum do Canto shared.[27] This proximity resulted in governmental support for the project and it explains the positive reception of the film when it was released.

In an interview published in *Notícias* magazine in 1950, Brum do Canto stated that both Salazar and the General Agency of the Colonies approved of his plans to film *Chaimite*, a backing that materialized in the financial assistance for the production of the movie dispensed by the National Cinema Fund.[28] The 4 April 1953 premiere at the movie theater Monumental was attended by several politicians, and the film was extremely well received by the press, which stressed its relevance as a way of making Portugal's civilizing mission in Africa known to a larger audience. *Chaimite* was also advertised through a note by the SNI printed in several newspapers, which applauded the greatness of the movie's subject matter and labeled it "a must-see."[29]

The film was commercially distributed throughout the country and even in the colonies, which testifies both to the authorities' interest in its dissemination and to the public's fascination with the events of the plot. In 1954, the movie was awarded the Grand Prize of the SNI, and one of the film's protagonists, Emílio Correia, received the Best Actor Award. After the year of its premiere, *Chaimite* continued to be screened during New State's military and cultural initiatives, including the commemoration of official dates like Salazar's rise to power, the Day of the National Revolution, and Portugal Day.[30] It appears that, as Seabra claims, "we are not looking at a 'regime film' […] but above all a 'film of the regime.' Although it was not the result of an official initiative, it was not without interest to the New State due to its topic and the goals of its authors."[31] Brum do Canto's movie presents an image of Portuguese colonization pervaded by the values of spirituality that, according to the New State ideology, guided Portuguese action in the overseas territories.

Figure 7.1 Maria (Maria Lourdes Norberto) and Daniel (Artur Semedo) in *Chaimite*

The first scenes of *Chaimite* allow us to identify its main themes. The film opens with a close-up of a group of rifles and battle shields, and then cuts to a group of Africans in a circle moving to the rhythm of warlike singing. These initial moments highlight the black population's belligerence, which contrasts with the peaceful disposition of the Portuguese, represented in the opening sequence by Aunt Rosa (Maria Emília Vilas) and her niece Maria (Maria Lourdes Norberto). The two are tending the fields when António (Emílio Correia) warns them that a rebellion has broken out and recommends that they take refuge in Lourenço Marques. The native population's cruelty is emphasized through the depiction of the murder of a white woman and her child, who are killed by several Africans as these men chaotically run after the Portuguese settlers fleeing from the insurrection.

The audience is confronted from the outset with the black fighters' violent inclinations and with the laborious, orderly society that Portugal implanted in Africa. The movie highlights the way the settlers adapted to life in Mozambique, cultivating the land and developing commercial activities—an idea that echoes the official discourse of the regime. Salazar praised the Portuguese people's malleability, their capacity to adapt to the climate and the native culture of the regions they colonized without great difficulty: "The Portuguese probably owe their reputation of being excellent colonizers to their unique ability to adapt. Indeed, it is very easy for them to acclimatize under the most inhospitable skies, and they quickly understand the mentality, the life, the customs and the activities of peoples who are foreign to them."[32] Salazar thus reproduced the thesis of Brazilian sociologist Gilberto Freyre, according to whom the Portuguese propensity to interact with other populations resulted in a fusion of cultures in the various regions of the world where they settled.[33]

The notion that the Portuguese were particularly well suited to be colonizers goes hand in hand with the idea that Portuguese colonization was more benevolent than that of other European nations. As Salazar told Christine Garnier, "[e]veryone knows that Portuguese domination was always exercised with kindness, and respected both men and their customs. We never had racial biases. […] traces of violent actions cannot be found in the places where we have been […]."[34] Although he recognized in this statement that the Portuguese occupation of African territories was a form of domination, Salazar emphasized that this process took place without violence or racial biases, and implied that this occupation had been advantageous for the Africans, who were able to elevate themselves spiritually through contact with European civilization.[35]

The Portuguese characters in *Chaimite* subscribe to the New State's vision of the colonial project as a way of bringing civilization and progress to the African continent. However, the absence of discrimination that Salazar proclaimed is contradicted by the movie, beginning with its aesthetic and narrative choices. As Robert Stam and Louise Spence emphasize in their study of colonialism and racism in cinema, the film industry has, throughout its history, used several techniques to express the inferiority of the colonized. These include encouraging the spectator to identify with the colonizer's perspective through the point of view of the camera, negating the subjectivity of the colonized, and creating a negative image of non-Western characters. Several of these techniques are used in *Chaimite* in order to delegitimize the Africans' revolt against European rule and to convey that the insurgents are in the minority. Unlike the settlers, the majority of the Africans that appear in the film are not given a name, their personalities are not developed, and their participation in the plot is restricted to a reduced portion of the narrative.[36]

In the movie, the African population is divided into two groups: the insurgents, who are indiscriminately called traitors, incapable of recognizing the moral superiority of the colonizers; and those collaborating with the Portuguese by providing them with information about acts of sedition, who are portrayed in a positive light.[37] These two categories correspond to the distinction between two types of natives established by Armindo Monteiro: "But a part of black societies, all over Africa, remains steadfast within the patterns of their old organization. [...] Their external nudity mirrors their moral nudity. [...] within a few dozen years, the black races that cannot climb the rough paths of civilization will have disappeared from the face of the earth."[38] The Africans who do not accept Portuguese domination, who refuse to assimilate, and who fight the empire react in this way because of their "moral nudity," which prevents them from recognizing the spiritual superiority of the Portuguese. The New State's discourse is thus essentially contradictory in its attitude towards the native inhabitants of the colonies, a contradiction that, as we have seen in the previous chapter, is mirrored in films like *Feitiço do Império* and *Chaimite*. On the one hand, the European characters in the films argue for the need to respect African customs and traditions. On the other hand, the movies suggest that Africans should support Portuguese colonialism as a means for their spiritual improvement, which they could never hope to achieve on their own.

Despite their supposed benevolence and devotion to peace, the Portuguese do not fail to show their courage when they fight those who rebel against the ideals of spirituality. The military leaders depicted in *Chaimite*—Mouzinho de Albuquerque (Jacinto Ramos), Paiva Couceiro (Jorge Brum do Canto) and Caldas Xavier (Augusto de Figueiredo)—are historical figures that actually fought in Africa at the end of the nineteenth century.[39] These officers are elevated to the rank of national heroes who embody the virtues of bravery and patriotism characteristic of the colonizers. In battle, army leaders remain calm and face danger without hesitation, an attitude emulated by the soldiers, who stand firm while the hordes of African combatants that chaotically attack Portuguese troops charge at them.[40]

Brum do Canto's skill as a filmmaker shines through in these war sequences, which sometimes echo the westerns of John Ford, since the battle between the two armies stands for a clash of cultures.[41] Throughout the plot, the film offers evidence of the Portuguese technological superiority, which leads to the Africans' defeat in battle even when they have a numerical advantage. Significantly, these victories are interpreted as miracles that attest to the divine mandate of the colonizers to govern the native population, and not as the result of possessing better arms and more advanced combat techniques. The film thus suggests that the Portuguese technological and material advantage is due to their moral superiority. According to this perspective, the serenity and courage with which the Portuguese army confronts the native fighters results from the Europeans' unwavering faith in the great spiritual truths of religion, patriotism, and family values.

Mouzinho de Albuquerque states several times that he would like to give his life for his nation. Such a death would not only be heroic but would also certainly be rewarded by God because it would contribute to the expansion of Christian values in pagan lands.[42] *Chaimite* suggests that the Africans must abandon their moral confusion and acknowledge the value of the spiritual ideals defended by the Portuguese, thereby simultaneously recognizing their own inferiority, from which they can be freed only if they give in to the colonizers. Here, one can see an extension of the above-mentioned, distorted neo-Kantian logic: if the Portuguese become freer the more they surrender to the principles of the New State, the colonized achieve this freedom by embracing the same ideas, this time mediated by Portuguese colonization.

Figure 7.2   The imprisonment of Ngungunhane in *Chaimite*

The cinematic representation of the colonizers' moral superiority culminates in Chaimite, the town where Ngungunhane, one of the main rebel military commanders, is defeated. The Portuguese troops, led by Mouzinho de Albuquerque, break into the fortress where the insurgents are hiding. The movie highlights Mouzinho's imposing presence: the Africans, despite being armed, flee from the Portuguese officer instead of shooting at him. When Ngungunhane, abandoned by his soldiers, is finally identified and apprehended, Mouzinho orders the captive to kneel in front of him. Ngungunhane first stares defiantly at the colonizer, refusing to obey. For several seconds the camera moves from one man to the other while they look each other in the eyes. At the end of the scene, Ngungunhane lowers his gaze, a movement that signals the moment when he becomes conscious of his unworthiness upon seeing it externalized in the European's stare. Ngungunhane accepts not only the military superiority of the Portuguese but also their moral victory. When he surrenders, the rest of the Africans salute in what Mouzinho interprets as a manifestation of happiness due to the imprisonment of their leader. The Portuguese thereby suggests that the Africans were oppressed by their own rulers and that, once freed, they would hail the advantages that colonization brings.

In *Chaimite*, Portuguese patriotism spans all social classes, and the settlers frequently display their eagerness for combat by enthusiastically enlisting in the army. This love for the fatherland can be seen not only in war, but also in the intervals between battles. The soldiers sing and play melodies evocative of Portugal that contrast with the Africans' warlike drumming, and Portuguese piety is emphasized when the troops celebrate Christmas.[43] The positive traits of the settlers are juxtaposed to a negative image of both the Africans and the foreigners. The film often mentions other European nations, before which the Portuguese must look their best. Therefore, when the troops return to Lourenço Marques, tired and ragged after a battle, one of the commanders reminds the soldiers that they will be seen by foreigners, so they should straighten up and march confidently. On another occasion when the soldiers' morale is low, one of the army leaders gives a speech in the course of which he asks: "Wouldn't the foreigners scoff and the insurgents revel if our column stopped or turned around?"[44]

On the one hand, the preoccupation with the opinion of foreigners reflects the geopolitical situation of the late nineteenth century. After a British Ultimatum in 1890 ordered Portugal to give up its sovereignty over large parts of southern Africa, the Portuguese sought to cement their control over the African colonies they still possessed in areas coveted by other colonial powers. On the other hand, the relevance of the foreigners' perspective could be a reflection of the situation in 1950s Europe and the increasing international pressure on Portugal to democratize and grant independence to its overseas provinces. It is noteworthy that the foreigners are mentioned along with the rebels in the quote transcribed above, as if both were allied in their goal of destroying the Portuguese empire.⁴⁵

The hostile nature of foreigners is also mentioned in a conversation between Paiva Couceiro, Mouzinho de Albuquerque, his wife Maria José, and Caldas Xavier, during which it is narrated how Paiva Couceiro beat three foreign journalists because they had claimed, among other things, that the battle of Marracuene was a disaster and that the Portuguese were cowards. This dialogue is a modified version of the original script, which had included the filming of the scenes portraying the beating of the journalists. The sequence was cut by censors on the pretext that it could "raise international discord,"⁴⁶ a statement that once again should be understood in light of the international post-war political context. The foreigners' dishonesty in the film is a way of emphasizing that Portugal is the true heir of European spirituality, a value that was lost with the moral decadence of the rest of Europe.⁴⁷

Chaimite shows not only that the Portuguese people are devoted to peace—the eruption of war is merely a response to the Africans' rebellion—but also that the military confrontation is a the defense of their land, and its goal is to allow the settlers to return to commercial and agricultural activities. Therefore, the plot of the movie takes the unity of European Portugal and its overseas territories for granted, an idea that is also frequently mentioned by Salazar: "Under the sole authority of the State, Angola, Mozambique, and India are just like Minho or Beira. We are a juridical and political unit, and we hope to move towards economic unity [...]."⁴⁸ Portugal is a country whose territory is located in various continents, but this variety does not jeopardize the nation's sovereignty over its regions: "Among ourselves, we are a variety in unity [...] before other nations we are simply a unity, one and the same everywhere."⁴⁹ This unity is explained through a family metaphor:

> [We remain] united, by family ties, in economic and political life, in culture and faith, around the fireplace, in the old paternal home, when the world seems to crumble and certainly becomes divided in irreducibilities and hatreds. Amidst contemporary convulsions, we present ourselves as a brotherhood of peoples, cemented by centuries of peaceful life and Christian understanding, a

community of peoples that, whatever their differences may be, help each other, grow together, and rise up, proud to share the same name and essence of being Portuguese.[50]

Salazar extended his concept of the family to the relationship between European Portugal and the empire and applied his patriarchal vision of the ties uniting family members to the colonies. Even though he proclaimed that all the peoples joined together under Portuguese sovereignty were like brothers, they should gather "in the old paternal home" and obey Portuguese laws. He thereby subtly transformed the fraternal relationship between Portugal and its colonies into a hierarchical bond, with the colonizer being equated to a father who controls his children. In this paternalistic regime, filial rebellion is unacceptable, and any efforts towards independence will be brutally punished, as demonstrated in *Chaimite*.

Brum do Canto's film portrays the bond between Portugal and its empire using the perspective of several settlers in order to illustrate the Portuguese attachment to the African land. When Daniel (Artur Semedo) speaks with two friends who are going to enlist in the Colonial Army, they declare: "This land is ours; it's something that moves all of us. [...] It's the defense of our land invaded by those savages. [...] It's the defense of our families [...]."[51] Here the historical reality of colonization is inverted by classifying the Africans as "savages" who have invaded a region that legally belongs to the Europeans. As Salazar stated in his speech "O Império Colonial na Economia," the Portuguese who leave for the colonies recognize that "*Portugal is there.*"[52]

When Daniel, the owner of a bar in Lourenço Marques, meets Maria, a young woman who recently moved from a Portuguese village to Mozambique to be near her aunt, they both profess their desire to have "a house in the jungle, near a stream, with lands around it to farm,"[53] an expression that becomes a leitmotif in the film. Daniel and Maria get married and leave the city to pursue their dream of rural life in Africa. They move to an uninhabited area, build a house, farm the land, and after a few months the family is proud to have founded a new village. The plantations grow, Maria has a son, new settlers arrive, and a church is soon to be built.[54] Once again, in Salazar's words: "It is not that the land is being cultivated; it is Portugal that revives."[55]

The dedication to the land depicted in *Chaimite* results from a transfer of the Salazarist ideal of rural life from continental Portugal to its overseas territories. As we have seen in Chapter 3, the glorification of the countryside was

Figure 7.3 Maria (Maria Lourdes Norberto) and Daniel (Artur Semedo) with their son in their plantation in *Chaimite*

a fundamental characteristic of the New State that was mirrored in the filmography of the period. This idealization of rustic living dates back to Classical Antiquity, and was revived in Portuguese culture during the Renaissance. During this period, authors like Sá de Miranda portrayed bucolic lifestyle as a space of resistance to a generalized moral decadence caused in part by the quick profits resulting from overseas expansion.[56] Salazarism adopted this rural ideal and transplanted it to Africa. Traditionally considered to be the opposite of patriotic bucolic values, during the New State Africa becomes an offshoot of the Portuguese rural *ethos*. Brum do Canto's film documents this transmutation of the model of rural life now applied to the empire by accentuating the virtues of the colonizers—hardworking and honest, austere yet generous—who represent the perfect union between spirituality and matter.

Although *Chaimite* emphasizes the agrarian development of the overseas regions, which ties in with the rest of Brum do Canto's filmography,[57] the film also points out the progress made in trade under Portuguese rule. Daniel's café, the Chai-Chai, is the epitome of this growth. When Aunt Rosa and Maria take refuge there, Aunt Rosa develops it first into a restaurant and later also into a hotel. Brum do Canto says that his intention was to:

> [...] awaken, in the viewer's spirit [...] love for the land of Africa, just as Portuguese as the land here—through the constructive spirit that in the city elevates the Chai-Chai first from café to restaurant and later to a hotel—and that in the countryside prompts Daniel, a newlywed, to lay the foundations of a future city, transforming the untapped virgin jungle into the real value of prosperity [...].[58]

What stands out in this statement is the idea that both agriculture and trade would not be developed by the Africans themselves, which becomes yet another justification for Portuguese colonization. In the face of the local population's inability to take advantage of Africa's potential, the colonizers are an asset to the territory because they cultivate previously unproductive areas and foster local trade.

In the film, the engine of economic progress in the overseas provinces is the Portuguese people, in other words, the settlers who come from the Portuguese working classes, such as António, Maria, Daniel, and João Macário.[59] However, more than João Macário, a suitor whom Maria rejects, it is Daniel, whom she marries, who best symbolizes the ideal colonizer. In him, the warlike and agrarian impulses of the Portuguese—the two poles between which the action of the film oscillates—are reconciled. The confrontation of these two realities takes place even before the beginning of the narrative, since the music that accompanies the credits opens with an epic tone that later gives way to a lighter and happier melody. Likewise, the fighting of several battles against the African rebels is interspersed with the development of the young couple's love story. When they marry and are ready to depart for the village where they will build their home and establish a plantation, Mouzinho de Alburquerque makes a speech praising Daniel:

> [...] Daniel can serve as an example. Yes, because the problem is not just to defend Portuguese land from the Gaza invaders, it is also to use it, cultivate it, turn it into profit and prosperity. Daniel worked to defend the land; now he will work toward its glorification, thus completing the task he started. You are an example, young man, there is no doubt.[60]

Although war is frequently regarded as being opposed to both agriculture and trade during the period of Portuguese overseas expansion, these facets of colonization are reconciled in *Chaimite* through Daniel. He is a soldier, a settler, the owner of a café in Lourenço Marques and later of a plantation in the Mozambican backland.[61] The values of spirituality defined by Salazarism are thus embodied both in the warlike drive to defend a region considered to be Portuguese and in the cultivation of the land, an activity whose profits would in part revert to the state. The conquest precedes and creates the conditions for agriculture that, in turn, cements colonial domination achieved through military might:

> [...] but what has been done is more—it is a fusion of race and of land, extending the narrow borders of the peninsula to the edges of the backcountry, the Nation itself reproduced, soul and blood, like a Mother in her children. [...] The plow penetrates the soil more than the iron of the sword; sweat fertilizes the land more than blood from the veins; spirit molds and transforms men and nature more deeply than the material strength of conquerors.[62]

According to Salazar, the final goal of colonization, portrayed in *Chaimite*, is the transformation of the overseas provinces into a replica of European Portugal. This was made possible not only by the use of force but primarily through the transposition of Portuguese agrarian society to Africa.

To achieve the purpose of reproducing the material and economic structures of the New State and, more importantly, the values of spirituality in the colonies, it was necessary to keep the prevailing social order of Portugal in the overseas provinces. In *Chaimite*, there is a strict division between the people and the ruling class, represented by the army commanders and their families. This separation is expressed through consecutive scenes in which the leaders and the people perform the same activities in different places. Accordingly, Daniel, Maria, Aunt Rosa, and João's simple meal is followed by Paiva Couceiro, Caldas Xavier, Mouzinho de Alburquerque, and Maria José's elegant banquet. Daniel says goodbye to Maria immediately after Mouzinho says goodbye to his wife, and a scene in which Maria José reads a letter from Mouzinho precedes a scene during which a letter sent by Daniel from the front is read.

The emphasis on the parallelism between the leaders and the people is a way of underscoring national unity: all Portuguese fight for the same cause and act in a similar way.[63] However, class segregation in this film, as in others of the same period, reveals that, for Salazar, social hierarchy is essential for developing a prosperous society.[64] The members of the working class, who are responsible for the progress of the colonies, flourish to the extent that they obey their superiors, act subserviently, and are willing to follow the orders of their commanders, who are, in turn, the source of all knowledge, courage, and justice. Consequently, António and Daniel admire Paiva Couceiro's and Mouzinho de Albuquerque's patriotism, and say that they are willing to die in the service of their leaders. Mouzinho and his wife are the best man and the matron of honor at Daniel and Maria's wedding because their union should serve as an example for the newlyweds. Lastly, Maria learns from Mouzinho's wife how she can better serve her husband, since Maria José, who accompanies Mouzinho in war as a nurse, encourages Maria to do the same.[65]

Chaimite suggests that spiritual truths are disseminated vertically, permeating society from the top down. While these ideas are evident to some, an enlightened elite must reveal them to others, who are confused in their ignorance. As Salazar stated: "[…] the great national problems have to be solved, not by the people, but by the elites who direct the masses."[66] The spiritual values that emanate from religion and become embodied in the New State are transferred to the people by the best and the brightest of their leaders. The regime presupposes the existence of a hierarchical social chain of a paternalistic nature that begins with God, passes through political leaders, authority figures of the Church, and military commanders, to end with the lower classes. Spirituality reaches the native populations of the African provinces, which are at the bottom of the imperial social ladder, through colonization. This social order is the materialization of Portuguese moral values and, at the same time, the necessary condition for material progress. The connections established between the different levels of the hierarchy represented in the film reveal the ties that united all members of the nation, from European Portugal to the colonies, ties forged by the "great truths" of the spirit.

Chaimite reflects the New State's ambition of creating a politics of the spirit that would make the principles upon which the regime was founded known in Portugal and in the colonies. In the words of the producer, Luiz Pinto Coelho, in a pamphlet that introduced the film: "The central role that Cinema can and should play in the creation, conservation, and development of the *spiritual and moral values that make men and nations great*, even those who are humble or small nations, was considered first."[67] The dissemination of spiritual truths that accompanied the development of the colonies presupposed the reproduction of Portuguese society—especially agrarian Portugal—in the overseas territories. This desire to transplant continental Portugal to Africa counted on the colonizers' ability to adapt, a skill embodied by Maria, who learns the African expression "maningue"—"many."[68] By making this the last word of the film, Brum do Canto stressed both the prosperity brought by the Europeans to the region, and the good will of the colonizers, who use the autochthonous language. In exchange for some concessions and tolerance for the more exotic elements of African culture, it is hoped that the antagonism of the colonized will fade away. Africans should recognize the moral superiority of the Portuguese and the advantages of surrendering to their rule. The Gaza revolt would then go down in history as just another glorious stage in the process of colonization, in the course of which European spirituality triumphed over disorder.

But if Portuguese sovereignty over the empire was a way of bringing spirituality to the Africans, the rebellion depicted in the film shows that the colonized were not ready to accept their inferior status. As Hegel writes, the movement of Spirit unfolds in human history through a dialectical progression. The philosopher justifies European dominance over Africa, insofar as he believes that the African continent does not possess a history and, therefore, Spirit is completely separated from itself in these circumstances. European colonization thus would be a way to violently introduce the historical dialectic of Spirit into that region. The implications of Hegel's theory, which he himself never developed, allow us to anticipate that the colonized will soon gain consciousness of the precariousness of the colonizer's position. The Africans will become aware that masters are dependent on slaves, and that the superiority of the rulers hinges upon the existence of the ruled. When the colonized thus appropriate Spirit, as they did during the colonial war that began in 1961, the Portuguese army will no longer be able to control their revolt. New State leaders, caught up in their belief in the universality of their spiritual values, could not predict such a development.

In the first scenes of *Chaimite* as the African rebellion erupts, António, a Portuguese settler, runs to the army headquarters in Lourenço Marques to warn the authorities that an insurrection has begun. The soldiers, sitting in a room with closed windows, are surprised by the news and seem to doubt that such an event would be possible. However, António only has to open the windows of the building for them to hear the shouts of the people and the insurgents outside. In wanting to protect the "great truths" of the regime from social upheaval, the New State shut itself behind locked windows, closed off to alternative truths both in European Portugal and in the overseas provinces. Brum do Canto's movie and many other films from this period reflect this disconnect. They portray Portugal and its African colonies through the filter of Salazarist ideology, as if filming reality from behind a closed window and only intermittently perceiving what is going on outside.

Notes

1 A first version of this chapter was published in the academic journal *Ellipsis* (no. 7: 71–107) under the title "O Espírito do Império: as Grandes Certezas do Estado Novo em *Chaimite*." We would like to thank the editor of *Ellipsis* for the permission to reproduce a revised version of this essay here.
2 "mundo está sobretudo doente do espírito." "A Nação na Política Colonial," in *Discursos (1928–1934)*, 236.
3 "Crise europeia, crise do espírito; crise do espírito, crise de civilização." Salazar, "Portugal perante a Crise," in *A Política Imperial e a Crise Europeia*, 48.
4 "[…] com a Revolução de 28 de Maio de 1926—*movimento puramente espiritual*, sem um tiro—uma aura de confiante expectativa bafeja e desperta todos os portugueses de lei." Almeida, *Política Colonial*, 20; emphasis added.
5 "mundo que se desagrega pela força dos erros ou das armas [...] é preciso refazer 'em espírito e em verdade.'" Salazar, "Problemas Político-Religiosos," in *Discursos e Notas Políticas (1938–1943)*, 237. Christine Garnier already pointed out the importance of spirituality for the New State in her book about Salazar: "Spirit? Here we have, perhaps, the key word. The one that best defines Salazar's politics. For him, whatever the area may be, everything is a projection of the spirit. He thinks that the spirit molds and transforms men more profoundly than the force of dominators. Did he not even say once that peace is mainly the work of the spirit?" ("L'esprit? Voici peut-être le mot clef. Celui qui définit le mieux la politique de Salazar. Pour lui, en quelque domaine que ce soit, tout est projection de l'esprit. Il pense que l'esprit façonne et transforme les hommes plus profondément que ne peut la force des dominateurs. N'a-t-il pas même dit, une fois, que la paix est surtout œuvre de l'esprit?") *Vacances*, 233–4. In another passage from the same book, Garnier cites Salazar as saying: "Civilization, as I understand it, should guarantee the predominance of spiritual power. It is, in its essence, the reign of the spirit." ("La civilisation, telle que je l'entends, doit assurer la prédominance du pouvoir spirituel. Elle est, dans son essence, la royauté de l'esprit.") 131.
6 "[…] a Europa tinha experimentado a maior crise mental dos últimos séculos. […] O filosofismo começara abalando nas inteligências a adesão às verdades eternas e corroendo nos espíritos as grandes certezas. [...] Negou-se Deus, a certeza, a verdade, a justiça, a moral, em nome do materialismo, do cepticismo,

do pragmatismo, do epicurismo, de mil sistemas confusos, em que o vácuo foi preenchido com dificuldades." Salazar, "A Escola," in *Discursos (1928–1934)*, 311.

7   Salazar believed that the values of the spirit justify the universality of European culture and its dissemination in various regions of the world through colonization: "That it [Europe] has expanded beyond the limits of our continent is nothing more than natural for a civilization that, not just because of the strength and splendor of its achievements, but above all because of the portion of truth that it comprises, can be considered the only universalist civilization among all that have been created on the face of the Earth." ("Que esta [a Europa] se tenha expandido para além dos limites do nosso continente nada mais natural numa civilização que, não só pela força e esplendor das suas realizações, mas sobretudo pela porção de verdade que contém, se pode considerer a única universalista entre as civilizações criadas à face da Terra.") "Portugal como Elemento," in *Discursos e Notas Políticas (1951–1958)*, 156. The New State presented itself as the heir to this European universality: "Portugal was not created nor was it unified in modern times, nor did it take its shape with the pagan and anti-human ideal of deifying a race or an empire. [...] The universality of idea and action in the course of Catholic and European evolution, directed to the material and moral elevation of the species, that is the characteristic of our Nation's history." ("Portugal não se fez ou unificou nos tempos modernos nem tomou a sua forma com o ideal pagão e anti-humano de deificar uma raça ou um império. [...] A universalidade de idea e de acção no curso da evolução católica e europeia, dirigida à elevação material e moral da espécie, eis a característica da história da nossa Pátria.") Salazar, "Espírito da Revolução," in *Discursos (1928–1934)*, 328–9.

8   For Salazar, the material side of the Portuguese people's life is under the guardianship of the state and should be administered by the regime, with freedom being restricted to the spiritual realm. The state, in the person of Salazar, would therefore take charge of administering the bodies of the citizens and of organizing society in order to free the Portuguese to devote themselves only to the spirit.

9   Ferro, *Entrevistas*, 55.

10 "Política do Espírito [...] é a que se opõe, fundamental e estruturalmente, à política da matéria. [...] é estabelecer e organizar o combate contra tudo o que suja o espírito [...] tudo o que é feio, grosseiro, bestial, tudo o que é maléfico, doentio, por simples volúpia ou satanismo. Política do Espírito é aquela que proclama, precisamente, a independência do Espírito, que o liberta da escravidão do materialismo tirânico, insinuante, que pretende constantemente suborná-lo, embriagá-lo. [...] Aquilo a que se chama espírito do Mal é satanismo, é materialismo. O Espírito do Bem é propriamente o Espírito." Ferro, *Política do Espírito e os Prémios*, 6–7.

11 "Mas que se faça uma Política do Espírito, inteligente e constante, consolidando a

descoberta, dando-lhe altura, significado e eternidade. Que não se olhe o espírito como uma fantasia, como uma ideia vaga, imponderável, mas como uma ideia definida, concreta, como uma presença necessária, como uma arma indispensável para o nosso ressurgimento. O Espírito, afinal, também é matéria, uma preciosa matéria, a matéria-prima da alma dos homens e da alma dos povos ..." Ferro, *Entrevistas*, 229.

12 "O dado essencial da colonização é de ordem humana—isto é, de *natureza espiritual*." Monteiro, "Directrizes," in *Conferência do Império Colonial*, 29; emphasis added.

13 "O Estado Novo [...] pôs com a máxima continuidade, como se de um prévio plano a cumprir se tratasse, a política moral e a política do espírito que haviam de conduzir e conduziram a uma consciência firme da obra do Império [...]." *Obra Colonial do Estado Novo*, 73. In the ninth point of his 1934 *Decálogo do Estado Novo*, João Ameal already associated Portuguese spirituality with the imperial project: "The New State wants to restore Portugal to its historical greatness, to the fullness of its universalist civilization of a vast Empire. It wants to turn *Portugal once more into one of the greatest spiritual powers of the world*." ("O Estado Novo quer reintegrar Portugal na sua grandeza histórica, na plenitude da sua civilização universalista de vasto Império. Quer voltar a fazer *de Portugal uma das maiores potências espirituais do mundo*.") 79; emphasis added.

14 "manifestações do espírito"; "desenvolvimento da ciência e da cultura"; "aperfeiçoamento da língua"; "incremento das artes". Almeida, *Política Colonial*, 5.

15 Salazar, "O Império Colonial na Economia da Nação," in *Discursos e Notas Políticas (1935-1937)*, 158-9.

16 "Crescemos tanto em potência material [...] como em força espiritual [...]." Almeida, *Política Colonial*, 8.

17 "Se, por exemplo, nos sentimos indissoluvelmente presos ao Estado português na Índia, não é pelos interesses materiais [...] mas porque constitui, com Macau, um padrão do espírito do Ocidente que tivemos a glória, cometemos a audácia, dizemos o sacrifício de implantar ali [...]." Salazar, "A Nação Portuguesa Irmandade," in *Discursos e Notas Políticas (1943-1950)*, 284.

18 "Enquanto fomos espiritual e materialmente superiores e enquanto nos guiaram governos autoritários e tivemos em vista apenas dilatar a Fé e o Império, a chefia do país era idónea e a sua vontade reflectia-se beneficamente em todos os departamentos da vida nacional." Almeida, *Política Colonial*, 7.

19 Hegel, *Reason in History*, 22.

20 "É da essência orgânica da Nação Portuguesa, desempenhar a função histórica de possuir e colonizar domínios ultramarinos e de civilizar as populações indígenas que neles se compreendam, exercendo também a influência moral que lhe é

adstrita pelo Padroado do Oriente." *Obra Colonial*, 83. The civilization and spiritual elevation of the colonized populations are associated with the evangelization brought about by the Portuguese: "[…] we consider ourselves fortunate to be able to *spiritually elevate* the colonies and reinforce the moral unity of continental and overseas Portugal with new conditions of missionary work." ("[…] consideramo-nos felizes por nos ser possível *elevar espiritualmente* os domínios e reforçar com novas condições de trabalho missionário a unidade moral de Portugal de Aquém e de Além-Mar.") Salazar, "Problemas Político-Religiosos," in *Discursos e Notas Políticas (1938–1943)*, 241; emphasis added. In the book *Como se Levanta um Estado*, Salazar also claims: "This universalist, deeply humane tendency of the Portuguese nation, could be defined as a missionary calling due to its spirituality and its detachment from material interests." ("Vocação de missionário se pode chamar a esta tendência universalista, profundamente humana do povo português, pela sua espiritualidade e pelo seu desapego de interesses.") *Como se Levanta*, 129.

21 Faith in political leaders complements religious faith, given that the conjunction of both is indispensible for the good governance of the empire: "What is fundamentally necessary for the construction of an Empire? Creative thought and unbreakable faith in leaders inspired by the spirit." ("O que é necessário, fundamentalmente, à constituição de um Império? Um pensamento criador e uma fé inquebrantável nos dirigentes pelo espírito.") *A Obra Colonial*, 24. This statement implies that the regime's policies may seem unfathomable, like God's designs, but, like divine commandments, the directives of political leaders should be obeyed without question.

22 "[…] devemos organizar cada vez mais e mais eficazmente e melhor a protecção das raças inferiores cujo chamamento à nossa civilização cristã é uma das concepções mais arrojadas e das mais altas obras da colonização portuguesa." Salazar, "Nação na Política Colonial," in *Discursos (1928–1934)*, 241.

23 Salazar, "Problemas Político-Religiosos," in *Discursos e Notas Políticas (1938–1943)*, 233, 237. In this speech Salazar mentioned more than once the correlation between the material side and the spiritual side of power: "What is this about? Merely completing the political work of the Colonial Act with the sanction of our spiritual hold conferred by the Vatican and with the nationalization of missionary work, which is definitively part of the Portuguese colonial action." ("De que se trata? Simplesmente de completar a obra política do Acto Colonial com a sanção da posse espiritual conferida pela Santa Sé, e com a nacionalização da obra missionária que se integra definitivamente na acção colonizadora portuguesa.") "Problemas Político-Religiosos," in *Discursos e Notas Políticas (1938–1943)*, 240. The spiritual hold over the colonies thus complements the political power exercised over these territories.

24 "[…] assim nos iremos aproximando daquilo a que eu ousarei chamar a

imperialização da vida portuguesa—quero dizer, a compreensão de que Portugal, sendo uma potência mundial, tem de dirigir-se em todos os momentos, de governar-se com o sentimento e a responsabilidade que esse facto importa." Monteiro, "Directrizes," in *Conferência do Império Colonial*, 15.

25 Seabra, "Imagens do Império," in *O Cinema sob o Olhar de Salazar*, 236.
26 Seabra, "Imagens do Império," in *O Cinema sob o Olhar de Salazar*, 245. The censors cut a scene from the script in which Daniel (Artur Semedo) rapes Maria. Another cut scene, which we will discuss later, showed how Paiva Couceiro (Brum do Canto) thrashed three foreign journalists for slandering Portugal (Seabra, "Imagens do Império," in *O Cinema sob o Olhar de Salazar*, 245–6).
27 Brum do Canto seems to glorify the African military campaigns that took place at the end of the nineteenth century: "Macontente, Chaimite, Manjacaze, Magul, Coolela, names marked by earth and blood, under the glare of glowing lances and burning huts, through the fog of gunpowder; barbaric names, with a simultaneously bitter and sweet taste, forever engraved in our grateful souls [...]." ("Macontente, Chaimite, Manjacaze, Magul, Coolela, nomes amassados de terra e sangue, ao clarão das lanças a luzir e de palhotas a arder, por entre o nevoeiro da pólvora, nomes bárbaros, de sabor simultaneamente ácido e adocicado, para todo o sempre gravados em nossa alma agradecida [...].") Cited in Seabra, "Imagens do Império," in *O Cinema sob o Olhar de Salazar*, 240. Brum do Canto's nationalism and his views on the colonial empire lead Jorge Seabra to nickname the filmmaker a "man of the 'spirit'" ("homem do 'espírito'") in an allusion to António Ferro's "politics of the spirit" (271).
28 Seabra, "Imagens do Império," in *O Cinema sob o Olhar de Salazar*, 255. The Ministry of the Armed Forces also provided support for the making of the film, which is dedicated "to the Portuguese army" (ao exército português).
29 Seabra, "Imagens do Império," in *O Cinema sob o Olhar de Salazar*, 255–60.
30 Seabra, "Imagens do Império," in *O Cinema sob o Olhar de Salazar*, 264–70, 273.
31 "não estamos perante um 'filme de regime' [...] mas sobretudo um 'filme do regime,' que, apesar de não provir da iniciativa oficial, pelo tema abordado e pelos objectivos que os autores se propunham concretizar, não deixava de interessar ao Estado Novo." Seabra, "Imagens do Império," in *O Cinema sob o Olhar de Salazar*, 271.
32 "Les Portugais doivent probablement leur renommée d'excellents colonisateurs à leur rare faculté d'adaptation. Ils ont en effet une grande facilité à s'acclimater sous les cieux les plus inhospitaliers, et ils comprennent très vite la mentalité, la vie, les coutumes et les activités des peuples qui leur sont étrangers." Garnier, *Vacances*, 153. In the speech "Aos Portugueses da América do Norte," Salazar also applauded the "formidable power of adaptation [of the Portuguese people] to the most varied local conditions of life and work." ("formidável poder de adaptação [dos portugueses] às

mais variadas condições locais de vida e de trabalho.") *Discursos e Notas Políticas (1938-1943)*, 168.

33 Gilberto Freyre claimed that Portuguese colonialism had a more benevolent nature than other forms of colonization. Freyre did not deny the cruelty of, for example, slavery, but he claimed that close relationships were established between masters and slaves, which made the institution less inhumane. The author developed the theory of Luso-tropicalism, according to which the characteristics of the Portuguese allowed them to easily adapt to tropical regions, which contributed to the intense miscegenation that took place throughout the Portuguese empire. Salazar also states, along this line of thought, in an interview with Christine Garnier: "He [the Portuguese man] creates, then, through the fusion of races, other sorts of local populations that are better adapted to climatic conditions." ("Il crée, enfin, par des fusions de races, d'autres types de populations locales mieux adaptées aux conditions du climat.") *Vacances*, 154. For more information about the reception of Freyre's doctrines in the Portuguese New State, see Castelo, "*O Modo Português de Estar no Mundo. O Luso-Tropicalismo e a Ideologia Colonial Portuguesa (1933-1961)*," 69-107.

34 "[c]hacun sait que la domination portugaise s'est toujours exercée avec douceur, dans le respect des hommes et de leurs coutumes. Nous n'avons jamais eu de préjugés de race. […] on ne trouvera dans aucun des lieux où nous sommes passés trace de quelques violences exercées […]." Garnier, *Vacances*, 152. Salazar's words should be interpreted in light of the international pressure on Portugal to grant independence to its colonies. Salazar sought to convey the idea that Portuguese colonialism was not an imposition and that it was not violent. In the same interview with Garnier, he also stated that independence of the Portuguese colonies was out of the question: "Therefore you will understand the extent to which your question about the future emancipation of our colonies is beyond foreseeable reality." ("Vous comprenez ainsi à quel point votre question sur l'émancipation future de nos colonies est en dehors des réalités prévisibles.") *Vacances*, 158.

35 Salazar denied the existence of racism in the Portuguese Empire: "India has racial problems, but those cannot be held against us, for we do not have them in our territories and everywhere we stand up against the discrimination that affects that country's own sons." ("A Índia tem problemas raciais, mas não pode pô-los contra nós, que não os temos dentro dos nossos territórios e por toda a parte nos erguemos contra as discriminações de que os seus próprios filhos são vítimas.") "Questões de Políticas Interna," in *Discursos e Notas Políticas (1943-1950)*, 449.

36 Seabra, "Imagens do Império," in *O Cinema sob o Olhar de Salazar*, 244-5.

37 The Africans that rebel against the Portuguese are thus classified as traitors, while the Africans who betray other Africans by providing information to the colonizers about the revolt are paradoxically considered courageous and patriotic.

38 "Mas uma parte das sociedades negras, por toda a África, permanece imóvel dentro dos moldes da sua velha organização. [...] A sua nudez externa é o espelho da sua nudez moral. [...] dentro de poucas dezenas de anos, da face da terra terão desaparecido as raças negras que não puderam escalar as ásperas sendas da civilização." Monteiro, "Directrizes," in *Conferência do Império Colonial*, 28.

39 This glorification of the army reproduces the discourse of the New State. Salazar described the life of soldiers in the following manner: "For the soldier, however, there is no village or region, no province, no colony—there is the national territory. There is no family, relatives, friends, or neighbors—just the people who live and work in this territory: there is only, in one word, the Nation, in its whole material extension, in the entirety of its feelings and traditions, in all the beauty of its historical formation and its ideal future. [...] And it seems that it is because of this consumption of lives that the Nation goes on, increases its beauty and augments it power." ("Para o soldado, porém, não há a aldeia e a região, a província, a colónia—há o território nacional; não há a família, os parentes, os amigos, os vizinhos—há a população que vive e trabalha nesse território: só há, numa palavra, a Pátria, em toda a sua extensão material, no conjunto dos seus sentimentos e tradições, em toda a beleza da sua formação histórica e do seu ideal futuro. [...] E parece que é por esse consumo de vidas que a Pátria se mantém, e aumenta a sua beleza e engrandece o seu poder.") "Elogio das Virtudes Militares," in *Discursos (1928–1934)*, 108.

40 Salazar established a distinction between violence and force. The first is arbitrary, while the second seeks to establish legality in a situation of disorder. Salazar condemns violence but claims that force is necessary. "O Momento Político," in *Discursos e Notas Políticas (1935–1937)*, 70–1. In *Chaimite*, the army's actions are viewed as a manifestation of force but not of violence, since the rebels are considered to be a threat to Portugal's legitimate sovereignty over the African territories.

41 Avelar, "Echoes of John Ford's Westerns," in *Não Vi o Livro mas Li o Filme*. Mário Avelar lists the similarities between *Chaimite* and John Ford's westerns, which include structural parallels as well as direct citations. This connection between *Chaimite* and Ford's films had already been pointed out by João Mário Grilo (*O Cinema da Não-Ilusão*, 75).

42 Jorge Seabra highlights the fatalism of the character of Mouzinho de Albuquerque, whom Brum do Canto described in an interview as "a lover of death, an ingenious warrior and a man with a superior character." ("enamorado da morte, guerreiro genial e homem de superior carácter.") Cited in Seabra, "Imagens do Império," in *O Cinema sob o Olhar de Salazar*, 240.

43 When the rebels attack Lourenço Marques on Christmas Eve in 1894, the

Portuguese soldiers' remark "not even today" ("nem ao menos hoje") suggests that the insurgents were not only traitors but also heathens. On the other hand, António's house is decorated with a crucifix that is prominently displayed in the majority of the dialogues between him and his wife. António, one of the representatives of the Portuguese people, is a complex character. He was a deserter, but he later redeems himself through the courage he displays in the fight against the Africans. His piety and his patriotism allow him to overcome his past errors and be readmitted into the fold of the nation.

44 "O que não zombariam os estrangeiros e folgariam os rebeldes se a nossa coluna parasse ou voltasse para trás?"

45 On several occasions, the film implies that the foreigners were interested in the defeat of the Portuguese troops. However, the movie avoids references to the international situation surrounding Portuguese colonialism at the end of the nineteenth century, concentrating instead on the victories over the African rebels (Seabra, "Imagens do Império," in *O Cinema sob o Olhar de Salazar*, 244).

46 "levantar atritos internacionais." Seabra, "Imagens do Império," in *O Cinema sob o Olhar de Salazar*, 246.

47 Although Western Europe and the United States pressured the New State to grant independence to the overseas territories after the late 1940s, Salazar believed that the Soviet block was also a threat to the Portuguese empire: "Soviet communism, taking various forms in its doctrinal identity, preaches nationalism in Asia and internationalism in Europe. [...] If it triumphs there [in the Far East], it will not be long before it sets Africa on fire." ("O comunismo soviético, multiforme na sua identidade doutrinal, perfilha o nacionalismo na Ásia e o internacionalismo na Europa. [...] Se ali triunfa [no Extremo Oriente], não tardará muito que deite o fogo à África.") "O Meu Depoimento," *Discursos e Notas Políticas (1943–1950)*, 355. Communism is therefore a danger to the integrity of both continental Portugal and the colonies.

48 "Tal qual como o Minho ou a Beira é, sob a autoridade única do Estado, Angola ou Moçambique ou a Índia. Somos uma unidade jurídica e política, e desejamos caminhar para uma unidade económica [...]." Salazar, "Nação na Política Colonial," in *Discursos (1928–1934)*, 239.

49 "Entre nós, constituímos a variedade da unidade [...] perante os outros países somos simplesmente a unidade, um só e o mesmo em toda a parte." Salazar, "Nação na Política Colonial," in *Discursos (1928–1934)*, 239.

50 "[mantemo-nos] unidos, por laços de parentesco, de vida económica e política, de cultura e de fé, à roda da lareira, na velha casa paterna, quando o mundo parece se esboroa e decerto se divide em irredutibilidades e ódios. No meio das convulsões presentes nós apresentamo-nos como uma irmandade de povos, cimentada por

séculos de vida pacífica e compreensão cristã, comunidade de povos que, sejam quais forem as suas diferenciações, se auxiliam, se cultivam e se elevam, orgulhosos do mesmo nome e qualidade de portugueses." Salazar, "Nação Portuguesa Irmandade," in *Discursos e Notas Políticas (1943–1950)*, 282.

51 "Esta terra é uma coisa nossa, uma coisa que nos toca a todos [...] É a defesa da nossa terra invadida por esses selvagens. [...] É a defesa das nossas famílias [...]."

52 "*ali é Portugal.*" Salazar, "O Império Colonial na Economia," in *Discursos e Notas Políticas (1935–1937)*, 162.

53 "uma casa no mato, ao pé de um ribeiro, com terrenos à volta para cultivar."

54 Daniel and Maria's idyllic life on their plantation ends when the Africans burn the fields. This action, condemned in the film, is a sign that the Portuguese agrarian ideal cannot be easily implanted in African territory, where there were other forms of settlement that are not taken into consideration by the colonizers.

55 "Não é a terra que se explora: é Portugal que revive." Salazar, "Portugal perante a Crise," in *A Política Imperial e a Crise Europeia*, 43.

56 As Sá de Miranda writes in a famous letter to António Pereira: "I do not fear Castile, / From whence war does not yet sound / But I do fear Lisbon / That, upon smelling cinnamon, / Depopulates our Kingdom." (Não me temo de Castela, / Donde inda guerra não soa, / Mas temo-me de Lisboa / Que, ao cheiro desta canela, / O Reino nos despovoa.) *Poesia de Sá de Miranda*, 482.

57 In films like *The Song of the Earth* (*A Canção da Terra*, 1938) and *The Iron Cross* (*A Cruz de Ferro*, 1967), which we analyzed earlier, Brum do Canto stressed the bond between the Portuguese people and the land that they farm.

58 "[...] despertar, no espírito do espectador [...] o amor pela terra de África, tão portuguesa como a de cá—através do espírito construtivo que, na cidade, eleva o *Chai-Chai* primeiro de café a restaurante e depois a hotel—e que, no campo, impulsiona Daniel, recém-casado, a lançar os alicerces duma cidade futura, transformando o inaproveitado mato virgem em valor real de prosperidade [...]." Cited in Seabra, "Imagens do Império," in *O Cinema sob o Olhar de Salazar*, 242.

59 Seabra, "Imagens do Império," in *O Cinema sob o Olhar de Salazar*, 242.

60 "[...] o Daniel pode servir de exemplo. Sim, porque o problema não é só defender a terra portuguesa dos vátuas invasores, é também aproveitá-la, cultivá-la, transformá-la em rendimento e prosperidade. O Daniel trabalhou na defesa da terra, agora vai trabalhar na sua glorificação, completando assim a obra iniciada. És um exemplo, rapaz, não há dúvida."

61 Over the course of the history of colonization, the Portuguese vacillated between a model of overseas expansion based on the conquest of territories through force (as in Northern Africa), and an emphasis on trade, which would require less of a military presence.

62 "[...] mas o que está feito é mais—é a fusão da raça e da terra, o alargamento, até aos confins do sertão, das estreitas fronteiras da península, a mesma Pátria reproduzida, alma e sangue, ao modo de Mãe em seus filhos. [...] A charrua penetra o solo mais que o ferro da espada; o suor fertiliza a terra, mais que o sangue das veias; o espírito afeiçoa e transforma os homens e a natureza mais profundamente que a força material dos dominadores." Salazar, "Portugal perante a Crise," *A Política Imperial e a Crise Europeia*, 42.

63 In an interview with Jorge Seabra, Brum do Canto said that he wanted to show "portugueseness" (portuguesismo) in *Chaimite*, that is, "that which makes all of us Portuguese and not French" ("aquilo que faz que sejamos portugueses e não sejamos franceses"). Cited in Seabra, "Imagens do Império," in *O Cinema sob o Olhar de Salazar*, 242. In the film, "portugueseness" is common to all social classes and it promotes national unity.

64 One example is *Costa of the Castle* (*O Costa do Castelo*, Arthur Duarte, 1943). Despite the reconciliation of different social classes at the end of the narrative, the theme of segregation pervades the entire movie. When Rita (Maria Olguim) and Januário (João Silva), representatives of the lower classes, move into the home of aristocrats Mafalda (Maria Matos) and Simão (Manuel Santos Carvalho) to accompany Luisinha (Milu), they stay in the servants' quarters. The homeowners' actions on the upper floor mirror the development of the story of the poorer characters on the lower floor.

65 *Chaimite* includes several proto-feminist moments. Mouzinho de Albuquerque's wife finds it unfair that women cannot fight alongside men. Later, she decides to follow her husband to the battlefield as a nurse, convincing Maria to do the same. Aunt Rosa says that, if she could, she would fight the Africans with a rolling pin, in an allusion to other Portuguese female figures involved in heroic war actions, like the Padeira de Aljubarrota and Maria da Fonte. However, the initiatives of these Portuguese women never call into question their main role as companions of the male characters, who are the true protagonists in the battle against the insurgents. The courage of Portuguese women makes the humiliation of African women even more conspicuous. Ngungunhane's mother begs Mouzinho de Albuquerque to kill her instead of her son, a request to which the soldier responds by saying that Ngungunhane's life is in the hands of the King of Portugal.

66 "[…] os grandes problemas nacionais têm de ser resolvidos, não pelo povo, mas pelas elites, enquadrando as massas." Ferro, *Entrevistas*, 183.

67 "Considerou-se em primeiro lugar a alta função que o Cinema pode e deve desempenhar na criação, conservação e desenvolvimento *dos valores espirituais e morais que fazem grandes os homens e os povos*, mesmo os humildes e os povos

pequenos." Cited in Seabra, "Imagens do Império," in *O Cinema sob o Olhar de Salazar*, 242; emphasis added.

68 Salazar claimed that the success of Portuguese colonization stemmed from the Portuguese ability to adapt, which had a linguistic component: "The Portuguese man does not hesitate to vulgarize the words from his mother tongue and to enrich it with new expressions that he deems indispensable." ("Le Portugais n'hésite pas à vulgariser les mots de sa langue maternelle et à l'enrichir des nouvelles expressions qu'il juge indispensables.") Garnier, *Vacances*, 154.

Epilogue
New State Cinema Today

In May 2012 I was asked to introduce two emblematic New State propaganda films—*The May Revolution* and *Spell of the Empire*—before their screening at the Portuguese *Cinemateca* in Lisbon. Prepared to talk to a small group of film experts, I was pleasantly surprised to find that both sessions had been sold out. I was even more impressed when the vast majority of the audience sat through the roughly 135 minutes of *Spell of the Empire*, as the film was screened without its lost soundtrack.[1] After each session, several members of the audience approached me to ask questions about the movies. Many had watched these films for the first time and seemed eager to learn more about the filmography of the period.

My experience at the Portuguese *Cinemateca* was not an isolated incident. It was symptomatic of an ongoing re-assessment of the socio-political and cultural legacy of the New State. Almost forty years after the fall of the regime with the 1974 Carnation Revolution, Portuguese society is keen to get more information about the nearly five decades of authoritarian rule that determined the fate of the country in the last century. The variety of books published in recent years about the New State's charismatic leader, prime minister António de Oliveira Salazar, testifies to the fascination of present-day Portugal for its recent history. Ranging from veiled apologies of Salazar's authoritarianism to harsh criticism of his political positions, and dissecting both the leader's private life and his intellectual background, these publications reveal that Salazarism is still a contentious issue today.

This renewed interest in the New State and its leaders has extended to the cultural politics of the regime and its propaganda machine. How did Salazarism fashion itself? What face did it show to the public? In addition to historiography and literature, film has been a privileged medium for conveying the worldview of the New State to contemporary audiences. While fiction films have attempted to recreate this historical period in order to bring the atmosphere of those years back to life, documentaries have made extensive use of archival footage from the time in order to scrutinize the aesthetics of authoritarianism.

Starting in the end of the twentieth century, we have witnessed the release of an increasing number of historical fiction films that focused on the New State's final and most traumatic period, namely the protracted colonial war (1961–74) against the independence movements of the Portuguese African territories. For instance, *A Portuguese Goodbye* (*Um Adeus Português*, 1986) by João Botelho moves between war scenes set in Africa and the aftermath of the conflict in the 1980s, when a dead soldier's elderly parents visit his widow in Lisbon. Teresa Villaverde's *Alex* (*A Idade Maior*, 1991) depicts the homecoming of a Portuguese soldier who fought in Africa during Salazarism and *The Murmuring Coast* (*A Costa dos Murmúrios*, Margarida Cardoso, 2004), an adaptation of Lídia Jorge's homonymous novel, portrays the colonial war in Mozambique seen through the eyes of a soldier's wife who accompanied her husband to Africa.

Not only fiction films but also several documentaries have touched upon the topic of the colonial war. Margarida Cardoso's *Christmas 71* (*Natal 71*, 1999) is a telling example. It uncovers the history behind a record with Portuguese pop songs created as a Christmas present for the soldiers fighting in the war in 1971. Cardoso intersperses interviews with the various participants in the project of making the record with archival footage, including that of soldiers receiving the present. More recently, a series of TV documentaries on the colonial war have aired on RTP, the Portuguese Public Television channel, which also make extensive usage of archival footage from the New State.

Post-Salazar Portuguese cinema has focused not only on the colonial war but also on other aspects of the New State. For instance, the documentary *Aesthetics, Propaganda and Utopia in the Portugal of António Ferro* (*Estética, Propaganda e Utopia no Portugal de António Ferro*, Paulo Seabra, 2012) that also aired on National TV depicts the propaganda machine of the regime. It turns the viewers' attention to the leader of the SPN/SNI, Modernist intellectual António Ferro, whose politics of the spirit strove to create cultural artifacts—artworks, exhibitions, books, films—that would complement, on the artistic level, Salazar's socio-political reforms.

Susana Dias's short *Still Life: Visions of a Dictatorship* (*Natureza Morta: Visões de uma Ditadura*, 2005) and João Canijo's *Lusitan Phantasy* (*Fantasia Lusitana*, 2010) are two fascinating examples of a reworking of New State aesthetics.[2] Both movies are composed exclusively of archival footage from Salazarist propaganda documentaries, newsreels, war footage, and photographs that they transform in different ways. Dias employs techniques such as repetition, zooming, montage, and a slowing down of the normal pace of the film in order to highlight unnoticed details and to foster new interpretations of the images. Albeit less experimental than *Still Life*, *Lusitan Phantasy* also uses montage and, in particular, the superimposition onto archival footage of voice-over readings of texts by refugees who passed through Portugal during the Second World War. The juxtaposition of these disenchanted testimonies with the images of a prosperous nation disseminated at the time form an indictment of the country's neutrality during the conflict and of the deceitful tranquility of wartime Portugal.

Curiously, New State propaganda films had made extensive use of this technique of placing archival footage in a new context. As we saw in Chapters 1 and 6, both *The May Revolution* and *Spell of the Empire* insert documentary sequences into a fictional plot, so as to lend credibility to their propagandistic message. Contemporary movies appropriate this technique but ascribe to it a subversive function.[3] On the one hand, the films deploy these images to showcase Salazarist aesthetics and to highlight the regime's totalitarian discourse. On the other hand, the movies undermine the original meaning of propaganda footage and establish a critical distance between the viewers and the images. They invite the audience to reflect upon the mechanisms employed to forge an idealized picture of New State Portugal and of the country's African colonies.

In light of this growing interest in the New State and in the examination of Salazarism's aesthetic self-representation in film, one would expect that the cinema from the period would be readily available to a contemporary audience. Yet, this is not the case. With the notable exception of Portuguese-style comedies and films starring the fado singer Amália Rodrigues, New State filmography is by and large inaccessible. Some of the most emblematic Salazarist movies like *The May Revolution* and *Chaimite* can only be watched at the Portuguese National Film Archive, occasionally on public TV, and, in a few cases, online, though the copies available are of very poor quality.

One can only speculate about the reasons why there are no DVD editions of most New State films. If the comedies and fado movies present a mild, sometimes frivolous version of authoritarian Portugal, the other films are perhaps too heavily invested in disseminating the values of the regime. Could this propagandistic slant lead distributors to determine that these movies would be uncomfortable to watch? Are these films condemned because they do not afford the critical distance from Salazarist ideology inscribed in contemporary movies about this topic? Or is it simply easier to dismiss these films as meaningless propaganda than to analyze their rhetoric and aesthetics?

At a time when Portugal is still coming to terms with its history of authoritarianism, analyzing New State films through a critical prism might offer some insights into the country's recent past. These movies often reproduce the ideology of the New State and reveal the strategies used by the regime to spread its values. Furthermore, some of the films allow us to get a glimpse of the tensions inherent in Salazarist dogma and therefore trigger, even if unwittingly, a reassessment of the core tenets or the "great truths" of the New State—God, Fatherland, Family, Work, and Authority.

Portuguese Cinema, 1930–1960 offers a contribution to this reevaluation of New State filmography. A guiding threat through the various chapters was the analysis of how films portrayed the regime's vision of what Portuguese society should be like. Salazarist abstract values of religion, patriotism, and a traditional, hierarchically organized social structure were embodied in a series of figures that should guide the conduct of the Portuguese people: the male hero who works and fights for the glory of his country, the good housewife, the brave colonizer, the honest farmer, the law-abiding worker, and the spiritual, religious person, among others. These ideals, mentioned time and again in the speeches of Salazar and other leaders of the regime, were conveyed to the general public through literature, the fine arts, and also cinema. Salazarist movies were particularly effective in bringing these archetypal characters to life for a largely illiterate population that found in film the role models it should emulate.

In this study we looked at the cinematic reproduction of Salazarist ideology and at the portrayal of New State mythology and values in film. One of the tasks facing Portuguese society today is to undertake a thorough examination of the ideals of the regime. This book aims to contribute to the ongoing process of de-idealizing the emblematic heroes of Salazarism by analyzing their depiction in film. My experience at the Portuguese *Cinemateca* was an indicator that the Portuguese public is prepared to grapple with New State filmography as a step on the path toward establishing a critical relationship to the country's authoritarian past.

Notes

1 In addition, the film's first fifteen minutes were also lost.
2 Also interesting in this respect is Susana Dias's latest film *48* (2009), which refers to the forty-eight years of authoritarian rule in Portugal, comprising the military

dictatorship (1926–33) and the New State (1933–74). The film uses photographs of political prisoners taken by the political police and superimposes contemporary statements of these prisoners on to the old images. This eerie combination triggers a reflection about the long-lasting effects of Salazarism on Portuguese society.

3   The pioneer in this technique of critical usage of New State propaganda footage was Alberto Seixas Santos in his film *Gentle Ways* (*Brandos Costumes*, 1974). The movie, shot under the New State but released in 1975, after the Carnation Revolution, draws a parallel between the hierarchical political organization of the regime and the family structure prevalent at the time. The daily life of an upper middle-class family is set against a series of political events of Salazarism. The figure of the *pater familias* is compared to that of Salazar, through the juxtaposition of archival footage depicting the leader with scenes showing the father and head of the household.

Bibliography

Adorno, Theodor W. "Theory and the Pattern of Fascist Propaganda." In *The Culture Industry*, 132–57. Florence, KY: Routledge, 2001.
Almeida, António de. *Política Colonial Portuguesa no Passado e no Presente*. Lisbon: Agência Geral das Colónias, 1942.
Almeida, Miguel Valle de. "Marialvismo. Fado, Touros e Saudade como Discursos da Masculinidade, da Hierarquia Social e da Identidade Nacional." http://site.miguelvaledealmeida.net/wp-content/uploads/marialvismo.pdf Accessed 22 June 2011.
Ameal, João. *Decálogo do Estado Novo*. Lisbon: Secretariado da Propaganda Nacional, 1934.
Ameal, João and Luís Reis-Santos, eds. *Fátima: Altar do Mundo*. Vol. 1. Porto, Portugal: n.p., 1953.
António, Lauro. *Cinema e Censura em Portugal, 1926–1974*. Lisbon: Arcádia, 1978.
Avelar, Mário. "Echoes of John Ford's Westerns in Jorge Brum do Canto's *Chaimite*." In *Não Vi o Livro mas Li o Filme*, ed. Mário Jorge Torres, 115–23. Lisbon: Edições Húmus, 2008.
Azevedo, Cândido de. *A Censura de Salazar e Marcelo Caetano. Imprensa, Teatro, Cinema, Televisão, Radiofusão, Livro*. Lisbon: Caminho, 1999.
Azevedo, Manuel de. *Perspectiva do Cinema Português*. Porto: Clube Português de Cinematografia, 1951.
Baptista, Tiago. "Tipicamente Português. O Cinema Ficcional Mudo em Portugal no Início dos Anos Vinte." Master's thesis, Universidade Nova de Lisboa, 2003.
—*Os Filmes de Amália Rodrigues*. Lisbon: Tinta da China, 2009.
Barreto, José. *Religião e Sociedade. Dois Ensaios*. Lisbon: Imprensa de Ciências Sociais, 2002.
Barros, Leitão de, dir. *A Severa*. Sociedade Universal de Superfilmes, 1931.
—dir. *Maria do Mar*. Sociedade Universal de Superfilmes, 1930.
—dir. *As Pupilas do Senhor Reitor*. Tobis Portuguesa, 1935.
—dir. *Bocage*. Sociedade Universal de Superfilmes, 1936.
—dir. *Maria Papoila*. Lumiar Filmes, 1937.
—dir. *Ala-Arriba!* Tobis Portuguesa, 1942.
—dir. *Camões. Erros Meus, Má Fortuna, Amor Ardente*. Produções António Lopes Ribeiro, 1946.
Belo, Maria, Ana Paula Alão and Iolanda Neves Cabral. "O Estado Novo e as Mulheres." In *O Estado Novo. Das Origens ao Fim da Autarcia (1926–1959)*, 263–79. Vol. 2. Lisbon: Fragmentos, 1987.

Bhabha, Homi. *The Location of Culture*. New York: Routledge, 1994.
Botelho, João, dir. *Um Adeus Português*. 1986.
Brito, Joaquim Pais de. "A Cidade do Fado." *Penélope. Fazer e Desfazer a História*, no. 13 (1994): 177–91.
Brochado, Idalino da Costa. *A Missão de Salazar*. Lisbon: Companhia Nacional Editora, 1960.
—*Passado, Presente e Futuro*. Lisbon: Companhia Nacional Editora, 1960.
Campos, Henrique, dir. *Um Homem do Ribatejo*. Filmes Albuquerque, 1946.
—dir. *Ribatejo*. Filmes Albuquerque, 1949.
Canto, Jorge Brum do, dir. *A Canção da Terra*. Produção de Jorge Brum do Canto e Aquilino Mendes, 1938.
—dir. *Lobos da Serra*. Tobis Portuguesa, 1942.
—dir. *Fátima, Terra de Fé*. Filmes Portugueses César de Sá, 1943.
—dir. *Chaimite*. Cinal, Cinematografia Nacional, 1953.
—dir. *Fado Corrido*. Produções Felipe de Solms, 1964.
—dir. *A Cruz de Ferro*. Tobis Portuguesa, 1967.
Camões, Luís Vaz de. *Os Lusíadas*. Porto: Porto Editora, 2000.
Canijo, João, dir. *Fantasia Lusitana*. 2010.
Cardoso, Margarida, dir. *Natal 71*. 1999.
—dir. *A Costa dos Murmúrios*. 2004.
Carmona, Óscar. "A Mensagem do Chefe de Estado." In *A Política Imperial e a Crise Europeia*, António de Oliveira Salazar and Óscar Carmona, 31–8. Lisbon: Edições SPN, 1939.
Castelo, Cláudia. *"O Modo Português de Estar no Mundo." O Luso-Tropicalismo e a Ideologia Colonial Portuguesa (1933–1961)*. Porto: Edições Afrontamento, 1998.
Cerejeira, Manuel Gonçalves. *A Igreja e o Pensamento Contemporâneo*. Coimbra, Portugal: Coimbra Editora, 1924.
Cinema Português (O). Lisbon: Secretaria de Estado da Informação e Turismo, 1973.
Clark, Toby. *Art and Propaganda in the Twentieth Century: The Political Image in the Age of Mass Culture*. London: Weidenfeld and Nicolson, 1997.
Clemente, Manuel and António Matos Ferreira. *História Religiosa de Portugal*. Lisbon: Círculo de Leitores, 2002.
Colvin, Michael. "Images of Defeat: Early Fado Films and the Estado Novo's Notion of Progress." *Portuguese Studies*, no. 26.2 (2010): 149–67.
Costa, Alves. *Breve História do Cinema Português (1896–1962)*. Lisbon: Instituto da Cultura Portuguesa and Secretaria de Estado da Investigação Científica, 1978.
Costa, João Bénard da. *Histórias do Cinema*. Lisbon: Imprensa Nacional Casa da Moeda, 1991.
Cova, Anne and António Pinto Costa. "O Salazarismo e as Mulheres: Uma Abordagem Comparativa." *Penélope. Fazer e Desfazer a História*, no. 17 (1997): 71–94.

Cruz, Manuel Braga da. *O Estado Novo e a Igreja Católica*. Lisbon: Editorial Bizâncio, 1998.
Cunningham, Stanley B. *The Idea of Propaganda: A Reconstruction*. Westport, CT: Praeger, 2002.
Damásio, Manuel José, ed. *O Cinema Português e os seus Públicos*. Lisbon: Edições Universitárias Lusófonas, 2006.
Derrida, Jacques. *Of Grammatology*. Baltimore: Johns Hopkins University Press, 1998.
Dias, Susana, dir. *Natureza Morta: Visões de uma Ditadura*. 2005.
—dir. *48*. 2009.
Duarte, Arthur, dir. *O Costa do Castelo*. Tobis Portuguesa, 1943.
—dir. *A Menina da Rádio*. Companhia Portuguesa de Filmes, 1944.
—dir. *O Leão da Estrela*. Tobis Portuguesa, 1947.
Ellul, Jacques. *Propaganda: The Formation of Men's Attitudes*. 1962. Reprint, New York: Random House, 1973.
Félix, Padre José Maria. *Fátima e a Redenção de Portugal*. Vila Nova de Famalicão: Minerva, 1939.
Fernandes, António Teixeira. *O Confronto de Ideologias na Segunda Década do Século XX. À Volta de Fátima*. Porto: Afrontamento, 1999.
Ferreira, Carolin Overhoff, ed. *O Cinema Português através dos seus Filmes*. Porto: Campo das Letras, 2007.
Ferro, António. *Hollywood, Capital das Imagens*. Lisbon: Portugal-Brasil, n.d.
—*A Política do Espírito e os Prémios Literários do S.P.N.* Lisbon: Edições SPN, 1935.
—*Política do Espírito. Apontamentos para uma Exposição*. Lisbon: Edições SNI, 1948.
—*Teatro e Cinema (1936-1949)*. Lisbon: Edições SNI, 1950.
—*Entrevistas a Salazar*. Lisbon: Parceria A. M. Pereira, 2003.
Ferro, Marc. *Cinema and History*. Detroit: Wayne State University Press, 1988.
Fraga, Augusto, dir. *Sangue Toureiro*. Produtores Associados, 1958.
Freud, Sigmund. Sigmund Freud to Karl Abraham, 18 February 1909. In *The Complete Correspondence of Sigmund Freud and Karl Abraham 1907-1925*, ed. and trans. Ernst Falzeder, 82-4. New York: Karnac, 2002.
—"Fetishism." *International Journal of Psycho-Analysis*. no. 9 (1928): 161-6.
—"Three Essays on the Theory of Sexuality." In *The Standard Edition of the Complete Psychological Works of Sigmund Freud: A Case of Hysteria, Three Essays on Sexuality and Other Works*, ed. James Strachey, 123-246. Vol. 3. London: Hogarth, 1953-74.
—*Totem and Taboo*. London: Routledge and Kegan Paul, 1950.
—*Group Psychology and the Analysis of the Ego*. New York: W. W. Norton, 1959.
Freyre, Gilberto. *O Luso e o Trópico*. Lisbon: Comissão Executiva das Comemorações do V Centenário da Morte do Infante D. Henrique, 1961.
Garcia, Chianca de, dir. *Aldeia da Roupa Branca*. Tobis Portuguesa, 1939.
Garnier, Christine. *Vacances avec Salazar*. Paris: Grasset, 1952.

Garrido, Álvaro. "Coimbra nas Imagens do Cinema no Estado Novo." In *O Cinema sob o Olhar de Salazar*, ed. Luís Reis Torgal, 274–303. Lisbon: Temas e Debates, 2001.

Gaspar, José Martinho. *Os Discursos e o Discurso de Salazar*. Lisbon: Prefácio-Edição, 2001.

Geada, Eduardo. *O Imperialismo e o Fascismo no Cinema*. Lisbon: Moraes Editores, 1977.

Gil, José. *Salazar: A Retórica da Invisibilidade*, trans. Maria de Fátima Araújo. Lisbon: Relógio D'Água Editores, 1995.

Granja, Paulo Jorge. "A Comédia à Portuguesa, ou a Máquina de Sonhos a Preto e Branco do Estado Novo." In *O Cinema sob o Olhar de Salazar*, ed. Luís Reis Torgal, 194–223. Lisbon: Temas e Debates, 2001.

Grilo, João Mário. *O Cinema da Não-Ilusão. Histórias para o Cinema Português*. Lisbon: Livros Horizonte, 2006.

Guedes, Fernando. *António Ferro e a sua Política do Espírito*. Lisbon: Academia Portuguesa da História, 1997.

Hegel, G. W. *Reason in History: A General Introduction to the Philosophy of History*, trans. Robert S. Hartman. Upper Saddle River, NJ: Prentice Hall, 1997.

Horkheimer, Max and Theodor W. Adorno. *Dialectic of Enlightenment: Philosophical Fragments*. Stanford: Stanford University Press, 2002.

Horta e Costa, António. *Subsídios para a História do Cinema Português, 1896–1949*. Lisbon: Imprensa Literária Universal, n.d.

Husserl, Edmund. *The Crisis of European Sciences and Transcendental Phenomenology*. Evanston, IL: Northwestern University Press, 1970.

Jackall, Robert. Introduction to *Propaganda*, 1–9. London: Macmillan, 1995.

Jowett, Garth S. and Victoria O'Donnell. *Propaganda and Persuasion*. London: Sage Publications, 2006.

Kracauer, Siegfried. *From Caligari to Hitler: A Psychological History of the German Film*. 1947. Reprint, Princeton: Princeton University Press, 2004.

MacKenzie, John M. *Propaganda and Empire: The Manipulation of British Public Opinion 1880–1960*. Manchester: Manchester University Press, 1997.

Manique, António Pedro. "O 'Casal de Família'—Reflexões em Torno da sua Origem e Fundamentos Político-Ideológicos." In *O Estado Novo. Das Origens ao Fim da Autarcia (1926–1959)*, 221–9. Vol. 1. Lisbon: Fragmentos, 1987.

Martins, Moisés de Lemos. *O Olho de Deus no Discurso Salazarista*. Porto: Edições Afrontamento, 1990.

Matos-Cruz, José de. "Bocage." In *Textos da Cinemateca Portuguesa*, 245–7. Lisbon: Cinemateca Portuguesa, Folder 3, n.d.

—ed. *António Lopes Ribeiro*. Lisbon: Cinemateca Portuguesa, 1983.

—"Camões." In *Os Descobrimentos Portugueses e a Europa do Renascimento*, 43–6. Lisbon: Cinematica Portuguesa, 1983.

—ed. *Jorge Brum do Canto*. Lisbon: Cinemateca Portuguesa, 1984.

—*Prontuário do Cinema Português 1896–1989*. Lisbon: Cinemateca Portuguesa, 1989.
—*Cinema Português. O Dia do Século*. Lisbon: Grifo, 1998.
—*O Cais do Olhar. O Cinema Português de Longa-Metragem e a Ficção Muda*. Lisbon: Cinemateca Portuguesa, Museu do Cinema, 1999.
Melo, Daniel. *Salazarismo e Cultura Popular (1933–1958)*. Lisbon: Imprensa das Ciências Sociais, 2001.
Meneses, Filipe Ribeiro de. "Camões, Portuguese War Propaganda, and the Dream of a Safe Empire, 1914–1918." *NUI Maynooth Papers in Spanish, Portuguese and Latin American Studies*, no. 12 (2005): 1–25.
—*Salazar: Uma Biografia Política*. Lisbon: Dom Quixote, 2009.
Mira, Alberto, ed. *The Cinema of Spain and Portugal*. London: Wallflower Press, 2005.
Miranda, Armando de, dir. *Capas Negras*. Produtores Associados, 1947.
Monteiro, Armindo. "Directrizes duma Política Ultramarina." In *Conferência do Império Colonial*, António de Oliveira Salazar and Armindo Monteiro, 11–33. Lisbon: Agência Geral das Colónias, n.d.
—"Os Trabalhos da Conferência dos Governadores." In *Conferência do Império Colonial*, António de Oliveira Salazar and Armindo Monteiro, 34–41. Lisbon: Agência Geral das Colónias, n.d.
Morais, Armindo José Baptista de. "Vinte Anos de Cinema Português, 1930–1950: Conteúdos e Políticas." In *O Estado Novo*, ed. Fernando Rosas, 187–208. Vol. 2. Lisbon: Fragmentos, 1987.
Novo Cinema Português (1949–80) (blog). http://ncinport.wordpress.com/2007/ 07/16/ premios-de-cinema-premios-sni-1944-1953/ Accessed 27 July 2011.
Obra Colonial do Estado Novo (A). Lisbon: SPN and Agência Geral das Colónias, 1942.
Ó, Jorge Ramos do. *Os Anos de Ferro: O Dispositivo Cultural durante a "Política do Espírito" 1933–1949. Ideologia, Instituições, Agentes e Práticas*. Lisbon: Editorial Estampa, 1999.
Paulo, Heloísa. *Estado Novo e Propaganda em Portugal e no Brasil. O SPN/SNI e o DIP*. Coimbra, Portugal: Minerva, 1994.
Pereira, Wagner Pinheiro. "Cinema e Propaganda Política no Fascismo, Nazismo, Salazarismo e Franquismo." *História. Questões e Debates*, no. 38 (2003): 101–31.
Piçarra, Maria do Carmo. *Salazar vai ao Cinema. O Jornal Português de Actualidades Filmadas*. Coimbra, Portugal: Minerva-Coimbra, 2006.
—*Salazar vai ao Cinema II. A 'Política do Espírito' no Jornal Português*. Lisbon: DrellaDesign, 2011.
Pimentel, Irene Flunster. *História das Organizações Femininas no Estado Novo*. Lisbon: Círculo de Leitores, 2000.
Pina, Luís de. *A Aventura do Cinema Português*. Lisbon: Editorial Vega, 1977.
—*Documentarismo Português*. Lisbon: Edição do Instituto Português do Cinema, 1977.
—*História do Cinema Português*. Lisbon: Publicações Europa-América, 1986.

—*Estreias em Portugal (1918–1957). Filmes de Longa Metragem*. Lisbon: Cinemateca Portuguesa, 1993.

Pita, António Pedro. "Temas e Figuras do Ensaísmo Cinematográfico." In *O Cinema sob o Olhar de Salazar*, ed. Luís Reis Torgal, 42–61. Lisbon: Temas e Debates, 2001.

Portela, Artur. *Salazarismo e Artes Plásticas*. Lisbon: ICALP, Ministério da Educação, 1987.

Pratkanis, Anthony R. and Elliot Aronson. *Age of Propaganda: The Everyday Use and Abuse of Persuasion*. New York: W. H. Freeman and Company, 2001.

Proença, Maria Cândida, "O Conceito de Regeneração no Estado Novo." In *O Estado Novo. Das Origens ao Fim da Autarcia*, 251–62. Vol. 2. Lisbon: Fragmentos, 1987.

Pronay, Nicholas. Introduction to *Propaganda, Politics and Film, 1918–1945*, eds. Nicholas Pronay and D. W. Spring, 1–19. New York: Palgrave Macmillan, 2003.

Queiroga, Perdigão, dir. *Fado, História d'uma Cantadeira*. Lisboa Filme, 1947.

Quental, Antero de. *Causas da Decadência dos Povos Peninsulares*. Lisbon: Ulmeiro, 2001.

Ramos, Jorge Leitão. "O Cinema Salazarista." In *História de Portugal*, ed. João Medina, 387–406. Vol. 12. Lisbon: Ediclube, 1933.

Ramos, Rui, ed. *História de Portugal*. Lisbon: Esfera dos Livros, 2010.

Reeves, Nicholas. *The Power of Film Propaganda: Myth or Reality?* London: Continuum, 1999.

Reis, Bruno Cardoso. *Salazar e o Vaticano*. Lisbon: Imprensa de Ciências Sociais, 2006.

Ribeiro, António Lopes, dir. *Gado Bravo*. Bloco H. da Costa, 1934.

—dir. *A Revolução de Maio*. Secretariado da Propaganda Nacional, 1937.

—dir. *O Feitiço do Império*. Secretariado da Propaganda Nacional and Agência-Geral das Colónias, 1940.

—dir. *O Pai Tirano*. Produções António Lopes Ribeiro, 1941.

—"Planificação e Diálogos de *Feitiço do Império*." In *António Lopes Ribeiro*, ed. José de Matos-Cruz, 337–92. Lisbon: Cinemateca Portuguesa, 1983.

Ribeiro, Francisco, dir. *O Pátio das Cantigas*. Produções António Lopes Robeiro, 1942.

Ribeiro, M. Félix. *Filmes, Figuras e Factos da História do Cinema Português 1896–1949*. Lisbon: Cinemateca Portuguesa, 1983.

Rosas, Fernando. *O Estado Novo nos Anos Trinta (1928–1938)*. Lisbon: Editorial Estampa, 1996.

Sá de Miranda, Francisco de. *Poesia de Sá de Miranda*, ed. Alexandre M. Garcia. Lisbon: Editorial Comunicação, 1984.

Salazar, António de Oliveira. "Para Servir de Prefácio." In *Discursos (1928–1934)*, xliii–lxix. 5th edn, Vol. 1. Coimbra, Portugal: Coimbra Editora, n.d.

—"Os Problemas Nacionais e a Ordem da sua Solução." In *Discursos (1928–1934)*, 7–18. 5th edn, Vol. 1. Coimbra, Portugal: Coimbra Editora, n.d.

—"Política de Verdade, Política de Sacrifício, Política Nacional." In *Discursos (1928–1934)*, 21–42. 5th edn, Vol. 1. Coimbra, Portugal: Coimbra Editora, n.d.

—"Elogio das Virtudes Militares." In *Discursos (1928-1934)*, 97-112. 5th edn, Vol. 1. Coimbra, Portugal: Coimbra Editora, n.d.
—"As Diferentes Forças Políticas em Face da Revolução Nacional." In *Discursos (1928-1934)*, 159-84. 5th edn, Vol. 1. Coimbra, Portugal: Coimbra Editora, n.d.
—"Conceitos Económicos da Nova Constituição." In *Discursos (1928-1934)*, 185-213. 5th edn, Vol. 1. Coimbra, Portugal: Coimbra Editora, n.d.
—"'É esta a Revolução que Esperávamos?'" In *Discursos (1928-1934)*, 221-29. 5th edn, Vol. 1. Coimbra, Portugal: Coimbra Editora, n.d.
—"A Nação na Política Colonial." In *Discursos (1928-1934)*, 231-42. 5th edn, Vol. 1. Coimbra, Portugal: Coimbra Editora, n.d.
—"Propaganda Nacional." In *Discursos (1928-1934)*, 259-68. 5th edn, Vol. 1. Coimbra, Portugal: Coimbra Editora, n.d.
—"Educação Física e Desportos." In *Discursos (1928-1934)*, 269-75. 5th edn, Vol. 1. Coimbra, Portugal: Coimbra Editora, n.d.
—"A Escola, a Vida e a Nação." In *Discursos (1928-1934)*, 303-14. 5th edn, Vol. 1. Coimbra, Portugal: Coimbra Editora, n.d.
—"O Espírito da Revolução." In *Discursos (1928-1934)*, 315-32. 5th edn, Vol. 1. Coimbra, Portugal: Coimbra Editora, n.d.
—"O Estado Novo Português na Evolução Política Europeia." In *Discursos (1928-1934)*, 333-50. 5th edn, Vol. 1. Coimbra, Portugal: Coimbra Editora, n.d.
—"Constituição das Câmaras na Evolução da Política Portuguesa." In *Discursos (1928-1934)*, 369-93. 5th edn, Vol. 1. Coimbra, Portugal: Coimbra Editora, n.d.
—"Duas Palavras de Prefácio." In *Discursos e Notas Políticas (1935-1937)*, vii-xxiii. Vol. 2. Coimbra, Portugal: Coimbra Editora, 1937.
—"Funções e Qualidades do Chefe de Estado." In *Discursos e Notas Políticas (1935-1937)*, 1-12. Vol. 2. Coimbra, Portugal: Coimbra Editora, 1937.
—"Balanço da Obra Governativa. Problemas Políticos do Momento." In *Discursos e Notas Políticas (1935-1937)*, 19-40. Vol. 2. Coimbra, Portugal: Coimbra Editora, 1937.
—"'Na Ordem, pelo Trabalho, em Prol de Portugal.'" In *Discursos e Notas Políticas (1935-1937)*, 41-5. Vol. 2. Coimbra, Portugal: Coimbra Editora, 1937.
—"O Momento Político. Grandes e Pequenas Questões da Política Portuguesa." In *Discursos e Notas Políticas (1935-1937)*, 63-106. Vol. 2. Coimbra, Portugal: Coimbra Editora, 1937.
—"As Grandes Certezas da Revolução Nacional." In *Discursos e Notas Políticas (1935-1937)*, 125-41. Vol. 2. Coimbra, Portugal: Coimbra Editora, 1937.
—"Era de Restauração, Era de Engrandecimento." In *Discursos e Notas Políticas (1935-1937)*,143-9. Vol. 2. Coimbra, Portugal: Coimbra Editora, 1937.
—"O Império Colonial na Economia da Nação." In *Discursos e Notas Políticas (1935-1937)*, 151-71. Vol. 2. Coimbra, Portugal: Coimbra Editora, 1937.

—"O Suposto Arrendamento de Angola à Alemanha." In *Discursos e Notas Políticas (1935–1937)*, 255–64. Vol. 2. Coimbra, Portugal: Coimbra Editora, 1937.

—"A Embaixada da Colónia Portuguesa no Brasil e a nossa Política Externa." In *Discursos e Notas Políticas (1935–1937)*, 271–82. Vol. 2. Coimbra, Portugal: Coimbra Editora, 1937.

—"Portugal perante a Crise da Europa." In *A Política Imperial e a Crise Europeia*, António de Oliveira Salazar and Óscar Carmona, 39–55. Lisbon: Edições SPN, 1939.

—"Duas Palavras a Servir de Prefácio." In *Discursos e Notas Políticas (1938–1943)*, v–xv. Vol. 3. Coimbra, Portugal: Coimbra Editora, 1943.

—"A Educação Política Garantia da Continuidade Revolucionária." In *Discursos e Notas Políticas (1938–1943)*, 23–38. Vol. 3. Coimbra, Portugal: Coimbra Editora, 1943.

—"Revolução Corporativa." In *Discursos e Notas Políticas (1938–1943)*, 127–33. Vol. 3. Coimbra, Portugal: Coimbra Editora, 1943.

—"Aos Portugueses da América do Norte." In *Discursos e Notas Políticas (1938–1943)*, 165–9. Vol. 3. Coimbra, Portugal: Coimbra Editora, 1943.

—"Fins e Necessidade da Propaganda Política." In *Discursos e Notas Políticas (1938–1943)*, 191–211. Vol. 3. Coimbra, Portugal: Coimbra Editora, 1943.

—"Problemas Político-Religiosos da Nação Portuguesa e do seu Império." In *Discursos e Notas Políticas (1938–1943)*, 229–43. Vol. 3. Coimbra, Portugal: Coimbra Editora, 1943.

—"O Corporativismo e os Trabalhadores." In *Discursos e Notas Políticas (1938–1943)*, 353–76. Vol. 3. Coimbra, Portugal: Coimbra Editora, 1943.

—"Os Princípios e a Obra da Revolução no Momento Interno e no Momento Internacional." In *Discursos e Notas Políticas (1938–1943)*, 381–415. Vol. 3. Coimbra, Portugal: Coimbra Editora, 1943.

—*Para a Compreensão da Nossa Política*. Lisbon: Secretariado Nacional da Informação, 1950.

—"A Nação Portuguesa Irmandade de Povos." In *Discursos e Notas Políticas (1943–1950)*, 270–84. Vol. 4. Coimbra, Portugal: Coimbra Editora, 1951.

—"O Meu Depoimento." In *Discursos e Notas Políticas (1943–1950)*, 347–81. Vol. 4. Coimbra, Portugal: Coimbra Editora, 1951.

—"'A Regar! A Regar!'" In *Discursos e Notas Políticas (1943–1950)*, 395–400. Vol. 4. Coimbra, Portugal: Coimbra Editora, 1951.

—"Questões de Política Interna." In *Discursos e Notas Políticas (1943–1950)*, 423–55. Vol. 4. Coimbra, Portugal: Coimbra Editora, 1951.

—"Breves Considerações sobre Política Interna e Internacional a Propósito da Inauguração do Estádio de Braga." In *Discursos e Notas Políticas (1943–1950)*, 457–78. Vol. 4. Coimbra, Portugal: Coimbra Editora, 1951.

—"Governar Dirigindo a Consciência Nacional." In *Discursos e Notas Políticas (1943–1950)*, 479–511. Vol. 4. Coimbra, Portugal: Coimbra Editora, 1951.

—"Independência da Política Nacional—Suas Condições." In *Discursos e Notas Políticas (1951–1958)*, 47–72. Vol. 5. Coimbra, Portugal: Coimbra Editora, 1959.
—"O Plano de Fomento. Princípios e Pressupostos." In *Discursos e Notas Políticas (1951–1958)*, 89–126. Vol. 5. Coimbra, Portugal: Coimbra Editora, 1959.
—"Portugal como Elemento de Estabilidade na Civilização Ocidental." In *Discursos e Notas Políticas (1951–1958)*, 153–7. Vol. 5. Coimbra, Portugal: Coimbra Editora, 1959.
—"Governo e Política." In *Discursos e Notas Políticas (1951–1958)*, 301–21. Vol. 5. Coimbra, Portugal: Coimbra Editora, 1959.
—"A Atmosfera Mundial e os Problemas Nacionais." In *Discursos e Notas Políticas (1951–1958)*, 413–44. Vol. 5. Coimbra, Portugal: Coimbra Editora, 1959.
—"Caminho do Futuro." In *Discursos e Notas Políticas (1951–1958)*, 483–510. Vol. 5. Coimbra, Portugal: Coimbra Editora, 1959.
—*Como se Levanta um Estado*. Lisbon: Atomic Books, 2007.
Sapega, Ellen W. *Consensus and Debate in Salazar's Portugal. Visual and Literary Negotiations of the National Text, 1933–1948*. University Park, PA: Pennsylvania State University, 2008.
Schmitt, Carl. *Politische Theologie*. Berlin: Duncker & Humblot, 1979.
Seabra, Jorge. "Imagens do Império: O Caso *Chaimite* de Jorge Brum do Canto." In *O Cinema sob o Olhar de Salazar*, ed. Luís Reis Torgal, 235–73. Lisbon: Círculo de Leitores, 2000.
Seabra, Paulo, dir. *Estética, Propaganda e Utopia no Portugal de António Ferro*. 2012.
Sérgio, António. "O Reino Cadaveroso ou o Problema da Cultura em Portugal." In *Ensaios*, 25–61. Vol. 2. Lisbon: Livraria Sá da Costa, 1972.
Sevillano Calero, Francisco. *Propaganda y Medios de Comunicación en el Franquismo (1936–1951)*. Alicante: Publicaciones de la Universidade de Alicante, 1998.
Silveira, Paula. "Os Valores do Quotidiano no Estado Novo: Ruptura ou Continuidade?" In *O Estado Novo. Das Origens ao Fim da Autarcia (1926–1959)*, 303–20. Vol. 2. Lisboa: Fragmentos, 1987.
Stam, Robert and Louise Spence. "Colonialism, Racism, and Representation: An Introduction." In *Film Theory and Criticism: Introductory Readings*, eds. Leo Braudy and Marshall Cohen, 877–91. Oxford: Oxford University Press, 2004.
Telmo, Cottinelli, dir. *A Canção de Lisboa*. Tobis Portuguesa, 1933.
Torgal, Luís Filipe. *As "Aparições de Fátima." Imagens e Representações (1917–1939)*. Lisbon: Temas e Debates, 2002.
Torgal, Luís Reis. Introduction to *O Cinema sob o Olhar de Salazar*, 13–39. Lisbon: Círculo de Leitores, 2000.
—"Propaganda, Ideologia e Cinema no Estado Novo: A 'Conversão dos Descrentes.'" In *O Cinema sob o Olhar de Salazar*, ed. Luís Reis Torgal, 64–91. Lisbon: Círculo de Leitores, 2000.

—*Estados Novos, Estado Novo*. Vols. 1–2. Coimbra, Portugal: Imprensa da Universidade de Coimbra, 2009.

Valéry, Paul. "The Crisis of the Mind." In *The Outlook for Intelligence*, ed. Jackson Matthews, 23–36, trans. Denise Folliot and Jackson Matthews. New York: Harper and Row, 1962.

Vieira, Afonso Lopes. "Carta ao Realizador." In *António Lopes Ribeiro*, ed. José de Matos-Cruz, 140. Lisbon: Cinemateca Portuguesa, 1983.

Villaverde, Teresa, dir. *A Idade Maior*. 1991.

Winnicott, Donald. "Through Paediatrics to Psycho-Analysis." 1975. In *International Psycho-Analytic Library*, 1–325. Vol. 100. n.p., 1975.

—"Transitional Objects and Transitional Phenomena—A Study of the First Not-Me Possession." *International Journal of Psycho-Analysis*, no. 34 (1953): 89–97.

Index

"14 Years of Politics of the Spirit" ("14 Anos de Política do Espírito") 16–17n. 5
48 237n. 2

Adorno, Theodor 42, 54n. 64, 138, 140–1, 148n. 31
Afonso, Jorge 50n. 27
"Age of the Jazz-Band, The" ("A Idade do Jazz-Band") 52n. 47
agriculture 34, 51–2n. 44, 86–7, 90, 98–9, 105, 112–13n. 23, 118n. 49, 119, 123n. 76, 127, 218–19
Alão, Ana Paula 170nn. 6–9, 12
Albuquerque, Mouzinho de 66, 212–15, 220, 228n. 42, 231n. 65
Alcaide, Tomás 61–2
Alex (*A Idade Maior*) 234
Almeida, António de 178, 196n. 6, 203, 206–7 222n. 4, 234nn. 14, 16, 18
Almeida, Avelino de 22n. 50
Almeida, Miguel Valle de 172n. 24
Alvarez, Maria 128
Alves, Castro 74n. 22, 172n. 28
Amarante, Estêvão 193
Amaro, José 94, 167
Ameal, João 118n. 53, 149n. 37, 224n. 13
Amparo, Maria do 173n. 32
Aniki-Bobó 19n. 21
Animatógrafo 49n. 26, 190
António, Lauro 21n. 39
Aquinas, Thomas; Thomism 131–2, 134
Aristotle 103
Armed Forces; Army 11, 43, 199n. 27, 209, 212–14, 219, 221, 226n. 28, 228nn. 39–40
Aronson, Elliot 20n. 31
art for art's sake 10, 33–4
Atheism; atheist 120n. 60, 128, 130, 133, 135, 140
Authoritarianism; authoritarian 1, 15n. 1, 25, 39–44, 57, 103, 122n. 67, 123n. 72, 139, 141, 178, 196n. 6, 207, 233–6, 237n. 2
avant-garde 1, 44
Avelar, Mário 212n. 41
Azevedo, Alexandre de 51n. 36
Azevedo, Cândido de 21n. 39
Azevedo, Manuel de 5, 19nn. 26–7, 22n. 49

Baptista, César Moreira 16n. 5
Baptista, Tiago 113n. 27, 116n. 35, 163, 173n. 32, 174nn. 37–9, 175n. 44
Barreto, Bissaya 130–1, 144nn. 11–12
Barreto, José 150n. 45
Barros, Leitão de 6, 12, 14, 18n. 17, 49n. 24, 59, 62, 64, 66–7, 70–1, 74nn. 22–3, 75n. 28, 77n. 39, 82, 84, 86–7, 90, 92, 95–6, 154–5, 157–8, 172nn. 21, 24, 28, 175n. 45, 207
Bastos, Celita 68, 74n. 25
Battle of Alcácer-Quibir 63
Bela Flor, Elsa 85
Bergson, Henri 132
Best Film Award 62
Bhabha, Homi 192, 201n. 46
Bishop of Leiria 149n. 38
Bismarck 66
Black Mantels (*Capas Negras*) 12, 157, 160, 162–3, 172n. 29, 174nn. 37, 39
Bocage 14, 57–79, 207
Boer Wars 186
Bolshevik Revolution; Bolshevik 71n. 3, 101, 107
Bonucci, Caetano 59
Botelho, João 234
Branco, Graciete 171n. 14
Brandão, Nita 94, 160
Brazão, Eduardo 16n. 5
British Ultimatum 182, 198n. 16, 214–15
Brito, Joaquim Pais de 175nn. 46–7

Brum do Canto, Jorge 6, 12, 14, 15, 43, 49n. 24, 59, 66, 82, 86–7, 92n. 33, 105–8, 112n. 17, 115n. 33, 126–8, 130, 135, 137–9, 141–3, 144nn. 4, 13, 145n. 17, 149n. 40, 154, 160, 179, 187, 208, 209, 212, 216–18, 221–2, 226nn. 26–7, 228n. 42, 230n. 57, 231n. 63

Bucolism; bucolic 98, 217

Bullfighting Blood (*Sangue Toureiro*) 151, 160–1, 163–5, 167–8, 172–3n. 29, 173n. 32, 175n. 44

bullfighting; bullfighter 23n. 52, 94–5, 151, 158, 160–1, 163–5, 167–8, 172n. 24

Cabral, Iolanda Neves 170nn. 6–9, 12
Caetano, Marcelo 15n. 1, 21n. 39
Câmara, Eugénia de 172n. 28
Camões, Luís Vaz de 62–71, 75nn. 27–8, 30–2, 98, 189, 198n. 23

Camões, the Rabble-Rouser (*Camões, o Trinca-Fortes*) 6, 12, 14, 57–79, 207

Campos, Henrique 12, 82, 101
Campos, Luís de 187, 188, 194
Canijo, João 234
Cannes Film Festival 62, 74–5n. 26
Canonical Commission 143n. 1
Capitalism 82, 100–9, 115nn. 33, 122nn. 68, 71, 189
Cardinal Cerejeira *see* Cerejeira, Manuel
Cardoso, Margarida 234
Carlyle, Thomas 65
Carmona, Óscar 35, 40, 187, 191–2, 196n. 4
Carnation Revolution 15–16n. 1, 233, 237n. 3
Carvalho, Manuel Santos 231n. 64
Carvalho, Raul de 67, 68, 94, 159–60
Casal, Teresa 161
Casimiro, Mirita 96, 97, 154
Castelar, Maria 68
Castelo, Cláudia 227n. 33
Castro, Augusto de 48n. 16,
Castro, João de 79n. 51
Catholaicism (Catolaicismo) 134

Catholicism; Catholic 7, 14, 20n. 33, 39, 43–4, 73n. 11, 87, 123n. 72, 125–42, 143n. 1, 144nn. 5, 7, 145–6nn. 16, 18, 20, 148n. 30, 152, 154, 169n. 3, 233n. 7

"Causes of the Decadence of Peninsular Peoples" ("Causas da Decadência dos Povos Peninulares") 182

censorship 8–9, 11, 21n. 39, 27, 39, 89, 167, 174n. 37, 209, 215, 226n. 26

Censorship Committee 8–9
Center for Portuguese Cinema 18n. 17
Cerejeira, Manuel 133, 140, 143, 145nn. 15, 20
Chagas, Armando 128

Chaimite: The Fall of the Gaza Empire (*Chaimite. A Queda do Império Vátua*) 6, 12, 15, 43, 66, 115n. 33, 179, 187, 203–32, 235

Chamberlain, Austen 53n. 53
Christianity 15, 99, 121n. 65, 123n. 72, 132–4, 145n. 16, 153, 194, 204, 207–8, 213, 215–16

Christmas 71 (*Natal 71*) 234

Church 7, 11, 14, 43, 54n. 67, 83, 104, 123n. 72, 125–9, 133–7, 140, 142–3, 143n. 1, 145–6nn. 16, 18, 20, 24, 149n. 36, 154, 169n. 3, 199n. 27, 220

Church and Contemporary Thought, The (*A Igreja e o Pensamento Contemporâneo*) 133

Cinéfilo 17n. 8, 22n. 50
Cine-Jornal 131, 133, 143–4n. 4, 145n. 16
"Cinema and Dictatorships" ("O Cinema e as Ditaduras") 17n. 8

Cinema and the Christian Sense of Love and Family (*O Cinema e o Sentido Cristão do Amor e Família*) 145n. 16

Cinemateca 233, 236
Cinematografia Nacional (Cinal) 209
city 14, 81–2, 94–100, 102, 108–9, 113nn. 23, 27, 116nn. 35, 41, 44, 119n. 56, 128, 154, 167, 189, 194, 216, 218

City and the Mountains, The (*A Cidade e as Serras*) 98
civilization; civilize; civilized 3, 15, 18n. 14, 31, 41, 81–2, 110n. 5, 111n. 12, 115n. 33, 122n. 67, 177, 179, 185–6, 190–3, 196–7nn. 5, 8, 199n. 28, 200n. 38, 203, 207–9, 211–12, 222nn. 3, 5, 223n. 7, 224–5nn. 13, 20, 22, 228n. 38
Clara, Maria 29
Clark, Toby 53n. 56, 118n. 50, 170n. 9
Classical Antiquity 98, 217
Coelho, Luiz Pinto 220
collectivity; collective 22n. 46, 61, 64, 69–70, 75n. 35, 78–9n. 51, 87, 104, 111n. 11, 121nn. 65–6, 137, 148n. 30, 149n. 34
Colonial Act of 1930 177–8, 196n. 5, 197n. 9, 207, 225n. 23
Colonial University (Escola Superior Colonial) 178
colonialism; colonization 7, 15, 65, 75n. 32, 94, 115n. 33, 177–201, 203–4, 206–22, 223n. 7, 224–5nn. 12, 20, 22, 23, 227nn. 33, 34, 229n. 45, 234–6
Colvin, Michael 175n. 46
Communism 1–2, 28–9, 31–2, 35, 51n. 35, 54–5n. 68, 82, 100–9, 115n. 33, 119n. 57, 120n. 60, 122n. 67, 123n. 76, 131, 140, 149nn. 36, 38 203, 205, 229n. 47
Communist Party 120n. 60
community 42, 82–3, 85–6, 88–96, 100, 104–8, 112n. 23, 116n. 35, 118n. 50, 128, 136, 148n. 28, 163–4, 186, 215–16
Competition for the Most Portuguese Village of Portugal 84
Concordat (with the Vatican) 134–5, 146n. 21, 208
Conferência do Império Colonial 197n. 13, 198n. 17, 224n. 12, 226n. 24, 228n. 38
conversion 14, 29–30, 37, 50n. 28, 130–1, 133, 137–8, 140, 142–3, 149n. 38, 149n. 43, 187, 199n. 32
cooperation 62, 71, 102–8, 123n. 75

Cordeiro, Adriano Xavier 113n. 23
Corporatism 14, 82, 100–9, 110n. 8, 111nn. 10, 12, 122n. 70, 123n. 72,75–6, 189
Correia, Emílio 209–10
Correia, Manuel 128, 132
Correio Português 190
Costa Brochado, Idalino da 66, 75–6nn. 35–7
Costa of the Castle (*O Costa do Castelo*) 151, 155–6, 231n. 64
Costa, Alves 9, 21n. 41, 23n. 52, 49n. 26, 74n. 23
Costa, Alves da 101
Costa, Beatriz 13, 100, 109, 151, 154, 156
Costa, Fabrizio 126n. 3
Costa, João Bénard da 7, 9, 12, 16n. 2, 18n. 17, 20n. 35, 22n. 50, 172nn. 21, 23, 27, 174nn. 39,40, 175n. 45
Costa, José Manuel da 16n. 5
countryside 14, 62, 81–2, 86, 88, 94–100, 113n. 23, 116n. 44, 117n. 47, 154, 167, 192, 194, 216–18
Courtyard of the Ballads, The (*O Pátio das Cantigas*) 22n. 51, 157
Cousin Basil (*O Primo Basílio*) 59
Cova da Iria 125, 127
Cova, Anne 169n. 3, 170n. 8
Cruz, Manuel Braga da 134, 146n. 21
Cunningham, Stanley B. 20n. 31

D'Algy, Tony 155
d'Eça, Leonor 96
Damásio, Manuel José 22n. 49
Dantas, Júlio 12, 59, 157–8, 172n. 24, 175n. 44
decadence; decadent 67, 71, 79n. 51, 82, 94, 98, 179, 182–3, 196n. 8, 198n. 18, 203, 207, 215, 217
Decree No. 13 564 (Law of the 100 Meters) 3, 8, 21nn. 36–7
Decree No. 17 046-A 21n. 38
Decree No. 37 370 19n. 18
Department of the Interior 8
Derrida, Jacques 180–1
Diário de Notícias 127, 205
Diário Popular 63
Dias, Susana 234–5, 237n. 2

dictator 3, 15n. 1, 17n. 8, 35, 37–9, 41–3, 52n. 49, 54n. 60, 186, 234, 237n. 2
"Dictator and the Crowd, The" ("O Ditador e a Multidão") 37
"Directrizes duma Política Ultramarina" 197n. 13, 198n. 17, 224n. 12, 225n. 24, 228n. 38
discrimination 152, 180, 191–2, 211, 227n. 35
disenchantment (Entzauberung) 132
documentary films; documentaries 2, 4–6, 9, 12–14, 17n. 9, 19n. 21, 27–9, 34–7, 39–40, 49n. 26, 59, 82, 84, 90, 112n. 16, 114–15n. 30, 143n. 3, 187, 191–3, 195, 199n. 27, 234–5
dogma; dogmatic 2, 37, 45, 126, 134–5, 138, 236
Dolores, Cármen 68
Domestic Economy (Economia Doméstica) 153
domination 27, 180, 211–12, 219, 222n. 5, 227n. 34
Domingas, Maria 87, 154
Duarte, Arthur 12, 59, 143n. 3, 151, 155, 231n. 64

Echos da Via Sacra 147n. 27
economy 71, 87, 89, 94, 100, 102–4, 109, 120n. 58, 121n. 65, 123n. 75, 134, 153, 161, 173n. 33, 179, 181, 206
Éden Theater 187
education 2–4, 8, 17n. 9, 19n. 19, 21n. 37, 26–7, 33, 49n. 18, 82, 94, 120n. 58, 134, 139, 149n. 34, 153–4, 171n. 15, 173n. 33, 196n. 8, 198n. 15, 199n. 27
Eisenstein, Sergei; Eisensteinian 1
elite 54–5n. 68, 127–8, 130, 143, 220, 231n. 66
Ellul, Jacques 44
emigration 86, 89
empire 7–8, 12, 15, 23n. 52, 79n. 51, 177–201, 203–32
Enchanted Isles (As Ilhas Encantadas) 172n. 28

Enlightenment 71n. 3, 128–9, 132, 136, 138, 140–1, 147n. 28
Entrevistas a Salazar (Interviews with Salazar) 47n. 15, 51n. 38, 52n. 44, 53nn. 52, 54–5, 71n. 2, 77n. 45, 78–9nn. 47, 49–51, 53, 110nn. 5, 6, 8, 111n. 14, 117nn. 46–7, 121n. 65, 148n. 29, 169n. 5, 198n. 18, 223n. 9, 224n. 11, 231n. 66
equality; egalitarian 77n. 45, 122n. 67, 140, 152, 169, 179–80, 182, 191–2
Eugénia, Maria 155, 161
evangelization 20n. 33, 179, 185, 207–8, 225n. 20
Exhibition of the Portuguese World 112n. 15, 125, 186
Exhibition of the Portuguese World, The (A Exposição do Mundo Português) 2

fado 6, 12, 14–15, 23n. 52, 71, 78n. 51, 100, 151, 156–69, 172–3nn. 22, 24–5, 28–9, 174n. 37, 175nn. 43, 46–7, 49, 187, 235
Fado (O Fado) 172n. 22
Fado Corrido 160, 163, 173n. 30
fado singer 6, 14–15, 100, 151, 156–69, 172–3nn. 24, 28–9, 174n. 39, 235
Fado, Story of a Songstress (Fado, História de uma Cantadeira) 12, 70n. 51, 160–1, 172n. 29, 163–4, 174nn. 39–40, 166
faith 6–7, 14, 38–9, 47n. 15, 54n. 60, 77n. 45, 86, 126–43, 147n. 26, 149nn. 40, 43, 150n. 44, 197n. 8, 207, 213, 215–16, 225n. 21
family 2, 26, 32, 42, 83, 88, 96, 98, 100, 102–4, 109, 110n. 8, 112–13n. 23, 114n. 28, 121n. 62, 128, 131, 136–7, 145n. 16, 147nn. 26–7, 151–7, 160–2, 168, 169n. 2, 170n. 6, 173n. 33, 174nn. 34–5, 213, 215–16, 228n. 39, 236, 237n. 3
family couple (casal de família) 88, 112–13n. 23
Fascism 2, 7, 16n. 5, 21–2n. 46, 33, 42,

91, 99, 104, 139, 153, 161, 170n. 8, 186
Fascist Italy 2, 7, 33, 91, 99, 104, 139, 153, 161, 170n. 8
fatalism 71, 78n. 51, 165–9, 173n. 29, 175n. 45, 228n. 42
Fátima 143n. 3
Fátima e a Redenção de Portugal (*Fátima and the Redemption of Portugal*) 150n. 45
Fátima in the Middle East (*Fátima no Médio Oriente*) 143n. 3
Fátima, Altar do Mundo 149n. 37
Fátima, Hope of the World (*Fátima, Esperança do Mundo*) 143n. 3
Fátima, Land of Faith (*Fátima, Terra de Fé*) 12, 14, 43, 59, 73n. 11, 125–50
"Fátima's Miracle" ("O Milagre de Fátima") 133
feature-length film 2–5, 7–9, 27–8, 49n. 26, 84, 114n. 30, 126, 187, 208
Félix, José Maria 150n. 45
Female Portuguese Youth (Mocidade Portuguesa Feminina, MPF) 153, 162
femininity 151–7, 161–3, 168, 169n. 3
femme fatale 165–9
Fernandes, António Teixeira 144n. 7
Fernandes, Baltasar 50n. 27
Fernandes, Eduardo 96
Ferrari, Amadeo 59
Ferreira, Reinaldo 170n. 12
Ferro, António 1–6, 13–14, 16–17nn. 2, 5, 18n. 11–14,17, 19n. 18,20–4, 20nn. 29, 35, 29, 33–41, 44–5, 47n. 15, 50n. 27, 51n. 38, 52nn. 44,46–9,52, 53nn. 53–5, 54n. 60–1, 57–9, 62, 69, 71nn. 1–3, 72nn. 4, 6–9, 73nn. 12–17, 74–5nn. 22, 26–7, 77n. 45, 78nn. 47–51, 79n. 53, 81–2, 97–8, 109–10nn. 1–3,5–6,8, 111n. 14, 117nn. 46–7, 121n. 65, 134, 137, 148nn. 29,33, 152, 169n. 5, 198n. 18, 204–5, 223–4nn. 9–11, 226n. 27, 231n. 66, 234

Ferro, Marc 11, 22n. 48
"Fetishism" 198nn. 19–20
Fetishism; fetish 15, 177–201
Figueiredo, Augusto de 212
Film Archive 18n. 17, 235
film awards 5–6, 19n. 28, 20n. 30, 61, 62, 84, 163, 209
film subsidies 4–6, 8–9, 27, 58, 61, 105
Filme 149n. 40
Filmes Portugueses César de Sá 126
First Cinematographic Mission to the Colonies 191
First Conference of Colonial Governors 181
First Economic Conference of the Portuguese Colonial Empire 179
First Republic 1, 3, 14, 15n. 1, 25, 46n. 6, 65, 71, 75n. 32, 91, 125–8, 130, 133–4, 142, 144n. 7, 169n. 4, 177–8, 196n. 6, 203
First World War 17n. 8, 20n. 33, 65, 75n. 32
Fonseca, Artur 170n. 12
Ford, John 212, 228n. 41
foreigner 50n. 30, 151, 160, 182, 191–2, 211, 214–15, 229n. 45
Fraga, Augusto 151, 160
Franco, Francisco; Francoism 7, 17n. 9, 152, 161
freedom 32–3, 47n. 15, 50n. 30, 55n. 68, 89, 114n. 28, 130, 134–5, 137, 147n. 27, 148n. 30, 158, 162, 167, 173n. 32, 182, 207, 213, 223n. 8
Freemason 130
French Revolution 130
Freud, Sigmund 40–3, 54nn. 62, 67, 183–5, 192–3, 198nn. 19–22, 200n. 39, 201n. 47
Freyre, Gilberto, 211, 227n. 33
Friar Luís de Sousa (*Frei Luís de Sousa*) 6, 59
Friedrich, Caspar David 92
From Caligari to Hitler 21n. 45, 52nn. 49–51, 54n. 63

Gama, Vasco da 79n. 51

Gamboa, José 101
Garcia, Chianca de 18n. 17, 22n. 50, 49n. 24, 82, 100, 151
Garnier, Christine 1, 16nn. 2–3, 26, 47n. 14, 48n. 16, 51n. 37, 53n. 58, 71n. 5, 76n. 38, 79n. 51, 93–4, 115–16n. 34, 153, 166, 169, 170n. 10, 174n. 35, 175nn. 49–51, 179, 197n. 10, 199n. 26, 211, 222n. 5, 226n. 32, 227nn. 33–4, 232n. 68
Garrido, Álvaro 130, 144nn. 5, 11–12, 145n. 16
Gaspar, J. Natividade 17n. 8
Gaspar, José Martinho 47n. 13
Gaza (Empire) 208, 218, 221
Geada, Eduardo 22n. 49
Gebauer, Olly 94, 151, 159, 160
General Agency of the Colonies (Agência Geral das Colónias) 7, 73n. 11, 177, 179, 187, 206, 209
General Inspection of Entertainment (Inspecção-Geral dos Espectáculos) 8, 21n. 36
genius 62, 65, 67, 75–6n. 35
Gentle Ways (*Brandos Costumes*) 237n. 3
Gil, Cremilda 105
Gil, José 26, 47n. 12, 52n. 49
Gil, Rafael 143n. 3
Golden Age 98, 186
Gomes, Teresa 128, 151
Gonzalez, Eugénio 62
Graça, Maria da 151, 160, 164–5, 167, 175n. 42
Granja, Paulo Jorge 13, 54n. 66, 116n. 42, 119n. 57, 155, 172n. 20, 174n. 36, 175n. 50
Great Elias, The (*O Grande Elias*) 12
Great King, The (*Der Grosse König*) 66
"Great Tragic Actresses of the Silent Era, The" ("As Grandes Trágicas do Silêncio") 18n. 11, 34
great truths 26, 31, 83, 127, 136–41, 147n. 27, 151, 204, 220–1, 236
Grilo, João Mário 228n. 41
group psychology 40–1, 54nn. 62, 67
Group Psychology and the Analysis of the Ego 40, 54n. 67

Guedes, Fernando 16n. 5
Guimarães, Manuel de 8
Gulbenkian Foundation 18n. 17

Hegel, Georg Wilhelm Friedrich; Hegelian 64–5, 75n. 29, 106, 108, 207, 221, 224n. 19
Heiress of the Reeds, The (*A Morgadinha dos Canaviais*) 59
Henriques, Afonso 66
Henry the Navigator (Infante D. Henrique) 66, 75–6nn. 35, 37, 76n. 37, 78n. 50
hero 14, 59–71, 76n. 36, 78–9n. 51, 89, 113n. 25, 114n. 30, 143n. 3, 150n. 44, 193–4, 212–13, 231n. 65, 236
Heroic Plain (*Planície Heróica*) 143n. 3
Heron and the Serpent, The (*A Garça e a Serpente*) 143n. 3
hierarchy; hierarchical 13, 71, 82, 99, 101–3, 107, 110n. 6, 117n. 48, 121n. 66, 128, 135, 137, 140–1, 147n. 26, 152, 167–8, 180, 205, 216, 219–20, 236, 237n. 3
historical films 4, 6, 12, 19n. 21, 59–60
Historical Pageant of the Portuguese World 186
Hitler, Adolf; Hitlerism 10, 21n. 45, 38, 52nn. 49–51, 54n. 63, 99, 152, 170nn. 8–9
Hollywood, Capital das Imagens 18n. 11
Horace; Horatian 98
Horkheimer, Max 138, 140–1, 148n. 31
Horta e Costa, António 201n. 43
House of the People (Casa do Povo) 116n. 41
Husserl, Edmund 132, 204

identification 14, 40–2, 44, 61–3, 66, 68–9, 135
ideology 3–4, 7–12, 20n. 35, 21n. 42, 27, 29–33, 36–7, 43, 45, 51n. 35, 53n. 53, 57–8, 61, 64, 66, 76n. 37, 83, 90, 94, 100, 108–9, 113n. 23, 118n. 53, 119n. 55, 127, 131, 137–41, 144n. 5, 149n. 43, 156–7, 161–3, 167, 170n. 9, 178,

181, 198n. 23, 203–4, 206–7, 209, 221–2, 236
Ill-Fated Love (*Amor de Perdição*) 59
Imagem 22n. 50, 49n. 26
Images of Portugal (*Imagens de Portugal*) 2, 84
Inauguration of the National Stadium, The (*Inauguração do Estádio Nacional*, 1944) 2
industry 3, 18n. 17, 34, 52n. 44, 88, 98–100, 113n. 23, 118nn. 49–50, 119n. 55, 123n. 76, 161, 211
Integralism; Integralist 11, 112–13n. 23, 133
Iron Cross, The (*A Cruz de Ferro*) 82, 94, 105, 107–8, 230n. 57

Jackall, Robert 20n. 33
James, William 132
Jorge, Lídia 234
Jowett, Garth 6–7, 20nn. 31–2

Kamenesky, Eliezer 31
Kant, Immanuel; Kantian 136, 147n. 28, 205, 213
King John III 68
King Manuel I 69
King Sebastian; Sebastianist 76n. 38, 207
Kino 22n. 50, 49n. 26
Kracauer, Siegfried 10, 21n. 45, 36–7, 41, 52nn. 49–51, 54n. 63

Lady of Fátima, The (*La Señora de Fátima*) 143n. 3
Law 2 027 (Protection of National Cinema Law) 4–5, 19nn. 19, 27
Lemos Martins, Moisés de 143n. 43
Lemos, Óscar de 86, 161
Leviana 57
Liberalism 103, 121n. 62, 122n. 70, 189, 203
Lion of Estrela, The (*O Leão da Estrela*) 155
literature 14, 33, 57–9, 61–2, 65, 73n. 17, 78n. 48, 98, 137–8, 145n. 16, 233, 236
Lives Adrift (*Vidas sem Rumo*) 8
Living Museum 112n. 15

Lopes, António Luís 158
Lopes, Fernão 66
Lovers from the Tagus, The (*Os Amantes do Tejo*) 172n. 28
Lunacharsky, Anatoly 71–2n. 3
Lupo, Rino 143n. 3
Lusiads, The 64, 67, 75nn. 28, 30, 189
Lusitan Phantasy (*Fantasia Lusitana*) 234–5

MacKenzie, John M. 199n. 27
Maia, Leonor 62, 156
Man from Ribatejo, A (*Um Homem do Ribatejo*) 82, 86, 90, 92–3
Manique, António Pedro 113n. 23
Maria of the Sea (*Maria do Mar*) 12, 82, 84–5, 90, 92, 112nn. 16–17, 154
Maria Papoila 82, 96–8, 100, 119n. 56, 154
Marialvismo; Marialvan 172n. 24
Marialva, Count of 157–8, 160, 162, 172n. 24
Mariaud, Maurice 172n. 22
Martinez, António 29, 30
Marvelous Gale (*Vendaval Maravilhoso*) 74n. 22, 163, 172n. 28,
masculinity 152, 168–9, 172n. 24
Massis, Henri 84
materiality; materialism 15, 26, 94, 99, 101, 104, 115n. 33, 118n. 54, 120n. 60, 121n. 65, 133, 140, 203–6, 222n. 6, 222n. 10
Matos, Maria 231n. 64
Matos, Maria Helena de 68
Matos-Cruz, José de 9, 73n. 20, 77nn. 40–2, 144nn. 4, 13, 145n. 17, 149n. 40, 199n. 30, 200n. 38, 201nn. 42, 44
May Revolution, The (*A Revolução de Maio*) 1–2, 6–7, 13–14, 16n. 2, 25–55, 101, 105, 119n. 57, 131, 192, 199n. 32, 233, 235
Mello e Alvim 72n. 11, 126
Melo, Daniel 113n. 25, 116nn. 40–1, 43, 117n. 48, 120n. 60, 148–9n. 34
Meneses, Luís Filipe 66, 75nn. 31–2
"Mensagem do Chefe de Estado, A" 196n. 4, 201n. 41

Messiah; Messianism; Messianic 38, 143
metonymy; metonymic 62–4, 66, 163, 189, 193
Milú 151, 155, 156, 231n. 64
miracle 14, 53–4n. 59, 125–50, 212
Miraculous Fátima (*Fátima Milagrosa*) 143n. 3
Miranda, Armando de 12, 157
Missionary Agreement (with the Vatican) 135, 208
Moço, João 85
Modernism 2, 29, 34, 57, 66, 134, 234
Modernity 1, 13, 98–100, 118n. 53, 142, 141n. 41
Moita, António 86
Monarquia, A 133
Monteiro, Adolfo Casais 74n. 23
Monteiro, Armindo 181–3, 197n. 13, 198n. 17, 206, 208, 212, 224n. 12, 226n. 24, 228n. 38
Monteiro, Rosa Maria 85
Monumental 209
Morais, Armindo José Baptista 17n. 8, 21n. 46, 116n. 36
Mota Júnior, Joaquim Pereira 12, 73n. 11, 187–8, 200n. 33
Mothers' Work for National Education (Obra das Mães para a Educação Nacional; OMEN) 153–5
Mundo Literário 5
Muñoz, Eunice 62, 101
Murmuring Coast, The (*A Costa dos Murmúrios*) 234
Museum of Popular Art 84, 112n. 15
Mussolini 13, 27, 38, 44, 53n. 56, 99, 139, 152, 170n. 8, 171n. 14, 186
myth; mythology; mythological 22n. 46, 67, 74n. 23, 98, 130, 138, 140–1, 174n. 40, 236

National Assembly 135
National Cinema Fund (Fundo do Cinema Nacional) 8, 19n. 18, 58, 105, 209
National Secretariat of Information, Popular Culture, and Tourism 66, 76n. 38 (Secretariado Nacional da Informação, Cultura Popular e Turismo; SNI) 2, 4–8, 16–17nn. 4, 5, 7, 19–20nn. 27, 28, 30, 38, 57–60, 62, 81, 84, 163, 186, 205, 208–9, 234
National Stadium 2, 28
nature; natural 14, 27, 38, 78n. 50, 81–124, 131, 161, 193, 201n. 42, 204, 219, 223n. 7, 224n. 12, 231n. 62
Nazaré, a Fishermen's Beach (*Nazaré, Praia de Pescadores*) 84
Nazi; Nazism 2, 7, 10, 27, 35–7, 40–2, 66, 91, 99, 118n. 50, 139, 170n. 9
Neves, Cruz 145n. 16
New Cinema (Novo Cinema) 105, 124n. 77
New Man 31, 58
Nietzsche, Friedrich, 65
Nihilism, 14, 127, 137–43, 148n. 33
noble savage 92
Noblemen of the Moorish House, The (*Os Fidalgos da Casa Mourisca*) 59
Norberto, Maria Lourdes 210, 217
Noticiarios y Documentales Cinematográficos (NO-DO) 17n. 9
Notícias 209
Nova Geração A, 65
novel 12, 19n. 21, 57–61, 73n. 11, 95, 98, 116n. 37, 126, 187, 234

Ó, Jorge Ramos do, 18n. 13
O'Donnell, Victoria 6–7, 20nn. 31–2
Obra Colonial do Estado Novo, A 177, 196n. 5, 224n. 13
Old Regime 113
Olguim, Maria 231n. 64
Oliveira Martins 67, 85
On Heroes, Hero Worship and the Heroic in History 65
Ordinance 23054 186
Ordinance No. 22 966 3–4
Ordinance No. 36 062 19nn. 19, 27
Ordinance No. 37 369 19n. 18
Orpheu 2, 57
Otero, Carlos 87

overseas province 186–7, 199n. 29, 215, 218–19, 221

Paiva Raposo 62, 95
Passado, Presente e Futuro 76nn. 35–6
Pastoral Letter on the Cult of Our Lady of Fátima (*Carta Pastoral sobre o Culto de Nossa Senhora de Fátima*) 125, 143n. 1
Paula, Maria 96, 157
Paulo, Heloísa 16n. 5, 49nn. 22–3, 111n. 15, 114n. 30, 145n. 19, 199n. 28
Paz dos Reis Prize 5
peace 13, 29, 50n. 30, 96, 115n. 33, 117n. 48, 133, 136, 151, 191, 210, 212, 215–16, 222n. 5
Pena, Afonso 147n. 27
Piçarra, Maria do Carmo 16n. 2, 18n. 10
Pimentel, Irene Flunster 170n. 11, 171n. 15, 174n. 34
Pina, Luís de 9, 18n. 16, 63–4, 68, 73nn. 20–1, 74nn. 23–4, 75n. 28, 77n. 43, 200n. 32
Pinto, Ângela 172n. 21
Pinto, António Costa 169n. 3, 170n. 8
Pita, António Pedro 34, 52n. 45, 71n. 1
Plato; Platonic 26, 33
Poeira, Barreto 86, 128, 129, 132, 154
poetry 4, 14, 19n. 21, 51n. 41, 57–79, 98, 170n. 12, 172n. 28, 189
police 31, 37, 43, 51n. 36, 52n. 52, 54n. 66, 87, 237n. 2
Política do Espírito, Apontamentos para uma Exposição 17n. 5, 54nn. 60–1, 73n. 12
Política Imperial e a Crise Europeia, A 196n. 4, 201n. 41, 222n. 3, 230n. 55, 231n. 62
politics of the spirit 17n. 5, 18n. 13, 33–7, 51n. 43, 54n. 60, 57–9, 71, 139n. 33, 205–6, 208–22, 234
Politics of the Spirit and the Literary Prizes of the SPN (*Política do Espírito e os Prémios Literários do SPN*) 20n. 29, 148n. 33, 223n. 10
Pope Gregory XIII 20n. 33
Pope Gregory XV 6–7

Pope Leo XIII 123n. 72
Pope Pius XI, 125, 145n. 16
Pope Pius XII 143n. 2
Pope Urban VIII 20n. 33
Portuguese Catholic Center 134, 145n. 18, 148n. 30
Portuguese Federation of Educational and Recreational Organizations 139, 149n. 34
Portuguese Goodbye, A (*Um Adeus Português*) 234
Portuguese Journal (*Jornal Português*) 2, 18n. 10, 84
Portuguese National Radio (Emissora Nacional) 143n. 2, 170n. 12
Portuguese Public Television (RTP) 234
Portuguese Renaissance 52n. 47, 63, 98, 153, 183, 206, 217
Portuguese Youth (Mocidade Portuguesa) 7, 54n. 68
Portuguese-style comedy (comédia à portuguesa) 12–13, 54n. 66, 97, 100, 116n. 42, 119n. 57, 155–6, 171n. 16, 172n. 20, 174n. 36, 175n. 50, 235
poverty 8, 30, 88–9, 121n. 63, 170n. 12, 191
Pratkanis, Anthony R. 20n. 31
Princess Maria 68–9
Prize for Best Actor 5, 62, 209
Prize for Best Actress 5, 62
Proença, Maria Cândida 150n. 43
progress 18n. 17, 30–1, 34, 51n. 44, 64, 66, 81, 94, 98–100, 110n. 5, 113n. 23, 118nn. 50, 52, 128, 132, 149n. 41, 175n. 46, 182–3, 186, 189, 191, 199nn. 27–8, 207–8, 211, 217–21
propaganda 1–4, 6–10, 13, 16n. 4, 17nn. 7–9, 20nn. 31, 33, 35, 25–55, 57–8, 61, 63, 66, 71–2. 3, 83–4, 116n. 41, 127, 130, 133, 145n. 17, 153, 170n. 9, 177–9, 186–95, 199nn. 27–8, 205, 208–9, 233–6, 237n. 3
for António Ferro 1–4, 34, 38–41, 44–5, 49n. 26, 57–8, 71n. 3
definition of 6–7, 20nn. 32–3, 35

for Salazar 2, 17nn. 6–7, 26–9, 33, 43–5, 49nn. 18, 20–3, 71, 79n. 52, 130, 177, 196n. 5
in the New State 25–55, 61, 83–4, 116n. 41, 130, 133, 145n. 17, 177–9, 186–95, 199nn. 27–8, 205, 208–9, 233–6, 237n. 3
Protestantism 7
Providence 76n. 36, 88
psychoanalysis 12, 15, 41–2, 184–5, 201n. 47

Queiroga, Perdigão 12, 116n. 37, 143n. 3, 160
Queirós, Eça de 66, 98
Queluz Palace 61–2
Quental, Antero de 182

race; racial 65, 69–70, 71, 78nn. 48, 50, 98, 105, 179, 181, 185, 190–2, 196n. 8, 199n. 27, 207–8, 212, 219, 223n. 7, 227n. 33
Radio Girl, The (*A Menina da Rádio*) 155, 161
Ramos, Jacinto 212
Ramos, Jorge Leitão 7, 9, 21n. 43, 23n. 52, 31, 49nn. 24–5, 50n. 31
Ramos, Rui 22n. 47
Realpolitik 71
reason 14, 44–5, 75n. 29, 126–43, 147–8n. 28, 198n. 15, 224n. 19
Reason in History 75n. 29, 224n. 19
rebellion 101–2, 135, 210, 215–16, 221
Rector's Pupils, The (*As Pupilas do Senhor Reitor*) 59, 82, 95–6
Reeves, Nicholas 20n. 33, 72n. 3
Regaleira, Vasco 73n. 20
regional or folkloric films 14, 19n. 21, 59–60, 81–3, 89, 94, 104, 108, 116n. 35
Reis, Bruno Cardoso 146n. 21
Reis-Santos, Luís 147n. 37
religion; religious 14, 39–40, 50n. 28, 83, 89, 120n. 60, 122n. 67, 125–50, 167, 185, 205, 207–8, 213, 220, 225nn. 20–1, 23, 236
repression 137, 168, 184
Republican Period 63–4, 69, 83

Republicanism; Republican 11, 26, 63, 65, 69, 75n. 32, 76n. 37, 83, 91, 128, 130, 134, 140, 182
Rerum Novarum 123n. 72, 169n. 3
Restoration of 1640 63
revolt 101–2, 175n. 45, 203, 211, 221, 227n. 37
revolution; revolutionary 1–2, 6–7, 13, 15–16nn. 1–2, 25–55, 100–1, 105, 119n. 57, 130–1, 133, 135–6, 140, 192, 200n. 32, 203, 209, 233, 237n. 3
Ribatejo 12, 82, 101–3
Ribeiro, Alberto 157
Ribeiro, Ângela 105
Ribeiro, António Lopes 1–3, 6–7, 12–14, 16n. 2, 18n. 17, 22n. 50, 27–9, 31–3, 43–4, 49nn. 24, 26, 50nn. 27–8, 59, 62–3, 68, 73n. 11, 82, 143n. 3, 151, 156, 160, 179, 187, 191–2, 195, 199n. 30, 200nn. 33–4, 36–8, 201nn. 40, 42, 44–5, 208
Ribeiro, António Machado 105
Ribeiro, Francisco 22n. 51, 156, 157, 187
Ribeiro, M. Félix 18n. 17, 73nn. 18,20–1, 74nn. 23, 25, 75n. 27, 77n. 39, 112n. 17, 113n. 26, 144nn. 4, 6, 199n. 30, 191n. 44
Riefenstahl, Leni 40
Rodrigues, Amália 6, 151, 160–1, 163, 164, 165, 166, 170n. 12, 173nn. 29,32, 235
Rodrigues, Aurélio 126n. 4, 131–4, 143n. 4, 144n. 13, 145n. 16
Romanticism; Romantic 34, 62–3, 67, 92, 137, 165
Rosas, Fernando 118–19n. 55, 121n. 64
Rousseau, Jean-Jacques 92
Rumina, Elsa 86, 154
rurality; rural life; ruralism; rural 14, 81–124, 151, 153–4, 167, 216–17
Russian Revolution 140

Sá de Miranda, Francisco de 98, 217, 230n. 56
Sacra Congregatio de Propaganda Fide

(The Sacred Congregation for the Propagation of Faith) 6–7
Salazar, António de Oliveira
  colonialism 177–85, 195, 195n. 2, 196nn. 4, 7, 197nn. 9,11, 198n. 18, 199n. 26, 203–4, 206, 208, 211–13, 215, 216, 219–21, 222n. 2, 224n. 15, 225nn. 22–3, 227n. 33–4, 228n. 39, 229nn. 45,48, 232n. 68, 236
  communism 1–2, 28–9, 51n. 35, 54–5n. 68, 101–5, 115n. 33, 120n. 60, 122n. 67, 123n. 76, 140, 205, 229n. 47
  ideology 3–4, 7–12, 20n. 35, 21nn. 42,44, 27, 29–33, 43, 45, 51n. 35, 53n. 53, 61, 64, 66, 76n. 37, 83, 90, 94, 99–100, 109, 118–19nn. 53,55, 127, 131, 137–41, 144n. 5, 149n. 43, 156, 163, 167, 178, 181, 185n. 23, 203, 206–7, 209, 221–2, 236
  propaganda *see* propaganda, for Salazar
  speeches
    "'A Regar! A Regar!'" 54n. 65, 111n. 13
    "Aos Portugueses da América do Norte" 226n. 32
    "Atmosfera Mundial e os Problemas Nacionais, A" 196n. 8
    "Balanço da Obra Governativa. Problemas Políticos do Momento" 50n. 30, 123n. 71
    "Breves Considerações sobre Política Interna e Internacional a Propósito da Inauguração do Estádio de Braga" 114n. 28, 120n. 60
    "Caminho do Futuro" 122n. 70
    Como se Levanta um Estado 81, 110nn. 4, 7–8, 10, 112n. 20, 115n. 31, 119–20nn. 58–9, 122n. 71, 139, 147n. 26, 148n. 32, 149nn. 35,39, 169n. 2, 225n. 20
    "Constituição" 112nn. 21–2, 120n. 61, 121–2nn. 63, 66, 123nn. 74–5, 173n. 33
    "Constituição das Câmaras na Evolução da Política Portuguesa" 46n. 7
    "Corporativismo e os Trabalhadores, O" 110n. 8, 122n. 70
    "Diferentes Forças Políticas em Face da Revolução Nacional, As" 46n. 3, 51n. 41, 120n. 58, 146n. 20
    "Duas Palavras a Servir de Prefácio" 47n. 9, 116n. 39
    "Duas Palavras de Prefácio" 48n. 15, 111n. 9
    "É esta a Revolução que Esperávamos?" 115n. 32
    "Educação Física e Desportos" 117nn. 44–5
    "Educação Política Garantia da Continuidade Revolucionária A," 46n. 4, 49nn. 18–19, 77n. 44, 114n. 29
    "Elogio das Virtudes Militares" 228n. 39
    "Embaixada da Colónia Portugusa no Brasil e a nossa Política Externa, A" 115n. 33, 118n. 54
    "Era de Restauração, Era de Engrandecimento" 111n. 12
    "Escola, a Vida e a Nação, A" 223n. 6
    "Espírito da Revolução, O" 46nn. 3,6, 223n. 7
    "Estado Novo Português na Evolução Política Europeia, O" 47n. 11, 122n. 68, 123n. 75
    "Fins e Necessidade da Propaganda Política" 17n. 7, 49n. 17, 50n. 32
    "Funções e Qualidades do Chefe de Estado" 79n. 52
    "Governar Dirigindo a Consciência Nacional" 46n. 2, 51n. 35, 55n. 68, 122n. 69
    "Governo e Política" 51n. 33
    "Grandes Certezas da Revolução Nacional, As" 47n. 15, 48n. 16, 51n. 39, 136, 147nn. 25–6, 150n. 44, 169n. 1

"Império Colonial na Economia da Nação, O" 196n. 7, 206, 216, 224n. 15, 230n. 52
"Independência da Política Nacional — Suas Condições" 53n. 57, 114n. 29
"Meu Depoimento, O" 113n. 24, 146n. 20, 197n. 12, 198n. 14, 229n. 47
"Momento Político. Grandes e Pequenas Questões da Política Portuguesa, O" 45n. 2, 46n. 5, 195n. 2, 197n. 9, 228n. 40
"Nação na Política Colonial, A" 196nn. 4, 8, 222n. 2, 225n. 22, 229nn. 48–9
"Nação Portuguesa Irmandade de Povos, A" 197n. 11, 224n. 17, 230n. 50
Para a Compreensão da Nossa Política 51n. 34, 146–7n. 24, 197n. 8
"Para Servir de Prefácio" 47n. 11, 51n. 42, 53n. 56, 111n. 11
"Plano de Fomento. Princípios e Pressupostos, O" 77n. 46, 118n. 49
"Política de Verdade, Política de Sacrifício, Política Nacional" 46n. 8, 47n. 10
"Portugal como Elemento de Estabilidade na Civilização Ocidental" 118n. 52, 223n. 7
"Portugal perante a Crise da Europa" 222n. 3, 230n. 55, 231n. 62
"Princípios e a Obra da Revolução no Momento Interno e no Momento Internacional, Os" 77n. 45, 123n. 76
"Problemas Nacionais e a Ordem da sua Solução, Os" 47n. 10, 54n. 59, 169n. 6
"Problemas Político-Religiosos da Nação Portuguesa e do seu Império" 122n. 67, 146nn. 20, 23, 148n. 30, 222n. 5, 225nn. 20, 23

"Propaganda Nacional" 17nn. 6–7, 49nn. 20–1, 50n. 29, 79n. 52
"Questões de Política Interna" 227n. 35
"Revolução Corporativa" 123n. 73
"Suposto Arrendamento de Angola à Alemanha, O" 195n. 3
truth 13, 25–34, 43, 45n. 2, 47–8nn. 10–11, 15–16, 50n. 30, 52n. 52, 83, 116n. 40, 127, 136–7, 139–41, 151, 203–4, 220, 223n. 7
Santana, Vasco 13, 22n. 51, 62, 156, 157
Santos, Alberto Seixas 237n. 3
Santos, Sofia 151
São Luiz Theater 61–2
Sapega, Ellen W. 118n. 51
Sardinha, António 133
Schmitt, Carl 134–5, 142, 146n. 22, 149n. 42
Scholasticism 132, 204
Second Congress of the Portuguese Catholic Center, 145n. 18, 148n. 30
Second World War 13, 16nn. 4–5, 22n. 51, 199n. 27, 203, 235
Secretariat of National Propaganda (Secretariado da Propaganda Nacional; SPN) 1–2, 5–7, 16nn. 4, 5, 17n. 7, 26–7, 29, 31, 34, 38–9, 57, 59–60, 81, 84, 112n. 15, 126–7, 148n. 33, 153, 177, 186, 205–6, 208, 234
Secretariat of the State for Information and Tourism (Secretaria de Estado da Informação e do Turismo, SEIT) 5, 16n. 4, 19n. 28, 20n. 30
Século, O 112n. 17, 127
Selvagem, Carlos 191
Semedo, Artur 210, 216, 217, 226n. 26
Sequeira, V. M. 170n. 12
Sérgio, António 198n. 15
Severa (*A Severa*) 12, 59, 157–60, 162, 163, 165, 167, 168, 172nn. 21–2, 175nn. 44–6
short film; short 3, 27, 84, 187, 234
silent film 53n. 56

Silva, Hermínia 100, 167
Silva, João 231n. 64
Silveira, Paula 120-1n. 62, 121n. 63
Simões, Alberto Veiga 65
Sister Lúcia 140, 149n. 38
SNI *see* National Secretariat of Information, Popular Culture, and Tourism
social class 68-9, 90, 96, 99-104, 108-9, 118-20nn. 55, 58, 121n. 66, 122n. 70, 140, 151, 155, 160, 162, 164, 172-3n. 29, 214, 218-20, 231nn. 63-4, 237n. 3
Socialism 107, 111n. 8, 122n. 70, 123n. 76
Sociedade Universal de Superfilmes 61, 157
Song of Lisbon, A (*A Canção de Lisboa*) 12, 22n. 51, 151, 155-6, 157, 175n. 46
Song of the Earth, The (*A Canção da Terra*) 82, 86-7, 89, 92, 93, 104-5, 154, 230n. 57
Sotto, Madalena 187
sound film 3, 9, 12, 18n. 17, 157, 175n. 46
Sousa, António de 87, 171n. 13
sovereignty 67, 134, 142, 177, 183, 214-16, 221, 228n. 40
Soviet Union 31, 229n. 47
Spell of the Empire (*Feitiço do Império*) 7, 12, 15, 27-9, 50n. 28, 59, 73n. 11, 177-201, 233, 235
Spence, Louise 211
Spiguel, Miguel 143n. 3
Spirit (*Geist*) 64-5
spirit; spirituality 3, 15, 16-17n. 5, 18n. 13, 19n. 19, 20n. 29, 27, 31-7, 43, 46nn. 3, 6, 47n. 11, 49n. 19, 50n. 30, 51nn. 38, 43, 54-5nn. 60-1, 68, 57-9, 64-71, 73n. 12, 76-7nn. 39, 45, 92, 94, 97-101, 104, 111nn. 11-12, 114n. 28, 115n. 33, 117n. 48, 118n. 54, 123nn. 75-6, 127, 130-2, 135-6, 140, 143, 144n. 6, 145-7nn. 16, 20, 24-6, 148nn. 32-3, 150n. 43, 161, 203-32, 234, 236
SPN *see* Secretariat of National Propaganda

Stam, Robert 211
state of exception (Ausnahmezustand) 142
stereotype; stereotypical 1, 14, 151-75, 186-7, 192-3, 195
Still Life: Visions of a Dictatorship (*Natureza Morta: Visões de uma Ditadura*) 234-5
subalternity; subaltern 179-80
supplement 180-3, 189, 192, 195

Teatro e Cinema 18nn. 12, 14, 19nn. 18, 20-4, 72nn. 4, 6-9, 73nn. 13-17, 74-5nn. 22, 26-7, 78n. 48, 109-10nn. 1-3
Teixera, Virgílio 101
Telmo, Cottinelli 12, 125, 151
Ten Commandments of the New State (*Decálogo do Estado Novo*) 118n. 53
Teresa, Dina 157, 158, 172n. 23
Theater of the People 112n. 15
Third Congress of National Unity 114n. 29
Third Reich 41, 118n. 50
"Three Essays on the Theory of Sexuality" 201n. 47
Three Graces, The (*Las Tres Gracias*) 62, 73n. 21
"Through Paediatrics to Psycho-Analysis" 198n. 24
Tobis Klang Film 18n. 17
Tobis Portuguesa 4, 105
Torgal, Luís Filipe 143nn. 1-2, 144nn. 7-8, 145nn. 14-15, 149n. 36
Torgal, Luís Reis 9, 18n. 15, 21nn. 42, 44, 29, 50n. 28, 46nn. 46-8, 72n. 10, 75nn. 33-4, 76n. 37, 123n. 72, 145nn. 18, 20, 147n. 27, 170n. 12, 171n. 14, 175n. 48, 199n. 32, 200n. 33
Totalitarianism; totalitarian 10, 17n. 8, 27, 35-6, 39, 42, 120n. 60, 153, 170n. 11, 235
Totem and Taboo 41
Tovar, Isabel 188
"Trabalhos da Conferência dos Governadores, Os" 197n. 13

trade 217–19, 230n. 61
tradition 13, 14, 58, 66–7, 81–2, 87–8, 90–2, 98–102, 108, 112n. 23, 114–15nn. 29–31, 33, 117n. 48, 118n. 53, 120–1nn. 61–2, 128, 131, 137, 140–1, 145n. 20, 151, 153, 155–7, 162, 164–5, 167–9, 173n. 32, 190–1, 204, 212, 228n. 39, 236
transgression 15, 157–65, 169
transitional object 185, 198n. 25
Traveling Cinema (Cinema Ambulante) 2
Triumph of the Will (*Triumph des Willens*) 40
truth (in the New State) 6, 13, 21n. 42, 25–6, 29–34, 43–4, 45nn. 1–2, 47–8nn. 10–11,15–16, 50n. 30, 52–3n. 52, 70, 81, 83, 97, 127, 136–41, 147n. 27, 151, 203–4, 213, 220–1, 223n. 7, 236
Tyrannical Father, The (*O Pai Tirano*) 156

"Uma Casa Portuguesa" 170n. 12
unconscious 11, 44, 58
University of Coimbra 14, 95, 128, 130, 144n. 12
Up and Away! (*Ala-Arriba!*) 12, 82, 84–5, 89–90, 92, 112n. 17, 155

Vacances avec Salazar 16nn. 2–3, 47n. 14, 48n. 16, 51n. 37, 53n. 58, 72n. 5, 76n. 38, 79n. 51, 116n. 34, 170n. 10, 174n. 35, 175nn. 49, 51, 197n. 10, 199n. 26, 222n. 5, 226n. 32, 227nn. 33–4, 232n. 68
Valente, César 29
Valéry, Paul 2–3, 53n. 53, 204
Venice Biennale 84

Verde Gaio Ballet Company 84, 112n. 15
Verneuil, Henri 172n. 28
Victory in the West (*Sieg im Westen*) 52n. 49
Victory of the Faith (*Der Sieg des Glaubens*) 40
Vieira, Afonso Lopes 133, 189–90
Vieira, Tarquínio 69
Vigilanti Cura (Encyclical) 145n. 16
Vilar, António 62, 64, 75n. 28
Vilas, Maria Emília, 210
Village of White Clothes, The (*Aldeia da Roupa Branca*) 82, 94, 100, 109, 119n. 56, 151, 154, 167
Villardebó, Carlos 172n. 28
Villaverde, Teresa 234
Vimioso, Count of 172n. 24
Virgin Mary 125–9, 133, 140, 142, 143n. 3, 149n. 40, 185, 194
Viseu, Diamantino 160
Voltaire 129–30

War Office Cinematograph Committee, The 199n. 27
Weber, Max 132
White Telephone films 13
Wild Cattle (*Gado Bravo*) 12, 82, 94, 95, 100, 151, 159, 160, 162–3, 167, 168
Wilde, Oscar 34
Winnicott, Donald 185, 198nn. 24–5
Wolves of the Mountain (*Lobos da Serra*) 82, 86–90, 104–5, 154–5, 171n. 13
world-historical individuals (welthistorische Individuen) 65–6